Fundamentals of Production, Inventory and the Supply Chain

Nick T. Thomopoulos

ATLANTIC
PUBLISHERS & DISTRIBUTORS (P) LTD

Published by
ATLANTIC
PUBLISHERS & DISTRIBUTORS (P) LTD
7/22, Ansari Road, Darya Ganj,
New Delhi-110002
Phones: +91-11-40775252, 23273880, 23275880, 23280451
Fax: +91-11-23285873
Web: www.atlanticbooks.com
E-mail: orders@atlanticbooks.com

Branch Office
5, Nallathambi Street, Wallajah Road,
Chennai-600002
Phones: +91-44-64611085, 32413319
E-mail: chennai@atlanticbooks.com

Printed in India at Glorious Printers, A-13, D.S.I.D.C., Jhilmil Industrial Area, Delhi-110095

Preface

As I look back over my working years, I realize I was most fortunate with the background I gained as it happened to unfold from year-to-year in both industry and in academia. This included working in industry at International Harvester as supervisor of operations research in the corporate headquarters; as a consultant to international industry and government at IIT Research Institute (IITRI) as a senior scientist; as a professor in the Industrial Engineering Department at the Illinois Institute of Technology (IIT) and also in the Stuart School of Business at IIT. My stint with FIC Inc., a software company, enabled me to gain valuable knowledge of the software tools needed in industry, as well as the customers' call for user-friendly tools. For many of the years, I was privileged to serve as consultant to a wide variety of industries in the United States, Europe and Asia. These include: Wrigley Company, Wheelobrator Fry, Motorola Corporation, Florsheim Shoe Company, Clow Industries, Baxter Laboratories, Alberto Culver, International Harvester Corporation, Komatsu Dresser, International Truck and Engine, Olivetti, L.M. Erickson, Asea, British Motors, Citroen, Mitsubishi Heavy Industries, Suzuki, Toshiba, Hitachi Zosen, M-Focus, Unity Ltd, the Pentagon, the Office of Naval Research, the U.S. Army Aviation and Troop Command, the Federal Aviation Administration and the American Association of Railroads. At IIT, I was fortunate to be assigned an array of courses, widening my horizon with the variety of topics, and with the added knowledge I gained from the students and with every repeat of the course. The courses included: probability, advance data analysis, time series, queuing theory, simulation methods, data analysis, inventory management, inventory and production control, assembly methods, statistical methods, industrial forecasting, stochastic processing, statistical decision theory, supply chain methods, and operations research. I was also fortunate to serve as the advisor to many bright Ph.D. students as they carried on their dissertation research. Bits of knowledge from the various courses and research helped me in the classroom, in research, and also in my consulting assignments. Whenever I could, I used my industry knowledge in classroom lectures so that the students could see how some of the textbook methodologies are actually applied in industry. At the same time, the knowledge I gained from the classroom helped me to formulate and develop solutions to industry applications as they unfolded. The wide variety of experience allowed me to paint a picture on which quantitative tools are really useful in industry. This book is based on this total experience and also includes many of the quantitative methods that I found doable and useful to industry.

The book will be of immerse value to all concerned with business, particularly the quantitative methods in the supply chain.

Nick T. Thomopoulos

Acknowledgements

Thanks foremost to my wife, Elaine Thomopoulos, who has encouraged me to write this volume. She inspired and gave consultation very often as the need called. Thanks also to the many people who have helped and inspired me along the way. I can name only a few here. Deepak Bammi (Bammi Associates), Wayne Bancroft (Walgreens), Fred Bock (IIT Research Institute), Harry Bock (Florsheim Shoe Company), Randy Braun (Komatsu Dresser), Toemchai Bunnag (PTT Public), John Cada (Florsheim Shoe Company), Edine Dahel (Monterey Institute), John DeMotts (International Harvester), Shail Godambe (Motorola, Northern Illinois University), Mark Graham (International Truck and Engine), Scott Halligas (Florsheim Shoe Company), Jim Harrington (International Harvester), M. Zia Hassan (Illinois Institute of Technology), Willard Huson (Navistar), Dick Ilseman (International Truck and Engine), Chuck Jones (Illinois Institute of Technology), Arvid Johnson (Domenican University), Marsha Jance (Indiana University, Richmond), Rama Kishore (Walgreens), Tom Knowles (Illinois Institute of Technology), Tom Lewis (International Harvester), Carol Lindee (Panduit), Keith Mahal (Navistar), Nick Malham (FIC Inc.), Craig Marasek (Komatsu Dresser), Pissanu Manaspiti (Rangsit University), Pricha Pantumsinchai (M-Focus), Ted

Prenting (Marist College), Doloris Santucci (Navistar), Spencer Smith (Illinois Institute of Technology), Mark Spieglan (FIC Inc.), Manu Vora (Business Excellence, Inc.) and Jaimee Wu (International Truck and Engine).

Nick T. Thomopoulos

Contents

Introduction

Many companies in the trucking, construction, agriculture, footwear, food, beauty products, hardware, pharmacy, electronics, parts, components, tools and processing industries, hold millions of dollars worth of inventory on an ongoing basis. This inventory is constantly on the move: new shipments from suppliers are continually being received; orders to customers are being processed, picked and shipped to their destinations on a daily basis. Because the inventory of equipment and material in stock is costly, it is important to have available only those levels that are needed and economical. The international competition confronting these companies is fierce, and the better they manage their investment in facilities, equipment and inventory, the more profitable they will become. Moreover, those companies that manage poorly may not survive.

Distribution and manufacturing practices are undergoing extensive transition, striving to manage the supply chain, to minimize the time and cost and gain overall efficiency in the flow of the inventory from the suppliers to the customers. Their goal is to achieve a high level of service. A good inventory system accurately forecasts the demand for a product and thereafter determines the schedule of replenishment so that the suppliers can meet the ongoing demands. The book emphasizes the need for efficiency in the control of the inventory. Sensitivity relations are presented to stress the proper use of the methods. Examples of these sensitivity relations show how the cost increases when the order size is not economic; how the service level drops when the supplier is late in delivery; how sales are lost when the service level drops, and so forth.

The book contains sixteen chapters and a short description on each is given below.

Chapter 1, "The Supply Chain", describes the key locations that carry inventory along the supply chain. These are the facilities that play a role in the inventory as it is passing from one location to another until it reaches the customer. The inventory ingredients in the finished good item evolve from various earth commodities, and is passed from one supplier to another, and, along the way, value is added, as the inventory travels to manufacturing centers, distribution centers, retailers, and ends with finished goods received by the customer. Supply chain management seeks to minimize the overall time and cost of this flow. Optimal inventory levels are needed in all stages from the basic goods manufacturer to the retailer.

Chapter 2, "Forecasting", describes the various ways forecasts are generated for use in inventory and production facilities. Forecasts are needed for each of the items stocked in places like stores, dealers, distribution centers and service parts facilities. This is where inventory decisions are in continual need and the future demands are not known until they occur. The forecasts are used to make the inventory decisions on when and how much to buy. Forecasts provide estimates of future demands, and are generally revised at regular time periods, usually monthly. The forecasts are developed by generating an exact fit through the flow of demands from past time periods, and then projecting the fit throughout the future time periods.

This chapter shows how to generate the forecasts using the history of past demands. For simplicity, the demand history is assumed in monthly buckets, and thereby, each month new forecasts are obtained for each item. The methods presented here give higher weights to the more current demands in finding the forecast fit. The two forecast methods described are called 'discounting' and 'smoothing'. Discounting uses a fixed number of history demands to generate the new forecast. Smoothing revises the prior forecast with each most current demand to generate the new forecast.

Chapter 3, "Order Quantity", shows how to determine the quantity to buy for each item in the stocking facilities, such as in distribution centers, dealers, retailers and stores. The goal is to maintain adequate inventory to fill customer orders as they occur and also to buy the replenish stock that is economical with respect to hold and order costs. Because the model determines the particular quantity that yields the minimum order plus hold costs, the quantity is called the economic order quantity (EOQ). The chapter shows how to buy the stock in four different situations. First is when the buy quantity must be in equal month requirement increments. Second is when the supplier specifies a cost per unit for each part with no limitation on the buy quantity. Third is when the supplier offers a contract with price breaks, whereby the larger the buy quantity, the lower the cost-per-unit in increments. And fourth is the least-unit-cost that is used in the plants to find the lot size for the build schedule on the finished good items. The chapter also introduces the stocking rate that measures the hold plus order cost for each part.

Chapter 4, "Safety Stock", explains what safety stock is and why it is needed. It is the extra stock in the inventory to offset the uncertainty in demands. Safety stock is needed especially in the distribution and retail locations along the supply chain. The typical goal of inventory management is to achieve a high service level with minimum inventory investment. It is convenient, in planning, to partition the inventory into two segments, cycle stock and safety stock. The cycle stock is the inventory needed to fill the demands that are consistent with the forecasts; and the safety stock is the inventory needed for the demands that may fall above the forecast. A good inventory system will seek the minimum amount of safety stock that is needed to accomplish the service level goals of the management.

The chapter describes four methods to find the safety stock on a part. These methods are called the following: months-supply, availability, service level and Lagrange. Sometimes one method is more appropriate than another, depending on the type of inventory carried and the data available to calculate the safety stock.

Chapter 5, "Order Point and Order Level", are two measures that are computed for each part and location. The order point and order level are revised, typically, once a month and can be used each day to determine when to buy and how much. These quantities are obtained from the forecasts, lead time, safety stock and order quantity. This chapter shows how they are computed and gives examples on their use.

Chapter 6, "Low Demand Items", concerns parts in the inventory with low demand, and shows how to determine the order point and order level to satisfy the desired service level specified by the management. The model pertains to scenarios of lost sales and backorders. In many stocking facilities, like dealers, stores, retailers, etc. the monthly demands are low for most or all of the items in the inventory. Low volume items are particularly common when the items have many sizes and color combinations, like in shoes, clothing apparel and furniture where there are a variety of colors and sizes. In service part facilities (like automobiles and appliances), parts are held in stock awaiting any maintenance and repair needs on the finished good items. Some of the parts have high to moderate demands, but most have low demands. The Poisson distribution applies for these low volume items. This chapter shows how to determine the order point and order level to satisfy the service level specified by management.

Chapter 7, "Multi-Locations", concerns those distribution systems with two or more locations. Each location is assigned a region and is charged with filling the demands from the customers in the region. Often, one of the locations is designated as the master location, and holds inventory on all parts, and may serve as the source to all other locations. The locations hold just sufficient inventory to satisfy the regional demands. The goal is to achieve a high service level and maintain the minimum overall investment in inventory for the total system.

The stocking of the parts with multi locations require careful planning and some unique methods of distribution. These include network design, network replenishments, part-location assignment, and the allocation and transfer of stock between the locations.

Chapter 8, "Production", takes place at the part and component suppliers, and at the Original Equipment Manufacturers (OEMs) that produce the finished goods. The production planning and scheduling of the operations is a complicated process and requires careful coordination between materials, labor, machines and facilities. This chapter describes some of the main methods used in the production process. These include the production plan, the master production schedule, rough cut capacity planning, bill of materials and material requirements planning.

Chapter 9, "Assembly", describes single and mixed model assembly lines. In single model assembly, the chapter shows how to measure the cycle time, balance delay, and how these measures are important to determine the efficiency of the line. Also described is the concept of the precedence diagram, and how it is used with line balancing to assign the work elements to the station operators in a most efficient way. In mixed model assembly, the reader learns how line balancing takes place in mixed model assembly. The chapter also shows how to sequence the units down the line when they are produced on a make-to-stock basis and also when on a make-to-order basis. In the latter case, the customers specify the features and options that they desire on the individual units.

Chapter 10, "IOQ, EOQ and ATR", pertains especially to distribution centers that house parts for the repair and maintenance of finished goods items, like automobiles, appliances, printing presses, so forth. The chapter describes the three basic buy quantities on a part—IOQ, EOQ and ATR.

The IOQ (initial order quantity) is the first buy on a part and is called when the part is introduced and has no prior demand history to base the forecasts. This happens for service parts and concerns the new (never been used before) parts that are installed on the finished good units in assembly. These are the parts that are new due to engineering changes or are installed on new models.

The ATR (all-time requirement) is the last buy and is needed when the supplier will cease production on the part and calls for a final buy, and where the stocking location is obliged to continue stocking the part and thereby is forced to call for a final buy. This latter buy, a forecast on all future requirements on the part, is used to determine how much to buy.

The EOQ (economic order quantity) denotes all the buy quantities in between the IOQ and the ATR. All three of the buy quantities seek to replenish the part sufficiently, with the minimum stock to meet the oncoming flow of demands with a high service level.

Chapter 11, "Late Delivery and Lost Sales", describes two situations that concern the service level on a part. The first situation is when the supplier is late in delivery of replenish stock; and the second situation is when out-of-stock situation causes backorders or a loss in sales. This chapter shows how to measure these situations and how to cope with them.

Safety stock is needed to yield a desired service level (demand filled/ total demand). To determine the safety stock, the computations assume a planned lead time provided by the supplier. In reality, however, the actual lead time may vary from the planned lead time and often is longer. This chapter explores how the actual service level is effected when the lead time varies in this way; and shows how to determine the safety time stock needed to offset the longer than expected lead times.

The service level is measured in industry as the demand filled over total demand. Unfilled demand becomes a backorder or lost sales. Lost sales demand is often not known or measured by the management. This chapter describes how to estimate the lost sales demand and also shows how to measure the associated effective service level. Tables are provided for easy reference, and examples illustrate how to apply the results to industry situations.

Chapter 12, "Reusable Inventory", considers another form of inventory that is present in most firms but does not leave the firm's possession once a demand is fulfilled. This type of inventory demand takes place when a need occurs for use of the item and upon completion, the item remains in the inventory to meet the next demand. For purposes here, these items are labeled as reusable inventory items. If all of the reusable inventory items are occupied when a demand arrives and if the demand will wait, in essence, the demand is in a backorder state. Examples of reusable items with backorders are tools, lift trucks, pallets, molds, binding machines, order pickers, fixtures, and so forth. In the event the demand will not wait, the demand becomes a lost sale. Could be tables in a restaurant, pumps at a gas station, or items at a rental agency. Queuing theory is used to find the solutions to all situations described in this chapter.

Chapter 13, "Statistical Process Control", concerns any system that produces an output of a given product or service. Statistical process control (SPC) is the function that analyzes the outputs of such a process to take appropriate action to achieve and maintain a state of statistical control, and to improve the process capability. Process capability is a measure of the proportion of the output that conforms with the product specification tolerances.

Two important measures of a process are the quality and quantity of units produced. The key philosophy of SPC is that the quality has the highest importance, even at the risk of slowing down the quantity. This chapter describe the methods to control the quality of the manufactured items. These methods are commonly used at the parts and component suppliers and also at the plants. The goal is to produce items with zero defects. Two types of control measures are attribute and variable. Four control charts are described for attribute type data and four for variable type data.

Chapter 14, "Supply Chain Management", describes the typical role of the supply chain management (SCM) team in a company. The SCM staff studies the needs of their customer base and determines the associated flow of inventory from origin to customer. The goal is to provide a high level of service to the customers, while minimizing the time and cost of all activities involved in their products. The activities pertain to the procurement, transportation, storage and production, of any related raw materials, work-in-process and finished goods and often takes place within the company (in-house) and across (outside) companies, both upstream and downstream. For a successful supply chain management, cooperation and control is needed and planned between the in-house facilities, suppliers, third party service providers and retail outlets.

Some supply chain examples are described in the chapter. In the examples, the goal is to flow the inventory from one location (in the supply chain) to another in a way where the inventory needs are cost efficient at each location. To accomplish this, data sharing is needed from one location to another in both the upstream and downstream locations.

Chapter 15, "Software Along the Supply Chain", illustrates how software routines can be used in the various supply chain applications. A main routine is where the parts in each location are forecast and where the replenish computations are carried out. This is where the order quantity, safety stock, order point and order level are computed. A buy routine is run daily and seeks out any part that needs replenish stock and finds the quantity to buy.

When the inventory system has more than one location, an allocate routine and a transfer routine are used to spread the inventory properly across all the locations to avoid maldistribution. Another routine is used when buy quantities are needed for a group of parts to gain discount buys or truck-load buys. Other routines are used in the plants to generate master production schedules that level the future weekly work load from the aggregate of all parts in the plant. A utility routine measures the lost sales demand for a group of parts.

Chapter 16, "Transportation and Logistics", concerns the movement of goods from one location (plant, factory, shop) to another (warehouse, store, customer); whereas logistics is the management of the flow of goods, information and other resources between the point of origin and the point of consumption in order to meet the requirements of consumers. The transport may take place via air, water, rail, road, pipeline, or cable routes, using planes, boats, trains, trucks, or telecommunications equipment as the means of transportation. The goal for any business owner is to minimize transportation and storage costs while also meeting demand for products. These are important issues to transportation and to logistics and thereby this chapter describes the topics together.

Nick T. Thomopoulos

1

The Supply Chain

The key players along the supply chain are the manufacturing, distribution and retail facilities. The inventory originally evolves from earth commodities like lumber, fish and cotton, and as value is added, the inventory travels to manufacturing centers, distribution centers, retailers, and ends with finished goods received by the customer. Supply chain management seeks to minimize the overall time and cost of this flow. Optimal inventory levels are needed in all stages from the basic goods manufacturer to the retailer.

With local and worldwide competition so fierce, no firm can any longer afford inefficiency in management of inventory. Methods are continually being developed to achieve the goal of optimal inventory, and are now being applied by many firms. In the manufacturing industries, the goal is to control the inventory flow at each step in the production process. Concepts of just-in-time or zero-inventory are aimed at eliminating inventory altogether. The above goals of zero-inventory is somewhat achievable since most manufacturing orders are known in advance; much also depends on the integrity of the database and the proper execution of all stages of progression. However, in distribution and retail industries, most demands are not known until the moment they occur. An economical balance between inventory levels and customer service is the counterpart aim sought in the control of inventory.

A view of the facilities along the supply chain is given in this chapter.

Basic Goods Suppliers

Basic goods are products such as castings, sheet metal, steel bars, distilled oil and gas and rolls of rubber compounds. Manufacturers of these products are suppliers to manufacturers of whole goods and parts. Their suppliers are producers of raw materials, such as oil, coal, iron ore, rubber, leather, cotton, pulp and lumber. Costs of producing basic goods are high and competition is international, a major challenge is to keep operations costs down and produce quality products. Maintenance and repair of processing machinery and equipment is very costly and is a major concern to basic goods producers.

The primary purpose is to convert raw materials to homogeneous materials that will have applications in subsequent stages of manufacture. The uncertainty in the raw materials themselves, causes difficulty because their composition is subject to wide variations. Output batches may yield several grades of product, even when they emerge from the same combination of ingredients in the formulation. This unevenness may be caused by any of a number of factors, such as the composition or raw materials, the temperature, pressure, flow rate and the process machinery and equipment in use. Output products may be graded and separated by grade for particular end product uses or may be further processed when necessary. Some items of the output are waste and may have a high disposal cost.

Requirements by distribution centers and direct orders from manufacturers are totaled to determine demands on the basic goods product line. In addition, a forecast of other demands by line of product is used as the basic input to the MPS of the firm. Because of the high level of uncertainty with the yields from various production processes, producing their line of products to meet the exact schedule is difficult, and thus the role of material requirement planning is not as straightforward as in other manufacturing industries. Instead, MRP is generally reserved for the preparation of containers and packaging materials to meet the master production schedule.

Part and Component Suppliers

Original equipment manufacturers, OEMs, have facilities that fabricate many parts used in the whole goods. They also purchase parts from other firms specializing in the manufacture of individual products. These firms, called components manufacturers, usually do not have operation distribution centers as the OEMs do, but they receive orders on their line of products directly. The components manufacturer in essence is a supplier of parts for both OEM production lines and OEM distribution centers. Also, they can be a supplier to the all-makes distributors as well as to retail dealers and rebuild firms. A car dealer, for example, may bypass the distribution center of the OEM if he can receive stock at a lower cost from a components manufacturer. Doing so, however, usually requires a longer lead time and larger replenishment quantities.

A component manufacturer who receives orders from the dealer and rebuild firms, passes them on to the master scheduler of the production plant, and includes the orders with any product demands. These other demands may be open orders from OEMs for their production and service needs. All plant demands are combined with available inventory and the committed schedule to develop the production schedule for the lead time and planning weeks beyond. When the units are completed at the plant, they are delivered to each customer.

Packagers

Controlling the inventory at the packager is very challenging. A packager serves as a go-between for stock coming from a supplier and going to an OEM. This occurs for parts where the OEM orders the stock from the part supplier and when ready, the supplier ships the stock in bulk to the packager. The packager places the stock in containers with labels in a way that is storage friendly so the OEM can ship and store as needed.

The packager requires a wide inventory of packaging components to carry out the packaging process on the large variety of parts that it processes. An important task for the packager is to stock the packaging components in advance to meet the oncoming needs of parts to package. The packager buys this stock from the component suppliers. Each component has supplier procurement data like the lead time, cost per unit and the multiple quantity. Also needed is a part-packaging bill-of-material that specifies the packaging components, and also the quantity needed to package each part. It is the responsibility of the packager to have a systematic way to keep tract of the component inventory and to replenish this stock in an efficient way. The typical goal is to hold the minimum inventory on this component stock, and yet have sufficient stock to achieve a high service level. When the part stock comes in from the part supplier, the packager is obliged to package the parts quickly, and ship on to the OEM customer to meet the due date. This is a challenging task for many reasons. First, the packaging process of a part often requires two or more components and the lot quantity of all of the components must be available to finish the packaging process on a part. Second, many of the components are not dedicated to one part and thereby are shared on two or more parts. Third, the packaging schedule for oncoming parts comes periodically with due dates and in lumpy sizes. Fourth, the packager cannot start the packaging process on a part until they receive the shipment of raw stock from the part supplier. Fifth, the packager often has a short window of time to complete the packaging task to meet the part due date.

Willfitters

One kind of distributor of service parts to retailers, called willfitters, includes firms that concentrate on the manufacture and sales of high volume service and repair goods for a particular line of product. Willfitters copy (and sometimes improve) the design from the original part or component and produce imitation parts (generally of good quality) that can be substituted for the original part; often they can sell these components at a lower price. Willfitters do not require the large engineering staff to develop the product from the outset as does the original manufacturer. Typically they manufacture offshore in new industrial countries. Their salesmen seek out the retailers to promote their product line and to procure sales orders, as the willfitters are in competition with the OEMs for the retail share of orders.

Manufacturers

Manufacturers receive orders for their products from distributors. They sometimes receive order directly from retailers for the whole goods, such as autos, trucks and appliances. A government may also place orders, usually on a make-to-order basis. Manufacturers mostly produce goods to meet orders already received from distributors, retailers and governments. They also produce goods for stock to be warehoused in a distribution center, awaiting future orders. Each manufacturer strives to produce products with the maximum level of customer service (meeting due dates), with minimum investment in inventory, and with maximum efficiency of manufacturing resources.

In the production process, manufacturers are confronted with four distinct types of inventory: basic materials, parts and components, work-in-process and finished goods. The basic materials goods (chemicals, plastics, castings, rubber goods, steel bar products, so on) are partially purchased from basic materials manufacturers; parts and components are partially supplied from component manufacturers as describe below.

Several planning and production steps are followed in the manufacture of products, from beginning to the end of finished products.

Strategic Planning

Strategic Planning is where the top management gives direction in business, marketing, production and resources. These strategic plans are on a collective basis and may be developed by various divisions of the firm. Business planning pertains to projections of income, funds and expenditures. Market planning concerns the lines of products to produce and the markets to foster. Production planning schedules the level of production, inventories, shipment and backlogs over the future horizon by months. Resource planning sets the level of capacity appropriate to meet production needs, which may be stated in labor hours, machine hours, or other appropriate units.

Distribution Resource Planning

Distribution Resource Planning (DRP) pertains when a manufacturer of make-to-stock products has various locations in the distribution system. For each location, a forecast of finished good demands over the future year (in months, weeks, even days) is generated. This forecast is used—along with the safety stock, current on-hand and schedules due and on-order—to determine when replenishment is needed for each location.

Master Production Schedule

A Master Production Schedule (MPS) defines the number of end items to produce over the planning horizon. The sum of end items should equal the amount of production established and/or appropriated in the production plan by time period. An end item is any product with a bill of materials defined. A bill of material is a list of all parts and components, with quantities that are needed to produce one unit of the end item or one unit of a part or component item. The planning period should cover the time sufficient to meet the lead times of all items needed in the manufacturing process.

Final Assembly Schedule

The Final Assembly Schedule (FAS) is a detailed list of products and components released or to be released for manufacture on each production line. Here, the plans derived from the MPS are executed on the shop floor. In a make-to-stock environment the FAS and MPS are the same. The MPS states the number of end items to make, and the FAS may specify the number of end items to produce by assembly line. In both, the comprised sum of end items must equal the sum of production plan. Units produced from the assembly line are used to replenish the finished goods inventory.

In make-to-order situations, the FAS is the assembly line schedule that is set to satisfy specific customer orders. Customer orders represent end items that may be assembled with a wide variety of options for various features. The production plan is based on the number and mix of models and options to be produced on the assembly over future time periods. Over the near future, customer orders are available for specific models with feature options and with specific due dates.

Operations Scheduling

Operations Scheduling is the process of scheduling the work load to individual operations within each work center. Sometimes operations are scheduled by use of single machine scheduling techniques, flow shop scheduling techniques or job shop scheduling techniques. In any event the scheduling process considers the available and due dates of the lots along with the lot size quantities, processing times, queues, move time, production batch sizes and any set up times that may pertain.

Manufacturing Resource Planning

Manufacturing Resource Planning (MRP II), a detailed overall planning system refers to a combined process beginning with development of the production plan and ending with an acceptable capacity requirement plan. In between and included are the MPS and the MRP. MRP II pertains to all calculations and adjustments needed over these phases to allow the plant to carry out production needs efficiently with the resources available.

Demand Management

Demand Management is the function of recognizing and managing all demands for products to ensure that the master scheduler is aware of them. It includes the activities involved in forecasting, order entry, and service parts requirements. The forecast is the formalized request from sales to have manufacturing capability available to achieve the projected demands.

Just-in-Time

Just-in-Time (JIT) is a strategy used in production that is based on the concept of adding value and eliminating waste. Value is added only by work performed on the product and waste is anything, other that a minimal amount of necessary resources (material, manpower, capital equipment) that does not add value to the finished product. The ideal lot size is one, and the ideal output is for each worker to complete his product just before it is required. The philosophy is aimed at reducing all inventory queues of material, work-in-process and finished goods down to zero. Any excess stock cannot be tolerated.

Uniform Plant Loading

Uniform Plant Loading (UPL) is the starting point. To make the JIT production concept a reality, production must flow as smoothly as possible in the plant. The goal of uniform plant loading is to smooth out the production process by requiring that the same mix of products be built every production day. In this manner, the manufacturing operations become as predictable and repetitive as possible. Flow of materials and goods from upstream and downstream work stations or suppliers is level without any wide fluctuations.

Quality at the Source

Quality at the Source is needed because in JIT manufacturing, safety stock is not allowed, every piece is essential, and defects are not permitted. This standard entails that quality must be an integral part of each step along the way so that goods that inflow and outflow are defect free. Quality at the source is demanded, each worker inspects his own work. With this type of inspection, production may temporarily be stopped if a quality problem is detected. Mass production of defective goods is thus prevented, and having found and corrected the problem, workers resume manufacturing process. One method of performing these functions is called statistical process control which uses control charts with a statistical basis to monitor the output quality at the work station.

Kanban

Kanban is a JIT method that allows the stations in the plant to signal when new replenish inventory is needed by part and component. This is accomplished by a series of replenish type cards (called Kanbans) that have preprinted information with the following data: the station, part, quantity and a supplying station. When the inventory of a part (or component) at the station is at an order point level, the Kanban card is sent to the supply station signaling the supply station to send the quantity, accordingly. This is the way the stations in the plant communicate with each other and determine the station production needs by part and component. When all is achieved, the stations in the plant are replenished appropriately and the in-process-inventory is held to a minimum.

Minimum Set-up Times

Minimum Set-up Times are needed to coincide with the small production lot sizes called by JIT, UPL and Kanban. Smaller lot sizes in turn call for more frequent set-ups on the producing operations. This system becomes economically feasible when set-up times and costs are held to a minimum. Design and manufacturing engineers have the responsibility to integrate their activities to ensure minimum set-up times of all production operations. Holding down set-up times becomes necessary to yield small order quantities that are economical when both stocking and ordering costs are considered. When set-up times are reduced, lead times to the next work station are reduced accordingly. Even when lot sizes or order quantities cannot be made smaller, reduction in set-up time often results in reduction of production costs.

Cellular Manufacturing

Cellular Manufacturing is another JIT strategy intended to make the manufacturing processes smooth and synchronized in the complex job shop environment. This method applies when there are a large number of items and small order quantities. The concept is to manufacture families of products with the same characteristics from start to finish in one area using several operations manned in many cases by a single operator or by minimum manpower. A manufacturing work cell may be described as a group of functionally dissimilar operations, located together, and dedicated to the manufacturer of similar products called a cell family. The goal is to reduce the set-up time, lead time, material movement and work-in-process inventory. Included in the goals are a higher level of quality, and more flexibility to handle changes in production schedules, and changes to product design.

All Makes Service Parts Distribution Centers

Control of inventory for a service parts distribution center of an all makes distributor is much the same as that of an OEM. The main exception is that the all makes distributors carry the line of parts from whole goods produced by all manufacturers and thus carry a wider breadth of part numbers. All makes centers often specialize only in parts with certain functional uses, such as brakes, transmissions and tires. Frequently such centers are aligned with a chain of repair centers that perform repair and maintenance services for customers. An all makes distributor often operates its own rebuild facility to manufacture the cores (replaced components) from equipment serviced to level at, near or beyond original specifications. For these rebuilt items, any associated parts needed may be ordered from the OEM distribution center. Completed rebuilt components are then offered for sale at lowered prices.

To control the large number of parts that are carried, the inventory system generates forecasts, safety stocks and order points for every part and component. This system monitors the stocking position of all parts and components on a frequent basis. When a low stocking position is detected, the system determines the replenish order size that is economical, and which will provide the desired level of service.

Finished Goods Distribution Centers

Another major type of distribution center involves only the stocking and shipping of finished goods. These centers, associated with cooperatives, chains, franchises or manufacturers of finished goods, stock finished goods and receive orders from retailers for delivery; often the retailer expects next day or next week delivery. Examples would be drug store goods, grocery goods, hair styling goods, office equipment goods and so forth. This kind of distributor is sometimes faced with providing stock for goods, with ever changing styles and fluctuations of demand due to promotions of various types or due to seasonal needs, for example, Christmas tree lights. He furthermore is confronted with goods that are dated for various reasons, such as deterioration or expiration (food, dry cell batteries, so forth). In general, high turnover of stock is essential.

At a finished goods distribution center, stock is continually flowing in from manufacturers and out to retailers. Often the foods arrive and are stored in bins on a 24 hour basis. At the same time, retailer orders for delivery are given picking labels; order pickers promptly fill those orders for shipment, often using a scanning device to sort the picked goods by retail customer. Trucks are promptly filled and goods are delivered to the retailers.

Service Parts Distribution Centers

Controlling the part inventory at the distribution center (DC) is very challenging. The goal is to replenish the inventory in a systematic manner that will achieve a high service level, minimize the inventory investment, procure stock at the minimal prices and allow an increase in the sales. The DC carries a wide spectrum of parts and is often the main source for its customers. The typical customers are dealers, branches, and stores and with low lead times, the customers often buy in small quantities.

For a service part DC, the customer orders are mostly stock or emergency. Stock buys are when the customer fills their shelves to have available for their own customers needs; emergency buys are for immediate need generally for the repair or maintenance of a finished good item. Stock orders often are for larger quantities where the DC typically pays the freight; emergency orders are for immediate need and smaller quantities where the customer pays the freight.

Sometimes the suppliers to the DC offer promotions on their parts with lower prices and the DC passes the promotion prices on to the dealers. The dealers in turn are obliged to sell to their customers at lower prices. Promotions of this type cause a surge in demands for the promotion period and sometimes a small drop afterwards. When promotions are coming, the DC needs to properly increase its stock in advance to accommodate the projected rise in demands.

Some customers are other large outlets outside of the normal customer base—like an OEM. These customers buy from a particular set of parts, and usually in large quantities. This way the DC is the source to the outlet. The outlet buys from the DC with lower lead times than from the supplier. The DC buys from the supplier with the higher lead times. Some of these parts are common to both the DC customers and to the outlet. Stock is held at the DC for both uses. Other parts are unique only to the outlet.

Some parts are actually kits that are put together in a small assembly at the DC with other parts on the kit bill-of-material. The kits have a demand of their own, and the parts in the assembly also have demands of their own. The DC holds stock to meet the kit demands, and also holds stock on the parts to cover both the part independent demand, and also the part dependent demand from the kits.

Often customers place orders on parts for several weeks (or months) prior to the wanted delivery date. These advance orders are from regular customers but their demands are not yet in the history flow, and are missing when the forecasts are generated. Other orders for the future months are from non-regular customers like foreign countries, military or other OEM's. The DC adds these orders to the current forecasts on the future months and the total are the requirements on the parts.

A DC may be a lone location or may be one of several locations. When two or more locations, the DCs may buy stock together from the supplier to increase the buy quantity and receive quantity discounts. When stock comes in from the supplier, care in taken on how to split the new replenishment stock to the locations. In mal-distribution situations, stock may be transferred between locations as needed.

For a service part DC, on some occasions the supplier notifies the DC that it will stop supplying a part. The DC is then obliged to buy one last time for all of its future needs. The stock is held for long periods to satisfy the customer base future needs. These are called *all-time-buys*. On other occasions when new parts are introduced, the DC must buy stock—even when no demand history—in anticipation of future orders. These buys are called *initial-order-quantities*.

Dealers

Controlling the part inventory at the dealer is very challenging. The dealer often has limited storage space and budget for the parts inventory. The goal is to carry just the right parts and the quantity on each to achieve a high service level, and to do this with the minimum inventory investment; and whenever possible, the dealer wishes to buy the replenish stock at the minimal price.

Parts have two main roles at the dealer. First, is to serve the customers who buy stock over-the-counter for their own use at their own location. Second, is to have parts inventory available for customers who bring in the finished good item for maintenance or repair. In the event the stock on the part is not available when needed, the over-the-counter customer may buy elsewhere, and thereby this is a lost sale to the dealer. When maintenance or repair and a part needed is out, expediting costs at the dealer go up, goodwill is lost, and the customer suffers delay costs.

The typical replenish option on parts is from the *parts distribution center* (pdc). The pdc carries the parts for the finished goods that are sold by the dealer and this is the common place to replenish the stock of these parts. The dealer also may replenishes stock from *direct-ship suppliers* where the parts must be bought jointly to meet target goals to receive price discounts. They must buy in larger quantities than from the pdc and the lead time is often longer than from the pdc. Sometimes the dealer gets replenish stock from a *secondary supplier*. These may be parts that are available from a source that is closer to the dealer than the pdc and thereby has a lower lead time.

Considering the large number of parts at the dealer, the task of coordinating when to buy for a part, how much to buy, and from which source is very challenging. In addition, the replenish quantities must sometimes consider promotions, price breaks, job quantities and full bin quantities as well. The part inventory calls for a continual flow of replenishing decisions, and the actions taken play a major role in the profitability at the dealership.

2

Forecasting

This chapter describes the basic forecasting methods used for the parts and products held in the inventory. Forecasts are needed when customer demands are not known until they occur as in distribution centers, dealers and stores. The reader will learn the main demand patterns that occur are of the horizontal, trend and seasonal type. The two most common forecast methods are presented here, and are called discounting and smoothing. Both methods generate the forecasts by giving higher weights to the more recent demands of the past. Discounting uses all the past demands in generating the forecasts, while smoothing blends the most current demand with the prior forecast to generate a revised forecast. When more than one location holds the stock for an item, individual forecasts are needed for each location, and an aggregate forecast is needed for the whole. The chapter shows two ways to accomplish the forecasts of this type. These are by the top-down method and by the bottom-up forecast method. The chapter also shows some important sensitivity relations concerning the forecast accuracy and the way the forecasts are generated. The sensitivity relations allow the reader to see how the choice of the smoothing parameters and forecast model affects the accuracy of the forecasts.

Introduction

Forecasts are needed for each of the items stocked in places like retailers, stores, dealers, distribution centers and service parts facilities. This is where inventory decisions are in continual need to cope with future demands that are not known until they occur. The forecasts are used to make the inventory decisions on when and how much to buy. Forecasts provide estimates on future demands, and are generally revised at regular time periods, usually monthly. The forecasts are developed by generating a fit through the flow of the history demands and projecting the fit out to the future time periods.

This chapter shows how to generate the forecasts using the history of past demands. For simplicity in the examples of this chapter, the demand history is assumed in monthly buckets, and thereby, as each month passes, revised forecasts are obtained for every item in the inventory. The methods presented here give higher weights to the more current demands in finding the forecast fit by way of discounting and smoothing. Discounting uses a fixed number of history demands to generate the new forecast. Smoothing uses only the most current demand entry with the just prior forecast to generate the new forecast.

Demand Patterns and Forecast Models

The three basic demand patterns are horizontal, trend and seasonal. The figures below depict the pattern on each. The figures separate the history demands of the past from the forecast demands of the future.

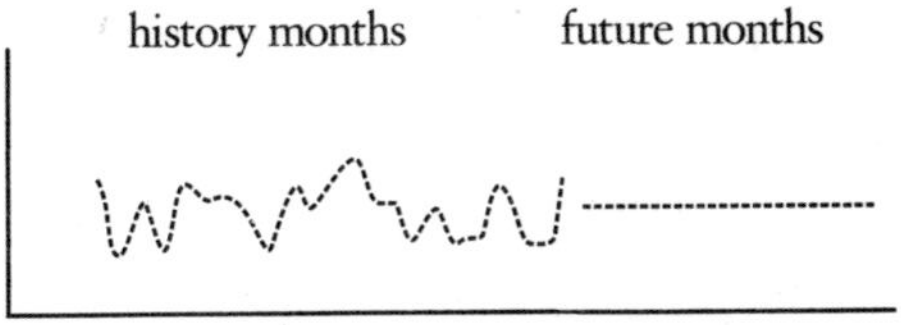

Horizontal demand pattern and forecasts

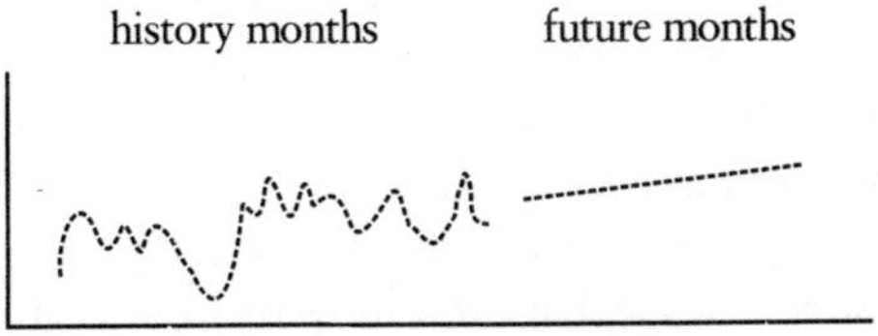

Trend demand pattern and forecasts

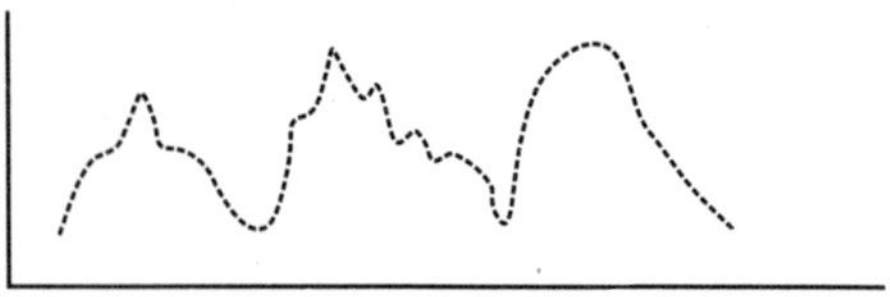

Seasonal demand pattern and forecasts

Figure 2.1: Horizontal, Trend and Seasonal Demand Patterns

Coefficient of Variation

The coefficient of variation (cov) is a relative measure of the forecast error. This is simply the ratio of the standard deviation of the one month ahead forecast error over the average one month forecast. This measure can be used to compare the forecast accuracy from one part to another, and the smaller the cov, the better. The data and calculations on the method are as follows:

f_τ = forecast for future month τ

f = average one month forecast

σ = standard deviation of one month ahead forecast error

cov = σ/f = coefficient of variation

When the cov is 0.33 or less, the monthly errors are assumed shaped like a normal distribution. When cov is one or larger, the shape is erratic and is more like an exponential distribution.

Demand History

A hardware distributor has 30,000 items in stock and maintains a database with a record on each part. The record includes the monthly demands for the most recent 24 months of history. The management wants to develop a forecasting system on each part that uses all the demand data available, and also one that gives more influence to the more recent demands. A consultant is called in, and upon review, recommends they use the discount forecasting models for parts with horizontal and trend demand patterns, and that they use the smoothing forecast model for parts with a seasonal demand pattern. This way they use all of their demand history with more weight assigned to the more recent months in computing the forecasts. As will be seen subsequently, the seasonal forecast model uses all the demand history to initialize the forecasts.

Discount Forecasts

When using the discount forecast model, all the history demands are utilized in a way where higher weights are assigned to the more current demands. The discounting parameter is denoted as β (beta). For the horizontal forecast model, the typical value of β is 0.90. For convenience, let β_H designate the discount parameter in use by the horizontal model, and so, the counterpart value for the trend model is $\beta_T = \beta_H{}^{0.5}$. Thereby, when $\beta_H = 0.9$, $\beta_T = .949$. Table 2.1 pertains to three candidate values of β (0.95, 0.90, 0.80), and for each parameter value, the table lists the assigned weights (w) by age of data. Note, the age of zero is associated with the most current demand.

Table 2.1: Discount Weights

Age	0.95 Weight	0.90 Weight	0.80 Weight
0	1.000	1.000	1.000
1	.950	.900	.800
2	.902	.810	.640
3	.857	.729	.512
4	.815	.656	.410
5	.774	.590	.328
6	.735	.531	.262
7	.698	.478	.210
8	.663	.430	.168
9	.630	.387	.134
10	.599	.349	.107
11	.569	.314	.086
12	.540	.282	.069
13	.513	.254	.055
14	.488	.229	.044

15	.463	.206	.035
16	.440	.185	.028
17	.418	.167	.023
18	.397	.150	.018
19	.377	.135	.014
20	.358	.122	.012
21	.341	.109	.009
22	.324	.098	.007
23	.307	.089	.006
24	.292	.080	.005

Note: β = smooth weight (0.95, 0.90, 0.80)
t = age of data (t = 0, 1, 2, ...)
$w_t = \beta^t$ = weight at age t

Horizontal Forecasts with Discounting

The example below demonstrates the horizontal forecast model when discounting is applied. In the example, the number months of history (nmh) is 12 months, and the discount parameter is $\beta = 0.90$. The method to generate the forecast is listed below in Figure 2.2. The example includes a plot of the demand history, the fit, and the forecasts. The history months are labeled as t = 1 to 12. When generating the forecast, the time scale uses $\tau = 0$ as the most current history month, and projects the future months as $\tau = 1, 2, ...$

The level is defined as the average value of the fitted relation for the most current time period. In this situation, the level is denoted as 'a' and is computed as below:

$$a = \Sigma x_t w_t / \Sigma w_t = 102.29/7.17 = 14.3 \text{ (level)}$$

For the horizontal forecast model, the level is used as the forecast for each of the future months. Thereby, the τ month ahead forecast becomes

$$f(\tau) = a = 14.3 \quad \tau = 1, 2, 3, \ldots$$

To measure the coefficient of variation, cov, the following three steps are applied. First, the variance (s^2) of the forecast error is computed by

$$s^2 = \Sigma(e_t^2 w_t)/\Sigma w_t$$

t	x	w	xw	f	* = x o = f
1	19	0.31	5.96	14.3	o *
2	15	0.35	5.23	14.3	o*
3	9	0.39	3.49	14.3	* o
4	14	0.43	6.03	14.3	*o
5	18	0.48	8.61	14.3	o *
6	14	0.53	7.44	14.3	*o
7	10	0.59	5.90	14.3	* o
8	17	0.66	11.15	14.3	o *
9	9	0.73	6.56	14.3	* o
10	11	0.81	8.91	14.3	* o
11	20	0.90	18.00	14.3	o *
12	15	1.00	15.00	14.3	o*
τ					
1				14.3	o
2				14.3	o
3				14.3	o
4				14.3	o
5				14.3	o
6				14.3	o
7				14.3	o
8				14.3	o
9				14.3	o
10				14.3	o
11				14.3	o
12				14.3	o
sum	171	7.17	102.29	171.1	cov = 0.26
	Σx	Σw	Σxw		

Figure 2.2: Horizontal Forecasts with Discounting

where $e_t = (x_t - a)$ is the residual error for history months, t = 1 to 12. Second, the square root of the variance is the standard error (s). Third, the coefficient of variation, cov, is obtained by

$$\text{cov} = s/a$$

where s is the standard error and a is the level. In the example, cov = 0.26.

Rounding the Forecast

It is common to convert the monthly forecasts to integers by rounding in a cumulative way. The fractional plus or minus portion of a forecast that is raised or lowered in the current month is carried on to the next month, and so forth. In the example above, the integer forecasts for the coming eight months, say, would be: 14, 15, 14, 14, 15, 14, 14 and 15.

Trend Forecasts with Discounting

The example below demonstrates the trend forecast model when discounting is applied. The number months of history (nmh) is 12, and the discount parameter is $\beta = 0.90$. The method to generate the forecasts is listed below. The example also shows a plot of the demand history as well as the fit and the forecasts. The history months are labeled as t = 1 to 12. The trend (b) and intercept at t = 0, a(0), are computed as below:

$$b = [\Sigma xw\Sigma tw - \Sigma xtw\Sigma w]/[(\Sigma tw)^2 - \Sigma w\Sigma t^2w] = 0.5$$

$$a(0) = [\Sigma xw - b\Sigma tw]/\Sigma w = 15.5$$

For simplicity, the level and trend (slope) coefficients above are listed in one decimal rounded values. Recall, the level is the fitted value of the most recent history month and, at t = 12, it is obtained by a(12) = a(0) + 12b, whereby, in the example, a(12) = 21.7. For convenience, the level is now denoted as *a*, i.e., *a* = a(12). The t month ahead forecast equation now becomes:

$$f(\tau) = a + b\tau = 21.7 + 0.5\tau \qquad \tau = 1, 2, 3, \ldots$$

The cov is computed in the same way as shown above for the horizontal forecast model. The forecast relation is reversed to give the fitted values over the history months (t = 1 to 12), and the fitted values are compared to the history demands to compute the monthly residual errors. The monthly errors are weighed by the corresponding monthly discount weights to generate the standard deviation of forecast error. In this example, cov = 0.10.

$\beta = w = 0.90$

t	x	w	x*w	t*w	x*t*w	t*t*w	f	
1	15	0.31	4.71	0.31	4.71	0.31	16.0	
2	18	0.35	6.28	0.70	12.55	1.39	16.5	
3	13	0.39	5.04	1.16	15.11	3.49	17.1	
4	19	0.43	8.18	1.72	32.72	6.89	17.6	
5	20	0.48	9.57	2.39	47.83	11.96	18.1	
6	16	0.53	8.50	3.19	51.02	19.13	18.6	
7	21	0.59	12.40	4.13	86.80	28.93	19.1	
8	22	0.66	14.43	5.25	115.47	41.99	19.6	
9	20	0.73	14.58	6.56	131.22	59.05	20.1	
10	18	0.81	14.58	8.10	145.80	81.00	20.7	
11	24	0.90	21.60	9.90	237.60	108.90	21.2	
12	20	1.00	20.00	12.00	240.00	144.00	21.7	
τ								
1							22.2	
2							22.7	
3							23.2	
4							23.7	
5							24.3	
6							24.8	
7							25.3	
8							25.8	
9							26.3	
10							26.8	
11							27.3	
12							27.9	
sum	226	7.18	139.86	55.42	1120.83	507.05	226.3	cov = 0.10
	Σx	Σw	Σxw	Σtw	Σxtw	Σt^2w		

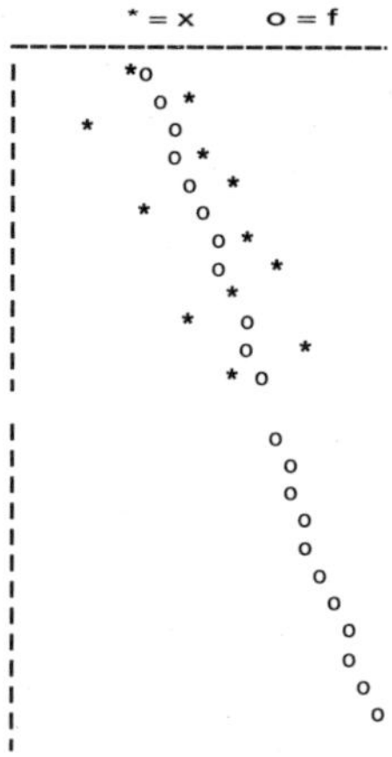

Figure 2.3: Trend Forecasts with Discounting

Discounting and the Standard Error

In forecasting by way of discounting, the symbol t sometimes represents the history months and sometimes the future months. Below is a short review on this matter.

To generate the forecasts, t represents the history months. In discounting, the forecasts are generated using the prior T history months of demand, x(t) for t = 1 to T, where x(T) is the most current demand. Discount weights, $w(t) = \beta^{T-t}$ for t = 1 to T, are applied to give higher weights to each more current demand. Recall β is the discount parameter.

In projecting the forecasts, t now represents the future months. The forecast models described above are the horizontal model where f(t) = a for future months $t \geq 1$. For the trend model, where a = the level, the forecast for the future months are f(t) = (a + bt) for $t \geq 1$.

To compute the standard error, t now designates the history months. To obtain a measure of the standard error of the one month ahead forecast error, σ, the forecasts are reversed to compute the fitted values of the past demands. For the horizontal model, the fit becomes x(t)′ = a for t = 1 to T; and for the trend model, (with a = level), it is x(t)′ = a – b(T – t) for t = 1 to T. So now, the residual errors for the history demands are measured by e(t) = [x(t)′ – x(t)] for t = 1 to T. Finally, the (weighted) variance of the forecast errors is $\sigma^2 = \Sigma[w(t)e(t)^2]/\Sigma w(t)$ for t = 1 to T. The standard error becomes $\sigma = \sqrt{\sigma^2}$. Note, here, t = 1 to T are history months.

Current Demand

Consider an office furniture store that maintains a database on the items they sell. They have a PC system with a database that holds one record on each item in the store. The only demand history they save is the demand from the most recent month of activity. At the beginning of each month, with the new entry of prior month demand, the inventory routine generates a revised forecast for each item in the store. The forecasts are based on smoothing, and the demand patterns are of the horizontal and trend type.

Smoothing Forecasts

Smoothing is used in forecasting when each new forecast is based on blending the most current demand entry with the prior forecast. As in discounting, more weight is assigned to the more current demands. A smoothing parameter α (alpha) is selected as a parameter. Typically for the horizontal forecast model, α = 0.10. For comparison sake, the table below lists three candidate values of α(0.05, 0.10, 0.20), and shows how much weight, and cumulative weight, is assigned to each month in the demand history by age of data. Note age = 0 is the most current month.

Table 2.2: Smoothing Weights

	Smooth Weights					
	0.05		0.10		0.20	
Age	Weight	Cum	Weight	Cum	Weight	Cum
0	.050	.050	.100	.100	.200	.200
1	.047	.097	.090	.190	.160	.360
2	.045	.143	.081	.271	.128	.488
3	.043	.185	.073	.344	.102	.590
4	.041	.226	.066	.410	.082	.672
5	.039	.265	.059	.469	.066	.738
6	.037	.302	.053	.522	.052	.790
7	.035	.337	.048	.570	.042	.832
8	.033	.370	.043	.613	.034	.866
9	.032	.401	.039	.651	.027	.893
10	.030	.431	.035	.686	.021	.914
11	.028	.460	.031	.718	.017	.931
12	.027	.487	.028	.746	.014	.945
13	.026	.512	.025	.771	.011	.956
14	.024	.537	.023	.794	.009	.965
15	.023	.560	.021	.815	.007	.972
16	.022	.582	.019	.833	.006	.977
17	.021	.603	.017	.850	.005	.982
18	.020	.623	.015	.865	.004	.986
19	.019	.642	.014	.878	.003	.988
20	.018	.659	.012	.891	.002	.991
21	.017	.676	.011	.902	.002	.993
22	.016	.693	.010	.911	.001	.994
23	.015	.708	.009	.920	.001	.995
24	.015	.723	.008	.928	.001	.996

Note: α = smooth weight (0.05, 0.10, 0.20)
t = age of data (t = 0, 1, 2, ...)
$w_t = \alpha(1 - \alpha)^t$ = weight at age t

Horizontal Forecasts with Smoothing

To apply smoothing for a horizontal forecast, consider the time periods, typically monthly, where the current time period is t, and the prior time period is (t – 1). The data to generate the forecasts are the following:

α = smoothing parameter

a(t – 1) = level from the prior time period

x(t) = demand from the current time period

The new level is computed as below,

$$a(t) = \alpha x(t) + (1 - \alpha)\ a(t - 1)$$

Since the forecast is based on the horizontal pattern, the forecast for each of the future time periods τ become,

$$f(\tau) = a(t) \qquad \tau = 1, 2, 3, \ldots$$

To illustrate, suppose $\alpha = 0.10$, $a(t - 1) = 10.0$, and $x(t) = 12$. The revised level is obtained by,

$$a(t) = 0.1 \times 12 + 0.9 \times 10.0 = 10.2$$

and so, the revised forecasts are,

$$f(\tau) = 10.2 \qquad \text{for } \tau = 1, 2, 3, \ldots$$

Trend Forecasts with Smoothing

To apply smoothing for a trend forecast, consider again the prior times where the current time period is denoted as t, and the prior time period is (t – 1). The data to generate the forecasts are the following:

α = smoothing parameter for the level

β = smoothing parameter for the trend

a(t – 1) = level from the prior time period

b(t – 1) = trend from the prior time period

x(t) = demand from the current time period

The revised value of the level and trend are computed as follows:

$$a(t) = \alpha x(t) + (1 - \alpha)\ (a(t - 1) + b(t - 1))$$

$$b(t) = \beta(a(t) - a(t - 1)) + (1 - \beta)\ b(t - 1)$$

Since the forecast follows a trend pattern, the forecast for future time period τ becomes,

$$f(\tau) = a(t) + b(t)\tau \qquad \text{for } \tau = 1, 2, 3, \ldots$$

To illustrate, suppose $\alpha = 0.10$, $\beta = 0.10$, $a(t - 1) = 10.0$, $b(t - 1) = 2.0$ and $x(t) = 15$. The revised level and trend are obtained as below,

$$a(t) = 0.1 \times 15.0 + 0.9(10.0 + 2.0) = 12.30$$

$$b(t) = 0.1(12.30 - 10.00) + 0.9 \times 2.0 = 2.03$$

and so, the revised forecasts are

$$f(\tau) = 12.30 + 2.03\tau \qquad \text{for } \tau = 1, 2, 3, \ldots$$

Seasonal Forecasts with Smoothing

The example below demonstrates the seasonal forecast model applied against a 12 month seasonal cycle. The model requires two stages, one to initialize the forecasts at the outset, and another to revise the forecasts as each new monthly demand is known. The model becomes $f(\tau) = [a(t) + b(t)\tau]r(t + \tau)$. Here, $a(t)$ = the level, and represents the seasonally adjusted average at time t, and $b(t)$ is the slope as of time t. In this situation, t is the most current time period and the future time periods are denoted as $t + \tau$. The model has 12 seasonal ratios $[r(t + 1), \ldots, r(t + 12)]$, representing the seasonality ratio for each of the future 12 months, and the seasonal ratios have an average near 1.00. The seasonally adjusted average for future month τ is $[a(t) + b(t)\,\tau]$. When $r > 1.00$ for future month τ, the month demand is projected to be above the seasonally adjusted average. When $r < 1$ for a month, the demand is projected below the seasonally adjusted average. The model uses three smoothing parameters, α to smooth the level, β for the slope, and γ is for the seasonal ratios. The example is based on ($\alpha = 0.10$, $\beta = 0.20$, $\gamma = 0.30$).

In this example, 24 months of demand history are used in the initial stage. In the initial stage, at month 24, the following 14 coefficients are estimated: $a(24)$, $b(24)$, $r(24 + 1), \ldots, r(24 + 12)$. Figure 2.4 demonstrates how the initial forecasts are generated. The history months are labeled as $t = 1$ to 24.

When generating the forecast, the time scale uses $\tau = 0$ as the most current history month, and projects the future months as $\tau = 1, 2, \ldots$ In the example, the forecast model as of $t = 24$ becomes $f(\tau) = (41.71 + 0.29\tau)r(24 + \tau)$ for $\tau = 1, \ldots, 12$. The 12 seasonal ratios are listed in the figure below. The example lists and depicts the demand history, the fit and the forecasts for the 12 future months. The fitted values are compared to the history demands to yield residual errors. In this example, cov = 0.16.

The following are the steps to initialize the forecasts. The example has 24 months of demand history ($x(t)$ $t = 1$ to 24).

X1 = average of $x(1)$ to $x(12)$, and X2 = average of $x(13)$ to $x(24)$

$b'(0) = (X2 - X1)/12 = 0.21$

$a'(0) = X1 - 6.5b'(0) = 36.73$

$a'(t) = a'(0) + b'(0)t \qquad t = 1 \text{ to } 24$

$r'(t) = x(t)/a'(t) \qquad t = 1 \text{ to } 24$

$r(t) = [r'(t) + r'(t + 12)]/2 \qquad t = 1 \text{ to } 12$

Do the following for $t = 1$ to 24:

$a(t) = \alpha[x(t)/r(t)] + (1 - \alpha)[a(t - 1) + b(t - 1)]$

$b(t) = \beta[a(t) - a(t - 1)] + (1 - \beta)b(t - 1)$

$r(t + 12) = \gamma[x(t)/a(t)] + (1 - \gamma)r(t)$

The initial forecasts are now completed. At $t = 24$, the forecasts for τ months ahead are:

$$f(\tau) = [a(24) + b(24)\tau]r(24 + \tau) \qquad \tau = 1, 2, 3, \ldots$$
$$= [41.71 + 0.29\tau]r(24 + \tau)$$

Note, the forecast for the first future month becomes: $f(1) = (41.71 + 0.29 \times 1)\ 0.58 = 24.36$.

alpha	beta	gamma
0.10	0.20	0.30

t	x(t)	a′(t)	r′(t)	r(t)	a(t)	b(t)	r(t+12)	f(t)	* = x o = f
0		36.73			36.73	0.21			
1	19	36.94	0.51	0.57	36.55	0.13	0.56	21.0	*o
2	29	37.15	0.78	0.67	37.36	0.27	0.70	24.9	o *
3	33	37.35	0.88	0.81	37.96	0.33	0.82	30.6	o*
4	44	37.56	1.17	1.20	38.14	0.30	1.18	45.7	*o
5	53	37.77	1.40	1.42	38.32	0.28	1.41	54.5	*o
6	48	37.98	1.26	1.45	38.06	0.17	1.39	55.1	* o
7	55	38.19	1.44	1.33	38.53	0.23	1.36	51.4	o *
8	42	38.40	1.09	1.19	38.40	0.16	1.16	45.9	* o
9	39	38.60	1.01	1.00	38.58	0.16	1.01	38.7	o *
10	41	38.81	1.06	0.94	39.24	0.26	0.97	36.9	o*
11	35	39.02	0.90	0.80	39.94	0.35	0.82	31.9	o *
12	19	23	0.48	0.61	39.35	0.16	0.57	24.1	* o
Ave = x1 = 38.1									
13	25	39.44	0.63		40.05	0.27	0.58	22.3	o*
14	22	39.65	0.55		39.42	0.09	0.66	27.6	* o
15	29	39.85	0.73		39.08	0.00	0.80	32.2	* o
16	49	40.06	1.22		39.31	0.05	1.20	46.6	o *
17	58	40.27	1.44		39.54	0.08	1.43	55.8	o*
18	66	40.48	1.63		40.40	0.24	1.46	56.2	o *
19	50	40.69	1.23		40.25	0.16	1.33	54.8	* o
20	53	40.90	1.30		40.92	0.26	1.20	47.7	o *
21	41	41.10	1.00		41.14	0.26	1.00	41.4	*
22	34	41.31	0.82		40.76	0.13	0.93	39.6	* o
23	29	41.52	0.70		40.33	0.02	0.79	33.1	* o
24	31	41.73	0.74		41.71	0.29	0.63	24.0	o *
Ave = x2 = 40.6									
1								24.4	o
2								27.8	o
3								34.1	o
4								51.6	o
5								61.6	o
6								63.6	o
7								58.0	o
8								53.0	o
9								44.4	o
10								41.5	o
11								35.5	o
12								28.2	o

Figure 2.4: Trend Season Initial Forecasts

Revised Forecasts

As each time period passes, a new demand x(t) becomes available, and the three forecast coefficients from the prior time period [a(t – 1), b(t – 1), r(t)] are revised in the following way:

$$a(t) = \alpha[x(t)/r(t)] + (1 - \alpha)[a(t - 1)+b(t - 1)]$$

$$b(t) = \beta[a(t) - a(t - 1)] + (1 - \beta)b(t - 1)$$

$$r(t + 12) = \gamma[x(t)/a(t)] + (1 - \gamma)r(t)$$

With the revised coefficients, the forecasts for the future time periods become,

$$f(\tau) = [a(t) + b(t)\tau]r(t + \tau) \qquad \tau = 1, 2, 3, \ldots$$

Smoothing the Standard Error

In smoothing, the forecasts are generated using the most current demand, x(t) and also the forecast coefficients from the past month. The coefficient for the horizontal model is a(t – 1) = level. For the trend model, the coefficients are: [a(t – 1) = level and b(t – 1) = slope]; and for the seasonal model, they are: [a(t – 1) = level, b(t – 1) = slope and r(j) = seasonal ratio for j = t to t + 11]. To measure the current standard error, $\sigma(t)$, the standard error from the prior month, $\sigma(t - 1)$, is needed in the computations. At the beginning of a month, when the just prior demand x(t) becomes known, the measure of the current forecast error is measured by using the forecast coefficients from the prior month. The one month ahead forecast for the horizontal model is f(1) = a(t – 1). The one month ahead forecast for the trend model is f(1) = [a(t – 1) + b(t – 1)]; and the corresponding one month ahead forecast for the seasonal model is [a(t – 1) + b(t – 1)]r(t). The associated one-month ahead forecast error becomes e(t) = [x(t) – f(1)]. So now, the variance of the one-month-ahead forecast error is updated in the following way: $\sigma(t)^2 = \alpha e(t)^2 + (1 - \alpha)\sigma(t - 1)^2$ where α is the smoothing coefficient used in the forecast model to update the level, a(t). Finally, the revised measure of the standard error becomes:

$$\sigma(t) = \sqrt{\sigma(t)^2}\ .$$

Outliers

Prior to generating a forecast on an item, it is good practice to search the demand history and filter out any outlier demands. A way to do this for the horizontal demands is described here. The first step finds the history demand with the maximum value, denoted as x_m. The second step collects all remaining demands, excluding x_m, and from these, compute the average ($\bar{x}_m$) and standard deviation (s_m). The third step measures $k = (x_m - \bar{x}_m)/s_m$. If $|k| > 3$, say, the demand x_m is called an outlier and is replaced with $\bar{x}_m$, prior to forecasting. In most outlier situations, $k > 0$.

A difficulty occurs since the above method applies well for demand patterns that are horizontal, but not for those that have trend or seasonal demand patterns. To overcome, the above test can be run using the residual errors instead of the past demands. Recall, the residual error for a history month is the difference between the demand and the fit (from the forecast relation for the history months). The residual errors from all demand patterns tend as horizontal with an average of zero, and thereby can be used to seek out any outlier demand. The month associated with the maximum absolute error is noted, and is checked as an outlier, and if so, the corresponding demand entry is modified to the average of its two closest neighbors.

Cov and Safety Stock

As stated earlier, a useful way to measure the accuracy of the forecast for a part is the coefficient of variation (cov). This measure is obtained by the ratio of the standard deviation σ of the one-month-ahead forecast error over the average one month forecast μ, i.e., cov = σ/μ. The cov can be measured for each part in a stocking location. The lower the cov, the better. Chapter 4 (Safety Stock) demonstrates that a 10% drop in the cov will, in general, result in a 15% decrease in the safety stock. In many locations, safety stock is almost half of the total inventory, and management is always seeking ways to reduce the inventory investment. So it is very important to obtain forecasts that yield the lowest possible cov's. Below are some examples on the sensitivity of the cov.

Sensitivity

The following sections demonstrate various sensitivities of the forecast accuracy. The sensitivity is measured by the cov and how it is affected by each of the following: the number of months of history, the forecast model selected, and the smoothing parameters. Sensitivity is also shown when outlier demands are included in the demand history.

Horizontal Model with Months of History

As the number of months of demand history (nmh) increases for a part, the forecasts become more accurate. To illustrate, the table below lists 36 months of simulated demands for a horizontal demand pattern generated from demands having a cov = 0.30. The horizontal smoothing forecast model using α = 0.10 is applied beginning when t = 1 (nmh = 1). Using this forecast against the demands for the future 12 months (t = 2 to 13), the cov of the forecast errors is computed. At t = 1, cov = 0.71. At t = 2 where two months of history are used in the forecast, the cov improves to 0.60. The smoothing model continues for 24 months and the cov is computed in the same way. Note how the cov decreases an nmh increases. When t = 24, (i.e., nmh = 24), the cov is 0.32.

Table 2.3: Sensitivity on Number Months History for the Horizontal Forecast Model

t	d	nmh	a	cov
1	15	1	15.0	0.71
2	5	2	14.0	0.60
3	10	3	13.6	0.55
4	10	4	13.2	0.50
5	9	5	12.8	0.45
6	12	6	12.7	0.46
7	10	7	12.5	0.56
8	10	8	12.2	0.55
9	7	9	11.7	0.45

10	8	10	11.3	0.43
11	7	11	10.9	0.38
12	9	12	10.7	0.36
13	13	13	10.9	0.38
14	5	14	10.3	0.31
15	11	15	10.4	0.31
16	11	16	10.5	0.32
17	10	17	10.4	0.34
18	10	18	10.4	0.36
19	3	19	9.6	0.27
20	9	20	9.6	0.28
21	14	21	10.0	0.31
22	7	22	9.7	0.28
23	9	23	9.6	0.28
24	13	24	10.0	0.32
25	10			
26	8			
27	13			
28	9			
29	8			
30	7			
31	14			
32	8			
33	5			
34	10			
35	9			
36	6			

Note: smooth weight α = 0.10
cov = coefficient of variation over next 12 months
nmh = number months of history
a = level t = month d = demand

Trend Model with Months of History

The table below lists 36 months of simulated demands for a trend demand pattern generated from demands having a cov = 0.30. The trend smoothing forecast model using $\alpha = 0.10$ and $\beta = 0.10$ is applied beginning when t = 1 (nmh = 1). Using this forecast against the demands for the future 12 months (t = 2 to 13), the cov of the forecast error is computed. When t = 1, cov = 0.58. The smoothing model continues for 24 months and the cov is computed in the same way. Again note, as nmh increases, cov decreases. When t = 24, (nmh = 24), the cov is 0.12.

Table 2.4: Sensitivity of Number Months History for the Trend Forecast Model

t	d	nmh	a	b	cov
1	7	1	7.0	0.00	0.58
2	5	2	6.8	0.02	0.59
3	13	3	7.4	0.04	0.54
4	9	4	7.6	0.06	0.53
5	17	5	8.6	0.15	0.45
6	7	6	8.6	0.13	0.46
7	15	7	9.3	0.20	0.41
8	15	8	10.1	0.25	0.35
9	14	9	10.7	0.29	0.32
10	12	10	11.1	0.30	0.31
11	13	11	11.5	0.31	0.32
12	17	12	12.4	0.37	0.27
13	19	13	13.4	0.43	0.21
14	12	14	13.6	0.41	0.22
15	19	15	14.5	0.46	0.18
16	17	16	15.2	0.48	0.16
17	22	17	16.3	0.54	0.13
18	17	18	16.9	0.55	0.12
19	20	19	17.7	0.57	0.12
20	17	20	18.1	0.56	0.14
21	19	21	18.7	0.56	0.14
22	20	22	19.3	0.57	0.14
23	25	23	20.4	0.62	0.14

24	18	24	20.7	0.59	0.12
25	19				
26	24				
27	21				
28	21				
29	19				
30	25				
31	27				
32	31				
33	23				
34	24				
35	30				
36	28				

Note: smooth weights (α, β) = 0.10
cov = coefficient of variation over next 12 months
nmh = number months of history
a = level b = slope
t = month d = demand

Horizontal Demands with Smoothing and Forecast Model

Care is needed when choosing the parameters and forecast model to apply on the demand history of a part. This is demonstrated for a part with a horizontal demand pattern. The analysis is based on 100 samples where each sample has 24 months of randomly generated demand history. Each of the 24 monthly demands (per sample) is generated with an average monthly demand that varies with a coefficient of variation, cov = 0.30.

A forecast model is selected and 24 months of forecasts are generated along with the corresponding one month ahead forecast error. The cov of the 24 forecast errors is measured. The average of 100 covs is obtained and listed in Table 2.5.

The table shows three sets of forecasts: one set (of 6) with the horizontal smoothing model, and two sets (of 6) with the trend smoothing model. The horizontal forecasts (fH) are generated with smoothing parameters a = (.05, .10, .20, .30, .40, .50). The trend forecasts (fT) are generated with smoothing parameters, α = (.05, .10, .20, .30, .40, .50) and β = (.1, .2). With each set, the forecast error is computed and the average cov is listed in the table.

Note how cov of the forecast error is best as the smoothing weights are low and the forecast model (horizontal) is consistent with the horizontal demand pattern.

Table 2.5: Average cov of the Forecast Error When Horizontal Demands and the Forecast Models are Horizontal (fH) and Trend (fT)

	cov		
	fH	fT	fT
α		β = .1	β = .2
.05	.297	.300	.299
.10	.305	.311	.311
.20	.315	.311	.329
.30	.318	.329	.344
.40	.325	.328	.364
.50	.345	.355	.401

Trend Demands with Smoothing and Forecast Model

The sensitivity of the smoothing weight and the forecast model is now demonstrated for a part with a trend demand pattern. The analysis is based on 100 samples where each sample has 24 months of randomly generated demand history. Each of the 24 monthly demands (per sample) is generated with an upward trending demand pattern that varies with a coefficient of variation, cov = 0.30.

A forecast model is selected, the 24 months of forecasts are generated, and the corresponding one month ahead forecast errors are measured. The cov of the 24 forecast errors is computed. The average of 100 covs is obtained and listed in Table 2.6.

The table shows three sets of forecasts: six with the horizontal smoothing model, and twelve with the trend smoothing model.

The horizontal forecasts (fH) are generated with smoothing parameters α = (.05, .10, .20, .30, .40, .50). The trend forecasts (fT) are generated with smoothing parameters, α = (.05, .10, .20, .30, .40, .50) and β = (.1, .2). With each set, the forecast error is computed and the average cov is listed in the table.

Note how cov of the forecast error is best as the smoothing weights are low, and the forecast model (trend) is consistent with the trend demand pattern.

Table 2.6: Average cov of the Forecast Error When Trend Demands and the Forecast Models are Horizontal (fH) and Trend (fT)

	cov		
	fH	fT	fT
α		β = .1	β = .2
.05	.367	.306	.309
.10	.334	.314	.306
.20	.326	.318	.328
.30	.319	.337	.337
.40	.342	.341	.379
.50	.348	.357	.401

Seasonal Demands with Smoothing and Forecast Model

The sensitivity of the smoothing weight and the forecast model is now demonstrated for a part with a seasonal demand pattern. The analysis is based on 100 samples where each sample has 24 months of randomly generated demand history. Each of the 24 monthly demands (per sample) is generated with a seasonal demand pattern that varies with a coefficient of variation, cov = 0.30.

A forecast model is selected, the 24 months of forecasts are generated, and the corresponding one month ahead forecast errors are computed. The cov of the 24 forecast errors is measured. The average of 100 covs is obtained and listed in Table 2.7.

The table shows seven sets of forecasts: one set (of 6) with the horizontal smoothing model, two sets (of 6) with the trend smoothing model, and four sets (of 6) with the seasonal smoothing model. The horizontal forecasts (fH) are generated with smoothing parameters α = (.05, .10, .20, .30, .40, .50). The trend forecasts (fT) are generated with smoothing parameters, α = (.05, .10, .20, .30, .40, .50) and β = (.1, .2). The seasonal forecasts (fS) are generated with smoothing parameters, α = (.05, .10, .20, .30, .40, .50), β = (.1, .2) and γ = (.1, .2). With each set, the forecast error is computed and the average cov is listed in the table.

Note how cov of the forecast error is best as the smoothing weights are low and the forecast model (seasonal) is consistent with the seasonal demand pattern.

Table 2.7: Average cov of the Forecast Error When Seasonal Demands and the Forecast Models are Horizontal (fH), Trend (fT) and Seasonal (fS)

α	fH	fT β=.1	fT β=.2	fS β=.1 γ=.1	fS β=.1 γ=.2	fS β=.2 γ=.1	fS β=.2 γ=.2
.05	.443	.404	.407	.306	.316	.307	.312
.10	.429	.419	.423	.314	.317	.315	.329
.20	.424	.435	.441	.318	.325	.320	.333
.30	.423	.442	.457	.337	.338	.347	.357
.40	.409	.428	.448	.341	.351	.347	.360
.50	.400	.418	.438	.357	.366	.369	.383

Horizontal Demands with Outliers

Special care is needed prior to forecasting to detect and correct for outlier demands in the demand history. In the table below, this need is demonstrated for a part with a horizontal demand pattern. The demand history of 24 months is randomly generated using a cov = 0.30, not including the outlier demand. Three sets of demand history are listed. The first has no outlier demand in the history and the next two each has one outlier in the demand history. The three sets are from the horizontal smoothing model with α = 0.10. With each set, the forecast error is computed for the 24 month run and the corresponding cov is obtained. The covs are listed in the table below. As Table 2.8 shows, when the demand history has no outlier demand, the cov is 0.343. In the two examples when the history has one outlier demand, the cov increases significantly to 0.611 and 0.476.

Table 2.8: Cov of the Forecast Error When the Horizontal Smoothing Model is Applied with and without Outlier Demands in the History Months

forecast model:	H	H, O	H, O	H = horizontal
α	.10	.10	.10	O = outlier
cov	.343	.611	.476	

Regional Forecasting

Consider a truck manufacturer with five service part distribution center (DC) locations in the US. Each DC holds close to 100,000 parts. To control the inventory, forecasts are needed on each part by DC, and also for the aggregate of all DCs. The aggregate forecast is used to determine when to buy new stock, and if so, how much for the total DC system. This is a replenish buy from a supplier. The individual DC forecasts are needed to determine how much stock is needed on each part at every location. So, each month, forecasts are generated for the aggregate of every part and for each location.

When a part (product) is stocked in a multiple number of locations, each part-location combination is called a stock-keeping-unit (sku). Forecasts are needed both on a location basis and on an aggregate basis. The aggregate forecast is used to place orders with the supplier for replenishment to the total system. The local forecasts are used to determine how many units to stock by location. In top-down forecasts, the demands for all locations are gathered, and one forecast is generated for the total system. The location forecasts are found by allotting the location percent (of past demands) against the total forecast. In bottom-up forecasts, the demands for each location are used to separately generate each location's forecast, one-by-one. The sum of all location forecasts become the total forecast.

Sometimes a product (like shoes, sweaters, hats) comes in various colors and/or sizes and one forecast is generated for the total product. This forecast is not useful in itself since each size/ color is an sku and stocking decisions are needed on each sku. Of need is the forecast for each sku. To forecast the demands by sku, take the sku percent (from past demands) and allot the total forecast (with the percent) to the individual skus, accordingly. This method is the same as the top-down forecast, but the sku's are colors/sizes and not locations.

Top-Down and Bottom-Up Forecasts

Below is an example of demands for a part stocked in four distribution centers (DC). The history demands for 24 months are listed individually by DC and in total.

Table 2.9: Demand History for the 4 DC Example

	Demand History DC's				
t	1	2	3	4	all
1	1	2	3	4	10
2	2	4	6	8	20
3	2	5	7	10	24
4	2	5	7	10	24
5	2	5	7	10	24
6	3	6	10	13	32
7	4	9	14	18	45
8	3	6	9	12	30
9	2	4	7	9	22
10	2	5	8	11	26
11	1	2	3	4	10
12	1	2	3	5	11
13	1	2	3	5	11
14	0	1	2	3	6
15	3	6	9	13	31
16	3	7	11	14	35

17	5	10	16	21	52
18	6	12	18	24	60
19	5	11	16	22	54
20	4	9	14	19	46
21	4	8	12	16	40
22	3	7	11	15	36
23	2	4	6	8	20
24	2	4	7	9	22

Table 2.10 lists the forecasts for the 12 future months that are generated on a bottom-up basis, and also on a top-down basis. In both situations, the forecasts are generated for each DC and for the total of all DCs. For simplicity, the forecasts are rounded to integers.

Table 2.10: Bottom-Up and Top-Down Forecasts

	Bottom-Up Forecasts					Top-Down Forecasts (integer round)					
	DCs					DCs					
t	1	2	3	4	sum	all	1	2	3	4	sum
1	1	2	3	4	10	9	1	2	3	4	10
2	1	3	4	6	14	14	1	3	4	5	13
3	2	5	7	10	24	25	3	5	8	10	26
4	2	6	8	11	27	27	3	5	8	11	27
5	3	7	10	13	33	32	3	6	10	13	32
6	4	8	12	16	40	39	4	8	12	16	40
7	4	9	14	18	45	45	4	9	13	18	44
8	3	7	10	14	34	33	3	7	10	13	33
9	3	5	8	11	27	27	3	5	8	11	27
10	2	5	8	11	26	27	3	5	8	11	27
11	1	3	4	5	13	13	1	3	4	5	13
12	1	2	4	6	13	14	1	3	4	5	13

Note in the top-down method, the 'sum' is not always the same as 'all' because of integer rounding in the table. The column with 'all' represents the aggregate forecast.

Table 2.11 lists the covs of the fitted residual errors from history demands, by DC, and in total. The errors are from the individual seasonal fitted forecasts for each DC, and from the seasonal fitted forecast for the total of all DCs.

Table 2.11: Cov by Location

Location	Cov
DC 1	0.408
DC 2	0.380
DC 3	0.375
DC 4	0.364
All	0.351

Note in the above table, how the cov decreases as the demand size increases. These results demonstrate a general rule: as the size of the monthly demands increases, the forecasts tend to become more accurate.

Summary

The forecasting methods described in this chapter are based on either discounting or smoothing, thereby giving a higher weight to each more recent demand. Discounting is used when all of the past monthly demands are used together to generate the forecasts. Smoothing is used when the forecasts are revised each month using only the most current monthly demand and the just prior forecast coefficients. Three basic forecast patterns are described, the horizontal, trend and seasonal. The chapter also shows how to forecast when the parts are stocked in two or more locations. This is by the top-down, and bottom-up forecasting methods. The coefficient of variation (cov) is a relative measure of the forecast accuracy. The smaller the cov, the better. The chapter gives various examples showing the sensitivity of the cov with respect to the number months of history, the choice of the smoothing parameters, the choice of the forecast model and the presence of outlier demands.

References

Brown, Robert J., *Smoothing, Forecasting and Prediction of Discrete Time Series*, Prentice Hall, Inc, 1962.

Lady, Wilson, *Business Forecasting*, McGraw Hill Co., 2006.

Lewis, Colin, *Demand Forecasting and Inventory Control*, John Wiley & Sons, Inc, 1997.

Makridakis, S. and S. Wheelwright, *Time-Series Forecasting: Methods and Applications*, John Wiley and Sons, Inc, 1978.

Montgomery, D.C., and L.A. Johnson, *Forecasting and Time Series Analysis*, McGraw Hill Book Company, 1976.

Thomopoulos, Nick T., *Applied Forecasting Methods*, Prentice Hall, Inc, 1980.

3

Order Quantity

In this chapter, the reader will learn how to determine the optimal buy quantity for each part in the inventory. The goal is to find the quantity that yields the minimum order plus hold cost. This is called the economic order quantity and is denoted as the EOQ, and the chapter shows four ways to obtain the EOQ. The first way is more instructional and applies when the buy quantity is limited to sizes of equal monthly requirements, i.e. one month requirements, two months requirements, so forth. The next two ways are used mostly in distribution and retail facilities to control the part inventory. The second way is when the supplier contract specifies one cost per unit for the part and no restrictions on the quantity size. Third is when the supplier offers price breaks on a part, whereby the more you buy, the lower the cost per unit, in increments. Finally, the fourth method, called the least-unit-cost, is more common in plants and is used to find lot build sizes when the part requirements are of the lumpy type over the future weekly time horizon. The reader will also learn how the measure called the stocking rate is computed, and how it is a relative assessment of the cost to order plus hold the part in the inventory. The stocking rate is used with the procurement cost per unit to determine the effective cost per unit on each part.

Introduction

The simple lot size model is used to determine the quantity size to buy for the items in stocking facilities, such as distribution centers, dealers, retailers and stores. The goal is to maintain adequate inventory to fill customer orders as they occur, and also yield quantities that are economic with hold and order costs. Because the model determines the particular quantity that yields the minimum order plus hold costs, the quantity is called the economic order quantity (EOQ).

Order Quantity and Related Measures

This section describes how to determine the buy quantity (Q) on a part that yields the minimum cost to order and hold the part. The method shown restricts the buy quantity to monthly buckets and thereby, the quantity to buy will be selected from one of the 12 cumulative monthly requirements from 1 to 12 months.

The goal is to find Q, the order quantity to buy. In addition to Q, a related measure is also shown here and is called the stocking rate, denoted as *s*. The stocking rate is a measure on the percent of added cost to the part due to the order plus hold cost. The stocking rate allows you to measure the effective cost, c′, for each unit by the relation: $c' = c(1 + s)$, where c is the procurement cost per unit.

To illustrate, suppose a part where the procure cost is $c = \$5.00$, and the stocking rate is $s = 0.142$, so the effective cost per unit becomes: $c' = c(1 + s) = \$5.71$. Thus, the "out-of-pocket" cost to procure one unit of the part is \$5.00, and the additional cost to order and hold the unit in the inventory is \$0.71.

The method to find the best order size and the corresponding stocking rate is described in the example below. The part data needed are the following:

A = annual demand

c = cost per unit

Co = cost per order

h = annual holding rate

The table below serves as a worksheet for this purpose, and a description on each column entry is below. Recall, in this method, the candidate buy quantities will be selected from one of the 12 cumulative requirement quantities.

m = month's supply

f = forecast per month = A/12

Q = m × f = order quantity using m

NR12 = A/Q = number receives per 12 months

cs = Q/2 = average cycle stock

Ko = A/Q × Co = annual order cost using Q

Kh = c × h × Q/2 = annual hold cost using Q

K = Ko + Kh = annual order + hold cost using Q

K/A = average order + hold cost per unit

s = K/(A × c) = stocking rate

c′ = c(1 + s) = effective cost per unit

Example 3.1. Assume the part data below.

A	c	Co	h
120	5.00	20	0.30

In the example, the monthly forecasts are assumed to be horizontal calling for 10 pieces a month. The table lists the computed results for the monthly buy quantities when m = 1 to 12 months.

Table 3.1: Worksheet for Example 3.1

					Annual Cost					
m	f	Q	NR12	cs	Ko	Kh	K	K/A	s	c′
1	10	10	12.0	5.0	240	8	248	2.063	0.412	7.06
2	10	20	6.0	10.0	120	15	135	1.125	0.225	6.13
3	10	30	4.0	15.0	80	23	103	0.854	0.171	5.85
4	10	40	3.0	20.0	60	30	90	0.750	0.150	5.75
5	10	50	2.4	25.0	48	38	86	0.712	0.142	5.71
6	10	60	2.0	30.0	40	45	85	0.708	0.142	5.71
7	10	70	1.7	35.0	34	53	87	0.723	0.145	5.72
8	10	80	1.5	40.0	30	60	90	0.750	0.150	5.75
9	10	90	1.3	45.0	27	68	94	0.785	0.157	5.78
10	10	100	1.2	50.0	24	75	99	0.825	0.165	5.82
11	10	110	1.1	55.0	22	83	104	0.869	0.174	5.87
12	10	120	1.0	60.0	20	90	110	0.917	0.183	5.92

The table shows that the minimum annual cost is K = \$85.00, and this occurs when m = 6 months and Q = 60 pieces. Note further, at Q = 60, the average order plus hold cost per unit is \$0.708, and thereby the stocking rate is s = 0.708/5.00 = 0.142. This indicates, the minimum hold plus order costs is 14.2% of the procurement cost. So the effective cost per unit is c′ = c(1 + s) = 5.00[1 + 0.142] = \$5.71.

Economic Order Quantity (EOQ)

This section shows how to find the economic order quantity, Q, on any part when no special constraints are included. For comparison, the cost relations are also shown when any buy quantity, say Q′, is selected. The part data and notation are the same as before. These are:

A = annual demand
c = cost per unit
Co = cost per order
h = annual holding rate
Q′ = any order quantity
Q = economic order quantity

The following are some relations that show how to compute the annual order plus hold cost. For notation sake, K(Q) will denote the annual order plus holding cost when the economic order quantity Q is in use. Also, K(Q′) will represent the corresponding cost when any other quantity Q′ is in use. If Q′ = Q, then K(Q′) = K(Q). Below shows how to compute the key measures from the part data listed above. Note when the buy quantity is Q′, the annual order cost = ACo/Q′, the annual hold cost = chQ′/2, and this gives K(Q′) as below. Using calculus, the value of Q′ that yields the minimum order plus hold cost, K(Q′), is Q = EOQ as listed below.

12 month order plus hold cost using Q′: $K(Q') = ACo/Q' + chQ'/2$

economic order quantity (EOQ): $Q = \sqrt{2ACo/ch}$

12 month order plus hold cost using Q: $K(Q) = \sqrt{2AchCo}$

minimum stocking rate: $s = K(Q)/(Ac)$

effective cost per unit: $c' = c(1 + s)$

Example 3.2. Part data: A = 500, c = \$5, Co = \$15, and h = .30.

The quantity that yields the minimum order plus hold cost is the EOQ. For this part,

$$EOQ = Q = \sqrt{2 \times 500 \times 15 /(5 \times 0.30)} = 100 \text{ pieces}$$

Using Q = 100, some related measures are:

$$K(100) = \sqrt{2 \times 500 \times 15 \times 5 \times 0.30} = \$150.00,$$

$$s = 150/(500 \times 5) = 0.06,$$

$$c' = 5(1 + 0.06) = \$5.30.$$

If Q′ = 50 is selected as the buy quantity, K(50) = 500 × 15/50 + 5 × 0.3 × 50/2 = \$187.50. Note when the order size is 50 pieces, instead of the 100 pieces, the annual order plus holding cost rises from \$150.00 to \$187.50.

Sensitivity

Below are some sensitivity relations concerning the economic order quantity (EOQ), and also a list of the data associated with generating the EOQ. The data are the following: annual demand, cost per order, cost per unit, holding rate and the order quantity.

Annual Demand and EOQ

As shown above, the EOQ for a part is computed using the part data: (A, c, Co, h), and this quantity is denoted as Q. Now assume all the data remain the same except A changes to A′. When the annual demand changes from A to A′, the economic order quantity goes from Q to Q′. Using algebra, the mathematical relation between the annual demand and the order quantity becomes $Q'/Q = \sqrt{A'/A}$. This relation is listed in tabular form below for A′/A going from 0.1 to 2.0. Note when A′ = A, A′/A = 1.00 and Q′/Q = 1.00. The notation is as follows:

A = annual demand

Q = economic order quantity using: A, c, Co, h

A′ = another annual demand

Q′ = economic order quantity using: A′, c, Co, h

Table 3.2: Sensitivity of Annual Demand to Order Size

A′/A	Q′/Q	A′/A	Q′/Q
0.1	0.32	1.1	1.05
0.2	0.45	1.2	1.10
0.3	0.55	1.3	1.14
0.4	0.63	1.4	1.18
0.5	0.71	1.5	1.22
0.6	0.77	1.6	1.26
0.7	0.84	1.7	1.30
0.8	0.89	1.8	1.34
0.9	0.95	1.9	1.38
1.0	1.00	2.0	1.41

Note A could represent the annual forecast as well as the annual demand. When the annual forecast goes up by 50 percent, the order quantity increases by 22 percent; when the annual forecast goes down by 50 percent, the order quantity drops 29 percent (Q′/Q = 0.71), and so forth.

Example 3.3. Suppose part ABC has an annual demand of 480 units and the EOQ = 40 units. If the annual demand increases to 520 units, what will be the change in the EOQ, and in the associated inventory? Note, $Q' = Q\sqrt{A'/A}$ = $40\sqrt{520/480} \approx 42$ units, and thereby the inventory will increase 5.0%.

Cost per Order and EOQ

When the part data are (A, c, Co, h), the economic order quantity is Q. When all the part data are the same, but the cost per order changes from Co to Co′, then the economic order quantity changes to Q′. The relation between the cost per order and the order quantity is $Q'/Q = \sqrt{Co'/Co}$. This relation is listed below in tabular form for Co′/Co going from 0.1 to 2.0. The notation follows:

Co = cost per order

Q = economic order quantity using: Co, A, c, h

Co′ = another cost per order

Q′ = economic order quantity using: Co′, A, c, h

Table 3.3: Sensitivity of Cost per Order to Order Size

Co′/Co	Q′/Q	Co′/Co	Q′/Q
0.1	0.32	1.1	1.05
0.2	0.45	1.2	1.10
0.3	0.55	1.3	1.14
0.4	0.63	1.4	1.18
0.5	0.71	1.5	1.22
0.6	0.77	1.6	1.26
0.7	0.84	1.7	1.30
0.8	0.89	1.8	1.34
0.9	0.95	1.9	1.38
1.0	1.00	2.0	1.41

Notice when the cost per order goes up by 50 percent, the order quantity increases by 22 percent; when the cost per order goes down by 50 percent, the order quantity drops 29 percent (Q′/Q = 0.71), and so forth.

Example 3.4. Suppose part AAA has a cost per order of Co = \$20 and the EOQ is Q pieces. Assume a new system is in place and Co drops to \$5. What affect does this have on the average inventory for the part? Since $Q' = Q\sqrt{Co' / Co}$ = $Q\sqrt{5 / 20} = .50Q$, the average inventory will decrease by 50 percent. Note also, because the order size will be cut in half, the number of orders over a given time period will double.

Cost per Unit and EOQ

Consider again the part data (A, c, Co, h) and the associated economic order quantity Q. When the cost per unit changes from c to c′, and the remainder of the part data stays the same, the economic order quantity changes from Q to Q′. The mathematical relation between the cost per unit and the order quantity becomes $Q'/Q = \sqrt{c/c'}$. This relation is listed below in tabular form for c'/c going from 0.1 to 2.0. The notation is below:

c = cost per unit

Q = economic order quantity using: c, A, Co, h

c' = another cost per unit

Q' = economic order quantity using: c', A, Co, h

Table 3.4: Sensitivity of Cost per Unit to Order Cost

c'/c	Q'/Q	c'/c	Q'/Q
0.1	3.16	1.1	0.95
0.2	2.24	1.2	0.91
0.3	1.83	1.3	0.88
0.4	1.58	1.4	0.85
0.5	1.41	1.5	0.82
0.6	1.29	1.6	0.79
0.7	1.20	1.7	0.77
0.8	1.12	1.8	0.75
0.9	1.05	1.9	0.73
1.0	1.00	2.0	0.71

Notice when the cost per unit goes up by 50 percent, the order quantity decreases by 18 percent, (Q'/Q = 0.82); when the cost per unit goes down by 50 percent, the order quantity increases by 41 percent, and so forth.

Example 3.5. A firm buys several items from a supplier who announces a five percent increase in the price of its products. What affect will this have on the corresponding inventory at the firm? Since $Q' = Q\sqrt{c / c'} = Q\sqrt{1.00 / 1.05} = 0.975Q$, the ordered size and the number of pieces in the inventory will drop by 2.5 percent. But the dollar value of the inventory will increase by (1.05 × 0.975) = 1.025, or by 2.5 percent.

Holding Rate and EOQ

When the part data are (A, c, Co, h), the economic order quantity is Q. When the annual holding rate changes from h to h′, and all the other part data stays the same, the economic order quantity changes from Q to Q′. The mathematical relation between the annual holding rate and the order quantity is $Q'/Q = \sqrt{h/h'}$. This relation is listed in tabular form below for h′/h going from 0.1 to 2.0. The notation is below:

h = annual holding rate

Q = economic order quantity using: h, A, c, Co

h′ = another annual holding rate

Q′ = economic order quantity using: h′, A, c, Co

Table 3.5: Sensitivity of Holding Rate to Order Size

h′/h	Q′/Q	h′/h	Q′/Q
0.1	3.16	1.1	0.95
0.2	2.24	1.2	0.91
0.3	1.83	1.3	0.88
0.4	1.58	1.4	0.85
0.5	1.41	1.5	0.82
0.6	1.29	1.6	0.79
0.7	1.20	1.7	0.77
0.8	1.12	1.8	0.75
0.9	1.05	1.9	0.73
1.0	1.00	2.0	0.71

Note when the holding rate goes up by 50 percent, the order quantity decreases by 18 percent, (Q′/Q = 0.82); when the holding rate goes down by 50 percent, the order quantity increases by 41 percent, and so forth.

Example 3.6. A firm with \$10,000,000 in inventory, uses an annual holding rate of h = 0.20, and wants to lower the inventory to \$9,000,000. What change in the holding rate is needed to accomplish their goal? Since \$10,000,000/\$9,000,000 ≈ 1.11, then we want Q/Q′ = 1.11. Further, because $Q'/Q = \sqrt{h/h'}$, $h' = h(Q/Q')^2 = 0.20(1.11)^2 \approx 0.25$, and thereby the annual holding rate should increase to 0.25.

Order Quantity and Order Plus Hold Cost

When the part data are: (A, c, Co, h), the resulting economic order quantity is Q and the annual hold plus order cost is K, as shown earlier. Now if the order quantity Q′ is used instead of Q, and all the part data are the same as earlier, the annual order plus hold cost changes for K to K′. The mathematical relation between the order quantity and the annual hold plus order cost becomes K′/K = ½(Q/Q′ + Q′/Q). This relation is listed below for Q′/Q going from 0.1 to 2.0. The notation is below:

Q = economic order quantity using: h, A, c, Co
K = annual order + hold cost using Q
K = (Co × A/Q + c × h × Q/2)
Q′ = another order quantity
K′ = annual order + hold cost using Q′
K′ = (Co × A/Q′ + c × h × Q′/2)

Table 3.6: Sensitivity of Order Size to Hold Plus Order Cost

Q′/Q	K′/K	Q′/Q	K′/K
0.1	5.05	1.1	1.00
0.2	2.60	1.2	1.02
0.3	1.82	1.3	1.03
0.4	1.45	1.4	1.06
0.5	1.25	1.5	1.08
0.6	1.13	1.6	1.11
0.7	1.06	1.7	1.14
0.8	1.02	1.8	1.18
0.9	1.01	1.9	1.21
1.0	1.00	2.0	1.25

Note when the order quantity is 50 percent higher than the economic quantity, the annual cost of order plus hold increases by 8 percent; and when the order quantity is 50 percent lower than the economic quantity, the annual cost increases by 25 percent, and so forth.

Example 3.7. A firm currently uses one month buys for all parts, but an analysis shows that several parts should use an EOQ of four months. What is the added cost of hold plus order for these parts? Letting F = the average one month forecast, Q = 4F and Q′ = 1F. Hence, since K′ = K(½) (Q/Q′ + Q′/Q) = K(0.5) (4/1 + 1/4) = 2.125K, the current added cost of hold plus order is 2.125 times larger than the corresponding cost should the EOQ be in use.

Price Breaks

Below shows how to determine the order quantity when the supplier offers price breaks on a part. This is where the unit cost on the part goes down in increments as the buy quantity goes up.

Contract Data. The supplier contract data for the part consists of a finite number of tiers, where each tier i has three entries: [Q(i), c(i), Co(i)]. When the quantity falls in tier i, the buy quantity is Q(i) or larger, the cost per unit is c(i), and the cost per order is Co(i). With each successive tier, the quantity Q(i) increases, and c(i) or Co(i) (or both) decrease.

Part Data. The corresponding part data are the following: A = annual demand and h = annual holding rate.

Computations. The following computations are performed for each tier: Using the data: (A, h, c(i), Co(i)), find the EOQ and label it as Q′. The range of acceptable quantities for tier i is Q(i) to Q(i + 1) – 1. In the computations, the minimum quantity Q′ often falls outside this range. So in computing Q′ for tier i, if Q′ is below the range, set Q = Q(i); and if Q′ is above the range, set Q = Q(i + 1) – 1. At the last tier, Q(i + 1) = infinity.

Now using Q, find the annual order cost, hold cost and procure cost as below:

Ko = A/Q × Co(i) = annual order cost using Q

Kh = c(i) × h × Q/2 = annual hold cost using Q

Kp = c(i) × A = annual procure cost using Q

Now find the annual cost of order plus hold plus procure as below:

K = Ko + Kh + Kp = annual total cost using Q

Finally the tier with the minimum K yields the Q to use as the EOQ.

Example 3.8. The example below has part data of A = 360 and h = 0.30. The supplier contract includes five tiers. The table below shows the computations for each of the five tiers.

Table 3.7: Worksheet for Example 3.3

	Contract terms			Order size		Cost per year					
i	q(i)	c(i)	Co(i)	Q'	Q	Ko	Kh	Kp	K	s	c'
1	5-49	10.00	10.00	48	48	75	72	3600	3747	0.22	10.41
2	50-99	9.50	10.00	50	50	72	71	3420	3563	0.16	9.90
3	100-199	9.00	10.00	51	100	36	135	3240	3411	0.11	9.48
4	200-399	8.50	10.00	53	200	18	255	3060	3333*	0.09	9.26
5	400-	8.00	10.00	54	400	9	480	2880	3369	0.10	9.36

Note: * = optimal

The results show that tier 4 has the minimum annual total cost with K = 3333. Thereby, the economic order quantity is Q = 200, and the cost per unit is $8.50.

Note, the stocking rate, and the effective cost per unit for the part are:

s = stocking rate in tier using Q

s = (K-3060)/3060

c′ = effective cost in tier using Q

The table also shows for the optimal (tier 4), the stocking rate is s = 0.09, and the effective cost per unit is c′ = $9.26.

Least Unit Cost

In production facilities, the quantity to buy is often set in weekly or monthly buckets. The example below shows how to find the economic quantity for a part with monthly quantities. In these situations, the requirements per month are typically not smooth and often are of the lumpy type as in the example. The part data and computations to perform are listed below:

part data:

c = cost/unit
h = holding rate per month
Co = cost/order
oh = on-hand
oo = on-order
ss = safety stock
t = time period
f_t = forecast per t

computations:

r = requirements ($r_t = f_t$ after month 1)
r_1 = $f_1 + ss - (oh + oo)$ (special for month 1)
Q = cumulative requirements
Ko = order cost when $Q = Co$
Kh = hold cost when Q
= $ch[0.5r_1 + 1.5r_2 + \ldots + (t - 0.5)r_t]$
K = $Ko + Kh$ = total cost when Q
K/Q = average cost per unit when Q

In the event the requirements at month 1 is less or equal to zero ($r_1 \leq 0$), set $Q = 0$ and proceed no further, since no buy is needed now. Otherwise, continue as below.

The example data and computations follow. Note, the forecasts for months 1, 2 and 3 are 40, 50 and 60 pieces, respectively; and the corresponding requirements are 38, 50 and 60 pieces. Here, the buy quantity will only be in monthly buckets, so the quantity to buy is associated with cumulative monthly requirements. If the buy is for one month, Q = 38 pieces; if the buy is for a two months quantity, set Q = 38 + 50 = 88 pieces; if three months, then Q = 38 + 50 + 60 = 148, and so forth.

The economic quantity is the quantity with the smallest average cost per unit. In the example, this occurs at month 3 with K/Q = 0.68 and thereby, the economic quantity is Q = 148 pieces.

Table 3.8: Worksheet for Least Unit Cost Example

t	f	r	Q	Ko	Kh	K	K/Q
1	40	38	38	40.00	4.75	44.75	1.18
2	50	50	88	40.00	23.50	63.50	0.72
3	60	60	148	40.00	61.00	101.00	0.68
4	80	80	228	40.00	131.00	171.00	0.75
5	50	50	278	40.00	187.25	227.25	0.82
6	40	40	318	40.00	242.25	282.25	0.89
7	70	70	388	40.00	356.00	396.00	1.02
8	100	100	488	40.00	543.50	583.50	1.20
9	30	30	518	40.00	607.25	647.25	1.25
10	20	20	538	40.00	654.75	694.75	1.29
11	0	0	538	40.00	654.75	694.75	1.29
12	10	10	548	40.00	683.50	723.50	1.32

Note: part = A123   c = 10.00   h = 0.025   Co = 40.00
oh = 17   oo = 0   ss = 15

Summary

This chapter describes how to determine the order size that yields the minimum cost to hold and order the stock, called the economic order quantity (EOQ). A related measure to the order size is called the stocking cost, and this is a measure that gives the added cost per unit to order and hold the inventory. The chapter also shows sensitivity relations between the EOQ and the data used to compute the order quantity, i.e. the forecasts, the holding rate, the cost per unit and the cost per order. The chapter also shows how to compute the EOQ when the supplier offers price breaks for the parts. Another way to determine the order size is called the least unit cost. This latter method finds the best lot size on a part when the future demands are of the lumpy type, and is particularly used in manufacturing facilities.

References

Lipman, Burton, *How to Control and Reduce Inventory*, Prentice Hall, Inc., 1972.

Magee, John F. and D.M. Boodman, *Production Planning and Inventory Control*, McGraw Hill Education, 1982.

Narasimham, Sam and Dennis McLeavey, Peter Billington, *Production Planning and Inventory Control*, Prentice Hall, Inc., 1995.

Thomopoulos, Nick T. *Strategic Inventory Management and Planning*, Hitchcock Publishing Co. Carol Stream, II. 1990.

Wright, O.W. and G.W. Plossl, *Production and Inventory Control*, Prentice Hall, Inc., 1967.

4

Safety Stock

In this chapter, the reader will become acquainted with the standard normal distribution and also the relevant data used in setting the safety stock needs for the parts in the inventory. The four basic safety stock methods are described, and are here called the following: months-supply, availability, service level and Lagrange. The comparison on the safety stock needs from the four methods are shown for an example part. Tables are presented to guide the reader on the data sensitivity in the safety stock with respect to the coefficient-of-variation, the order size, the lead time and the desired service level.

Introduction

For convenience in the following discussion, the inventory on a part is partitioned into two segments: cycle stock and safety stock. The cycle stock is the inventory needed to fill the demands that are consistent with the forecasts. The safety stock is the inventory needed for demands that may fall above the forecast. A good inventory system will seek the minimum amount of safety stock to accomplish the service level goal of the management.

Sometimes, as in production facilities, all of the future demands are known in advance, and no safety stock is needed. However, in retail and service parts facilities, the future demands for the items are not known in advance and the inventory planning is driven by a forecast of the future demands. The stock level for the items depend on the size of the order quantity and the safety stock. The amount of safety stock is derived from various data associated with the item, such as the forecast error, the lead time, the order quantity, and the desired service level.

This chapter describes four typical methods to find the safety stock on a part. Sometimes one method is more appropriate than another, depending on the type of inventory carried, and the data available to calculate the safety stock.

Standard Normal Distribution

The standard normal distribution is the most commonly used probability distribution in materials management as well as in many other scientific developments. The primary use in inventory applications occurs when future demands on an item are not known and a forecast of these demands is generated for inventory decision making. Actual demands are generally assumed to follow a normal distribution with the mean and standard deviation estimated by the forecast of the demands.

In the normal distribution, the variable x is symmetrically shaped with a bell shaped density, and has mean μ and standard deviation σ. A companion distribution—the standard normal distribution—has a mean of zero, a standard deviation of one, and the same shape as the normal distribution. For notation, the variable x is denoted as $N(\mu, \sigma^2)$, and its counterpart, z as $N(0, 1)$. The variable z is the standard normal variable and is related to x by the relation: $z = (x - \mu)/\sigma$. In the same way, x is obtained from z from: $x = \mu + z\sigma$.

If k represents a particular value of z, the probability density at k is $f(k) = 1/\sqrt{2\pi}\exp(-k^2/2)$. The probability that z is less than k is denoted as F(k) and is computed by $\int_{-\infty}^{k} f(z)dz$. The partial expectation is labeled as E(k), sometimes denoted E(z>k), and is computed by $\int_{k}^{\infty}(z - k)f(z)dz = f(k) - k(1 - F(k))$. Table 4.1 lists the key measures of the standard normal distribution sorted by F(k) from 0.01 to 0.99. For each F(k), the corresponding values of k, E(k) and f(k) are listed.

Table 4.1: Measures from the Standard Normal Distribution

F(k)	k	E(k)	f(k)	F(k)	k	E(k)	f(k)
0.010	-2.327	2.330	0.027	0.510	0.025	0.387	0.399
0.020	-2.054	2.061	0.048	0.520	0.050	0.374	0.398
0.030	-1.881	1.893	0.068	0.530	0.075	0.363	0.398
0.040	-1.751	1.767	0.086	0.540	0.100	0.351	0.397
0.050	-1.645	1.666	0.103	0.550	0.125	0.339	0.396
0.060	-1.555	1.581	0.119	0.560	0.151	0.328	0.394
0.070	-1.476	1.507	0.134	0.570	0.176	0.317	0.393
0.080	-1.405	1.442	0.149	0.580	0.202	0.306	0.391
0.090	-1.341	1.383	0.162	0.590	0.227	0.296	0.389
0.100	-1.282	1.329	0.175	0.600	0.253	0.285	0.386
0.110	-1.227	1.280	0.188	0.610	0.279	0.275	0.384
0.120	-1.175	1.234	0.200	0.620	0.305	0.265	0.381
0.130	-1.126	1.192	0.212	0.630	0.331	0.255	0.378
0.140	-1.080	1.152	0.223	0.640	0.358	0.245	0.374
0.150	-1.036	1.114	0.233	0.650	0.385	0.236	0.370
0.160	-0.994	1.079	0.243	0.660	0.412	0.226	0.366
0.170	-0.954	1.045	0.253	0.670	0.439	0.217	0.362
0.180	-0.915	1.013	0.262	0.680	0.467	0.208	0.358
0.190	-0.878	0.982	0.271	0.690	0.495	0.199	0.353
0.200	-0.841	0.953	0.280	0.700	0.524	0.191	0.348
0.210	-0.806	0.925	0.288	0.710	0.553	0.182	0.342
0.220	-0.772	0.898	0.296	0.720	0.582	0.174	0.337
0.230	-0.739	0.872	0.304	0.730	0.612	0.165	0.331
0.240	-0.706	0.848	0.311	0.740	0.643	0.157	0.324
0.250	-0.674	0.823	0.318	0.750	0.674	0.149	0.318
0.260	-0.643	0.800	0.324	0.760	0.706	0.141	0.311
0.270	-0.612	0.778	0.331	0.770	0.739	0.134	0.304
0.280	-0.582	0.756	0.337	0.780	0.772	0.126	0.296
0.290	-0.553	0.735	0.342	0.790	0.806	0.119	0.288
0.300	-0.524	0.715	0.348	0.800	0.841	0.112	0.280
0.310	-0.495	0.695	0.353	0.810	0.878	0.105	0.271
0.320	-0.467	0.675	0.358	0.820	0.915	0.098	0.262
0.330	-0.439	0.657	0.362	0.830	0.954	0.091	0.253

0.340	-0.412	0.638	0.366	0.840	0.994	0.084	0.243
0.350	-0.385	0.621	0.370	0.850	1.036	0.078	0.233
0.360	-0.358	0.603	0.374	0.860	1.080	0.071	0.223
0.370	-0.331	0.586	0.378	0.870	1.126	0.065	0.212
0.380	-0.305	0.570	0.381	0.880	1.175	0.059	0.200
0.390	-0.279	0.554	0.384	0.890	1.227	0.053	0.188
0.400	-0.253	0.538	0.386	0.900	1.282	0.047	0.175
0.410	-0.227	0.523	0.389	0.910	1.341	0.042	0.162
0.420	-0.202	0.508	0.391	0.920	1.405	0.036	0.149
0.430	-0.176	0.493	0.393	0.930	1.476	0.031	0.134
0.440	-0.151	0.479	0.394	0.940	1.555	0.026	0.119
0.450	-0.125	0.465	0.396	0.950	1.645	0.021	0.103
0.460	-0.100	0.451	0.397	0.960	1.751	0.016	0.086
0.470	-0.075	0.438	0.398	0.970	1.881	0.012	0.068
0.480	-0.050	0.424	0.398	0.980	2.054	0.007	0.048
0.490	-0.025	0.412	0.399	0.990	2.327	0.003	0.027
0.500	-0.000	0.399	0.399				

Note in the table, z ~ N(0, 1) and k is a particular value of z, f(k) = probability density when z = k; F(k) = cumulative distribution = probability of z less than k, and E(k) = partial expectation of k.

Four Safety Stock Methods

Safety stock is the extra amount of stock to hold (for a part) in the event the demands exceed the forecast. The typical management in distribution and retail facilities carry the safety stock to ensure the customer demands are filled as they arrive and in a timely matter. The part data needed to determine the amount of safety stock includes the desired service level (a parameter set by the management), and the forecast, standard deviation, lead time, order quantity, and cost per unit. This section describes the four common methods used to set the amount of safety stock on a part. These methods are denoted as: months-supply, availability, service level, and Lagrange. A common confusion in the literature exists, since the service level method described here is sometimes called the percent fill method;

and the availability method described here is sometimes called the service level method.

The notation for the part data are the following:

f(t)	forecast for future month t (t = 1, 2, ...)
σ	standard deviation of one month forecast error
L	lead time in months
Q	ideal order quantity
c	cost per unit
F12	12 month forecast

Safety Stock by Months-Supply

When the months-supply method is chosen, a parameter MS is set by the management to specify the number of future month forecasts to use as the safety stock. For example, if MS = 1.5, the safety stock for the item should be the sum of the forecast for future month 1 and half of the forecast for future month 2.

Parameter:

MS = months-supply (of safety stock)

Data per part:

f(t) = forecast for future month t

Computations by part:

If $MS \le 1$, $ss = MS \times f(1)$

If $MS \le 2$ $ss = f(1) + (MS - 1) \times f(2)$, and so forth

Example 4.1. Suppose a part where the months-supply parameter is set to 1.25 months, and also the forecasts for the coming months are 10 pieces per month. The safety stock for this part becomes: $ss = 1 \times f(1) + 0.25 \times f(2) = 1 \times 10 + 0.25 \times 10 = 12.5$.

Safety Stock by Availability

Availability is a common way to set the safety stock. The management states a parameter AV that specifies the probability that the future demand will not exceed the on-hand inventory over the order cycle duration. Recall an order cycle is the time span between two successive arrivals of new stock for a part. To carry out this method, the following parameter and part data are needed:

Parameter: AV = availability = probability the demand does not exceed the on-hand inventory over an order cycle. This is sometimes called the 'service level'.

Data per part:

L = lead time (months)

σ = standard deviation of one month forecast error

f(t) = forecast for future month t

To find the safety stock needed, the computations on each part are listed below:

Computations: The four steps below show how to find the safety stock with this method.

1. Set F(k) = AV.
2. From Table 4.1, locate F(k), and find the corresponding k, where k = safety factor.
3. Compute, FL and σ_L, where,

   FL = sum forecasts for lead time duration, and

   $\sigma_L = \sqrt{L}\sigma$ = standard error for the lead time forecast.
4. Now, ss = k × σ_L = safety stock.

Application: To apply this method, the following data is also needed on each part:

Q = desired order size (usually the EOQ), and

oh + oo = current on-hand plus on-order inventory.

The order point (op) and the order level (ol) for the part are computed in the following way:

op = FL + ss = order point, and

ol = op + Q = order level.

In the event, (oh + oo) ≤ op, a replenish buy of size q is called to bring the (oh + oo) back up to the order level. Thus, the buy quantity becomes: q = ol – (oh + oo).

Rational: Note, the quantity q will not be available to fill demands until a lead time (L) after it is ordered. The lead time demand is not known in advance and is here denoted as DL. DL is assumed to be normally distributed with a mean of FL, and standard deviation σ_L. Thereby, the order point ensures the probability, $p(DL \le op) = F(k)$ where $F(k) = AV$. For the lead time duration, this is the probability specified by the management as the availability.

Example 4.2. Assume a part where the availability parameter is set to AV = 0.95, the lead time is L = 2 months, and the standard deviation of the one month forecast error is $\sigma = 3.0$. The standard error for the lead time forecast is $\sigma_L = \sqrt{L}\sigma = \sqrt{2} \times 3 = 4.24$. With AV = 0.95, Table 4.1 is searched at F(k) = AV = 0.95 to find the associated safety factor, k = 1.645. So now the safety stock becomes: $ss = k \times \sigma_L = 1.645 \times 4.24 = 6.97$.

Safety Stock by Service Level

Service level is also a common way to set the safety stock for parts in distribution centers, dealers and retailers. A parameter SL is specified and represents the desired percent of future demand that is filled by the stock on-hand. To carry out this method, the following parameter and part data are used:

Parameter: SL = service level = ratio of (demand filled)/(total demand). This parameter is sometimes referred as the percent fill.

Data per part:

- L = lead time (months)
- σ = standard deviation of one month forecast error
- f(t) = forecast for future month t
- Q = desired order size (usually the EOQ)

Computations: The computations required on each part are listed below:

Computations by part:

1. Calculate FL and σ_L, where,

   FL = sum forecasts for lead time duration, and

   $\sigma_L = \sqrt{L}\sigma$ = standard error for the lead time forecast.

2. Now compute the partial expectation,
   $E(k) = (1 - SL) \times Q/\sigma_L$
3. From Table 4.1, locate the associated E(k), and the corresponding k, where k = safety factor.
   Set k = max(k, 0), i.e., not negative.
4. Now, $ss = k \times \sigma_L$ = safety stock.

Application: To apply the method, the following data is needed on each part:

oh + oo = current on-hand plus on-order inventory.

With the part data and the computations, the order point (op) and the order level (ol) for the part are computed in the following way:

op = FL + ss = order point

ol = op + Q = order level

In the event, (oh + oo) ≤ op, a replenish buy of size q is called to bring the (oh + oo) back up to the order level. Thus, the buy quantity becomes: q = ol – (oh + oo).

Rational: Note, the order cycle for the part is defined as the time duration between two order receipts of new inventory. The expected demand in the order cycle is Q, the desired order size. Further, when the actual order quantity q is placed, it will be received a lead time (L) duration in the future. The demand over the lead time is DL, and DL is assumed to be normally distributed with a mean FL and standard deviation σ_L. The expected demand beyond the order point is E(demand short in the order cycle) = $E(k)\ \sigma_L$. Thereby, the expected percent demand filled in the order cycle is $SL = [1 - E(k)\ \sigma_L/Q]$. For the order cycle duration, this is the same as the service level parameter specified by the management.

Example 4.3. Assume a part where the service level parameter is set to SL = 0.95, the lead time is L = 2 months, the order quantity is Q = 20 pieces, and the standard deviation of the one month forecast error is σ = 3.0. The standard error for the lead time forecast becomes $\sigma_L = \sqrt{L}\sigma = \sqrt{2} \times 3 = 4.24$. The partial expectation is now computed by the relation: E(k) = (1 – SL) ×

$Q/\sigma_L = (1 - 0.95) \times 20/4.24 = 0.2358$. So now, Table 4.1 is used to find the safety factor k that corresponds with E(k) = 0.2358. The table shows when E(k) = 0.236, k = 0.385. So now the safety stock becomes: $ss = k \times \sigma_L = 0.385 \times 4.24 = 1.63$.

Safety Stock by Lagrange

The Lagrange method is a cost-benefit way to set safety stock over a group of parts. This method is particularly applicable to the parts in distribution centers, dealers and retailers. A Lagrange parameter (LG) is selected for a group of parts. The parts from the group are run and all use the same parameter LG. At the end of processing all parts with the parameter LG, the service level for the group is measured. If the service level for the group is too low, LG is lowered, and the parts are rerun; if the service level for the group is too high, LG is raised, and so forth. This cycle continues until the desired service level for the group is achieved.

With this method, each part is assigned a safety stock in accordance with the cost and service level benefit to the total group. Some parts will have a higher service level than others depending on the part data. For an individual part, the safety stock will decrease as the procurement cost goes up, and as the order quantity goes up, and as the forecast goes up, and as the lead time goes down. After all parts are run, the service level is computed for the total group of parts. The advantage of this method is that it yields the minimum total investment in safety stock to achieve the aggregate service level for the group as desired by the management.

Parameter:

LG = Lagrange parameter

Data per part:

c = cost per unit

Q = order quantity

F12 = 12 month forecast

σ = standard deviation for one month ahead forecast error

L = lead time (months)

Computations per part: The following five steps are taken.

1. $\sigma_L = \sqrt{L}\sigma$ = standard deviation of the lead time forecast error.
2. F(k) = [1 – LG × c × Q/F12] = cumulative distribution. F(k) = max(F(k), 0.5) and min(F(k), 1.0).
3. From Table 4.1, locate F(k), and find the corresponding k and E(k) values.

   Note, k = safety factor, and E(k) = partial expectation.
4. The safety stock becomes: ss = $k\sigma_L$.
5. The service level is: SL = 1 – E(k) σ_L/Q.

Computations for all parts in the group: To compute the service level (weighed by cost per unit) for all parts (i) in the group, let g designate the group, and thereby the sum below measures the service level for the group:

$$SLg = \Sigma[c(i)F12(i)SL(i)]/\Sigma[c(i)F12(i)]$$

Example 4.4. Assume a part where the Lagrange parameter is set to LG = 0.05 and the lead time is L = 2 months, the standard error of the one month forecast is σ = 3.0. Also, the cost per unit is c = \$10.00, the order quantity is Q = 20, and the 12 months forecast is F12 = 120 pieces. The cumulative distribution is now computed by the relation: F(k) = [1 – LG × c × Q/F12] = [1 – .05 × 10 × 20/120] = 0.917. So now, Table 4.1 is used to find the safety factor k that corresponds with F(k) = 0.917. The table shows at F(k) = 0.920, k = 1.405; and at F(k) = 0.910, k = 1.341. With interpolation, the safety factor is k = 1.386. So now the safety stock becomes: ss = k × σ_L = 1.386 × 4.24 = 5.87.

Comparison on the Four Safety Stock Methods

Below is a comparison of the four safety stock methods for an individual part. With each method, three settings of the associated parameter are run to demonstrate the sensitivity between the parameters and the amount of safety stock. Also computed are the four measures: months supply (ms), availability (av) and service level (sl).

Parameters: The parameters selected for the run are the following:

The *months-supply* method uses parameter values of MS = 0.50, 1.00 and 1.50 months; the *availability* method uses AV = 0.90, 0.95 and 0.99, the *service level* method uses parameter SL = 0.90, 0.95 and 0.99, and the *Lagrange* method uses LG = 0.03, 0.05 and 0.10.

Notation: The notation is listed below:

F = forecast per month

F_L = forecast for lead time

σ = standard deviation of one month forecast error

σ_L = standard deviation of lead time forecast error

L = lead time (months)

F12 = 12 month forecast

M = months in buy

Q = order quantity

MS = months-supply parameter (in safety stock)

AV = availability parameter (probability not out of stock in order cycle)

SL = service level parameter (percent fill)
 = (demand filled)/(total demand)

LG = Lagrange parameter

ms = months supply computed

av = availability computed

sl = service level computed

F(k) = cumulative distribution

E(k) = partial expectation

k = safety factor

ss = safety stock

op = order point

ol = order level

Table 4.2: Worksheet for Four Safety Stock Methods

Data per part:

F	σ	L	M	F_L	σ_L	Q	F12
10	3	1	2	10	3	20	120

Computations:

MS	ss	op	ol	ms	av	sl
0.50	5.0	15.0	35.0	0.50	0.95	0.99+
1.00	10.0	20.0	40.0	1.00	0.99+	0.99+
1.50	15.0	25.0	45.0	1.50	0.99+	0.99+

AV	k	ss	op	ol	ms	av	sl
0.90	1.282	3.8	13.8	33.8	0.38	0.90	0.99
0.95	1.645	4.9	14.9	34.9	0.49	0.95	0.99+
0.99	2.327	7.0	17.0	37.0	0.70	0.99	0.99+

SL	E(k)	k	ss	op	ol	ms	av	sl
0.90	0.666	0.000	0.0	10.0	30.0	0.00	0.50	0.90
0.95	0.333	0.142	0.4	10.4	30.4	0.04	0.56	0.95
0.99	0.067	1.110	3.3	13.3	33.3	0.33	0.86	0.99

LG	F(k)	k	ss	op	ol	ms	av	sl
0.03	0.950	1.65	4.9	14.9	34.9	0.49	0.95	0.99+
0.05	0.917	1.38	4.1	14.1	24.1	0.41	0.92	0.99
0.10	0.833	0.96	2.9	12.9	32.9	0.29	0.83	0.98

Comments: Note, in the above examples, the difference between measures of the availability (AV) and the service level (SL). When AV = 0.95, sl = 0.99+; and when SL = 0.95, av = 0.56. Often, in practice, the safety stock is set by using the availability method, but in actuality, the measure that is most useful to the management is the service level measurement. When that is true, the safety stock should be computed by using the service level method and not the availability method.

Sensitivity of Safety Stock with Lead Time, Months-in-Buy, Coefficient of Variation and Service Level

This section shows how the safety stock is sensitive with changes in the lead time, the month-in-buy, the coefficient of variation, and the service level. The lead time is the elapsed time from the day of the buy until the day of the receive. The month-in-buy is a relative measure of the order size in months-supply. The coefficient of variation is a measure of the forecast error, and the (desired) service level is the parameter set by the management.

Table 4.3 lists the safety stock needs (in months supply) for typical ranges of input data: service level (SL), lead time months (L), months-in-buy (M), and the coefficient-of-variation (cov). The range of input data is below:

L = 0.25, 0.50, 1.00, 2.00, 3.00, 4.00

M = 0.25, 1.00, 3.00, 6.00

cov = 0.1, 0.3, 0.5, 0.7, 1.0

SL = 0.85, 0.90, 0.925, 0.95, 0.975, 0.99

Note, L = 0.25 is almost a week, and L = 1.00 is a month. The tables are separated into six partitions by lead time months: (0.25, 0.50, 1.00, 2.00, 3.00, 4.00). Each partition includes all combinations of months-in-buy, coefficient of variation and service level.

Table 4.3: Safety Stock (Months) by SL, L, M and cov

L	M	cov	SL	0.850	0.900	0.925	0.950	0.975	0.990
							SS		
0.25	0.25	0.10		0.00	0.00	0.00	0.02	0.04	0.06
0.25	0.25	0.30		0.05	0.09	0.12	0.15	0.20	0.26
0.25	0.25	0.50		0.17	0.23	0.26	0.31	0.39	0.49
0.25	0.25	0.70		0.30	0.38	0.43	0.49	0.60	0.72
0.25	0.25	1.00		0.53	0.63	0.70	0.79	0.93	1.10
0.25	1.00	0.10		0.00	0.00	0.00	0.00	0.00	0.02
0.25	1.00	0.30		0.00	0.00	0.00	0.02	0.09	0.17
0.25	1.00	0.50		0.00	0.00	0.05	0.12	0.23	0.34
0.25	1.00	0.70		0.00	0.09	0.16	0.25	0.38	0.53
0.25	1.00	1.00		0.11	0.25	0.34	0.45	0.63	0.83

0.25	3.00	0.10	0.00	0.00	0.00	0.00	0.00	0.00
0.25	3.00	0.30	0.00	0.00	0.00	0.00	0.00	0.07
0.25	3.00	0.50	0.00	0.00	0.00	0.00	0.05	0.20
0.25	3.00	0.70	0.00	0.00	0.00	0.00	0.16	0.35
0.25	3.00	1.00	0.00	0.00	0.00	0.11	0.34	0.58
0.25	6.00	0.10	0.00	0.00	0.00	0.00	0.00	0.00
0.25	6.00	0.30	0.00	0.00	0.00	0.00	0.00	0.00
0.25	6.00	0.50	0.00	0.00	0.00	0.00	0.00	0.09
0.25	6.00	0.70	0.00	0.00	0.00	0.00	0.00	0.21
0.25	6.00	1.00	0.00	0.00	0.00	0.00	0.11	0.40
0.50	0.25	0.10	0.00	0.01	0.02	0.04	0.07	0.10
0.50	0.25	0.30	0.12	0.17	0.21	0.25	0.32	0.40
0.50	0.25	0.50	0.31	0.38	0.43	0.50	0.61	0.73
0.50	0.25	0.70	0.52	0.62	0.69	0.78	0.92	1.08
0.50	0.25	1.00	0.87	1.00	1.09	1.21	1.40	1.64
0.50	1.00	0.10	0.00	0.00	0.00	0.00	0.01	0.05
0.50	1.00	0.30	0.00	0.00	0.02	0.08	0.17	0.27
0.50	1.00	0.50	0.00	0.09	0.16	0.25	0.38	0.54
0.50	1.00	0.70	0.10	0.24	0.33	0.44	0.62	0.82
0.50	1.00	1.00	0.32	0.50	0.62	0.77	1.00	1.28
0.50	3.00	0.10	0.00	0.00	0.00	0.00	0.00	0.00
0.50	3.00	0.30	0.00	0.00	0.00	0.00	0.02	0.15
0.50	3.00	0.50	0.00	0.00	0.00	0.00	0.16	0.35
0.50	3.00	0.70	0.00	0.00	0.00	0.10	0.33	0.58
0.50	3.00	1.00	0.00	0.00	0.12	0.32	0.62	0.94
0.50	6.00	0.10	0.00	0.00	0.00	0.00	0.00	0.00
0.50	6.00	0.30	0.00	0.00	0.00	0.00	0.00	0.06
0.50	6.00	0.50	0.00	0.00	0.00	0.00	0.00	0.21
0.50	6.00	0.70	0.00	0.00	0.00	0.00	0.10	0.39
0.50	6.00	1.00	0.00	0.00	0.00	0.00	0.32	0.70
1.00	0.25	0.10	0.00	0.03	0.05	0.08	0.11	0.16
1.00	0.25	0.30	0.23	0.30	0.34	0.40	0.49	0.60

1.00	0.25	0.50	0.53	0.63	0.70	0.79	0.93	1.10
1.00	0.25	0.70	0.86	0.99	1.08	1.20	1.39	1.62
1.00	0.25	1.00	1.39	1.57	1.69	1.86	2.12	2.43
1.00	1.00	0.10	0.00	0.00	0.00	0.00	0.03	0.09
1.00	1.00	0.30	0.00	0.04	0.10	0.18	0.30	0.43
1.00	1.00	0.50	0.11	0.25	0.34	0.45	0.63	0.83
1.00	1.00	0.70	0.31	0.49	0.61	0.76	0.99	1.26
1.00	1.00	1.00	0.67	0.90	1.06	1.26	1.57	1.94
1.00	3.00	0.10	0.00	0.00	0.00	0.00	0.00	0.02
1.00	3.00	0.30	0.00	0.00	0.00	0.00	0.10	0.27
1.00	3.00	0.50	0.00	0.00	0.00	0.11	0.34	0.58
1.00	3.00	0.70	0.00	0.00	0.12	0.31	0.61	0.93
1.00	3.00	1.00	0.00	0.22	0.42	0.67	1.06	1.49
1.00	6.00	0.10	0.00	0.00	0.00	0.00	0.00	0.00
1.00	6.00	0.30	0.00	0.00	0.00	0.00	0.00	0.15
1.00	6.00	0.50	0.00	0.00	0.00	0.00	0.11	0.40
1.00	6.00	0.70	0.00	0.00	0.00	0.00	0.31	0.69
1.00	6.00	1.00	0.00	0.00	0.00	0.22	0.67	1.17
2.00	0.25	0.10	0.04	0.08	0.11	0.14	0.19	0.24
2.00	0.25	0.30	0.41	0.50	0.56	0.64	0.76	0.91
2.00	0.25	0.50	0.87	1.00	1.09	1.21	1.40	1.64
2.00	0.25	0.70	1.37	1.55	1.67	1.83	2.09	2.40
2.00	0.25	1.00	2.19	2.43	2.59	2.81	3.17	3.60
2.00	1.00	0.10	0.00	0.00	0.00	0.01	0.08	0.15
2.00	1.00	0.30	0.04	0.16	0.24	0.34	0.50	0.68
2.00	1.00	0.50	0.32	0.50	0.62	0.77	1.00	1.28
2.00	1.00	0.70	0.66	0.89	1.04	1.24	1.55	1.92
2.00	1.00	1.00	1.23	1.54	1.74	2.01	2.43	2.93
2.00	3.00	0.10	0.00	0.00	0.00	0.00	0.00	0.06
2.00	3.00	0.30	0.00	0.00	0.00	0.04	0.24	0.46
2.00	3.00	0.50	0.00	0.00	0.12	0.32	0.62	0.94

2.00	3.00	0.70	0.00	0.21	0.41	0.66	1.04	1.47
2.00	3.00	1.00	0.25	0.64	0.90	1.23	1.74	2.32
2.00	6.00	0.10	0.00	0.00	0.00	0.00	0.00	0.00
2.00	6.00	0.30	0.00	0.00	0.00	0.00	0.04	0.30
2.00	6.00	0.50	0.00	0.00	0.00	0.00	0.32	0.70
2.00	6.00	0.70	0.00	0.00	0.00	0.21	0.66	1.15
2.00	6.00	1.00	0.00	0.00	0.25	0.64	1.23	1.89
3.00	0.25	0.10	0.08	0.12	0.15	0.19	0.24	0.31
3.00	0.25	0.30	0.56	0.66	0.73	0.82	0.97	1.15
3.00	0.25	0.50	1.15	1.31	1.41	1.56	1.79	2.06
3.00	0.25	0.70	1.79	2.00	2.15	2.34	2.65	3.02
3.00	0.25	1.00	2.83	3.11	3.31	3.58	4.00	4.53
3.00	1.00	0.10	0.00	0.00	0.00	0.04	0.12	0.21
3.00	1.00	0.30	0.13	0.27	0.36	0.48	0.66	0.87
3.00	1.00	0.50	0.51	0.71	0.85	1.03	1.31	1.63
3.00	1.00	0.70	0.95	1.22	1.40	1.63	2.00	2.44
3.00	1.00	1.00	1.70	2.06	2.29	2.61	3.11	3.72
3.00	3.00	0.10	0.00	0.00	0.00	0.00	0.00	0.10
3.00	3.00	0.30	0.00	0.00	0.00	0.13	0.36	0.62
3.00	3.00	0.50	0.00	0.10	0.28	0.51	0.85	1.24
3.00	3.00	0.70	0.07	0.43	0.66	0.95	1.40	1.91
3.00	3.00	1.00	0.55	1.01	1.31	1.70	2.29	2.99
3.00	6.00	0.10	0.00	0.00	0.00	0.00	0.00	0.02
3.00	6.00	0.30	0.00	0.00	0.00	0.00	0.13	0.43
3.00	6.00	0.50	0.00	0.00	0.00	0.10	0.51	0.95
3.00	6.00	0.70	0.00	0.00	0.07	0.43	0.95	1.53
3.00	6.00	1.00	0.00	0.19	0.55	1.01	1.70	2.47
4.00	0.25	0.10	0.11	0.16	0.19	0.23	0.29	0.37
4.00	0.25	0.30	0.69	0.81	0.88	0.99	1.16	1.36
4.00	0.25	0.50	1.39	1.57	1.69	1.86	2.12	2.43
4.00	0.25	0.70	2.16	2.40	2.56	2.78	3.13	3.56
4.00	0.25	1.00	3.38	3.71	3.93	4.23	4.72	5.33

4.00	1.00	0.10	0.00	0.00	0.01	0.07	0.16	0.25
4.00	1.00	0.30	0.21	0.36	0.47	0.60	0.81	1.04
4.00	1.00	0.50	0.67	0.90	1.06	1.26	1.57	1.94
4.00	1.00	0.70	1.21	1.51	1.71	1.98	2.40	2.90
4.00	1.00	1.00	2.11	2.52	2.78	3.14	3.71	4.39
4.00	3.00	0.10	0.00	0.00	0.00	0.00	0.01	0.13
4.00	3.00	0.30	0.00	0.00	0.03	0.21	0.47	0.75
4.00	3.00	0.50	0.00	0.22	0.42	0.67	1.06	1.49
4.00	3.00	0.70	0.23	0.63	0.88	1.21	1.71	2.29
4.00	3.00	1.00	0.83	1.34	1.68	2.11	2.78	3.57
4.00	6.00	0.10	0.00	0.00	0.00	0.00	0.00	0.04
4.00	6.00	0.30	0.00	0.00	0.00	0.00	0.21	0.54
4.00	6.00	0.50	0.00	0.00	0.00	0.22	0.67	1.17
4.00	6.00	0.70	0.00	0.00	0.23	0.63	1.21	1.86
4.00	6.00	1.00	0.00	0.43	0.83	1.34	2.11	2.98

Summary

Safety stock is the extra stock needed when the future demands on a part are not known in advance. This is added stock to the part inventory that is applied to ensure the customer demands are filled as they occur. The amount of safety stock to have depends on the level of service specified by the management. The chapter describes four ways to determine the safety stock size: months supply, availability, service level and Lagrange.

References

Brown, Robert J., *Smoothing, Forecasting and Prediction of Discrete Time Series*, Prentice Hall, Inc., 1962.

Minner, Stephan, *Strategic Safety Stocks in Supply Chains*, Springer Verlag, 2000.

Thomopoulos, Nick T., *Strategic Inventory Management and Planning*, Hitchcock Publishing Co., Carol Stream, II. 1990.

——, *Applied Forecasting Methods*, Prentice Hall, Inc., 1980.

Vollman, Thomas E., William L. Berry and D. Clay Whybark, *Manufacturing Planning and Control*, McGraw Hill, 1997.

5

Order Point and Order Level

This chapter describes the way the inventory is replenished on the individual parts that are housed in stocking facilities like distribution centers, dealers and retailers. The reader will learn how the order point and order level are used to determine when new stock is needed and how much. The chapter shows how these two quantities are computed and how often they are changed. A set of examples, from a one location part, are presented to illustrate how the part data is used to determine the buy quantities at the current time, and also for the projected times out through the future months. The reader will see how the projected replenish quantities are used for planning purposes at the stocking facility, and how they serve as the forecasts to the suppliers of the parts. Another set of examples pertain to parts stocked in multiple locations. The chapter shows how the part and location data are used to compute the order point and order level at each location. The reader will observe that an extra layer of stock is often needed for parts held in more than one location.

Introduction

One of the more important functions in an inventory system is scheduling the incoming replenishment of new stock. The goal is to have the minimum investment in inventory to satisfy customer demands and achieve a high service level, (demand filled/total demand). To accomplish, the inventory system needs a sound set of software routines to carry out the forecasting and replenishment functions. These routines are typically run at the beginning of each new month for every part and location. The routines refresh the forecasts, order quantities and safety stock using the latest data, and the results are used to compute the order point and order level for every part and location. The order point and order level are revised once a month. The inventory status on each part and location are monitored everyday to determine when and how much new replenish stock is needed. The integrity of these two measures (order point and order level) is essential for a sound inventory system. This chapter shows how they are computed and gives examples on their use.

Order Point and Order Level

For every part and location (sku) in the inventory, an order point (OP) and order level (OL) are obtained in the following way:

$$OP = FL + SS$$

$$OL = OP + Q$$

where, FL = lead time forecast

SS = safety stock

Q = order quantity

In most inventory systems, at the end of each month, new forecast are generated for each part and location, and this is when the OP and OL are recomputed. These quantities are saved in the database, and are used as needed throughout the month. The quantities remain fixed unless one of the ingredients: FL, SS, Q is changed. In the typical situation, OP and OL are rounded to the nearest integers. When the order quantity is small, the rounding may cause OP = OL, and should this happen, the order point is revised so that OP = OL – 1. The final result will have OP < OL.

When to Buy and How Much

For each part and location, the OP and OL are used to determine when to buy and how much. This happens on a daily basis, where the sum of the on-hand (OH) and on-order (OO) is compared to the OP and OL in the following way:

$$\text{if } (OH + OO) > OP, \quad buy = 0$$

$$\text{if } (OH + OO) \le OP, \quad buy = OL - (OH + OO)$$

For example, if OP = 10, OL = 16 and (OH + OO) = 15, then no new stock is needed, and buy = 0. However, if OH + OO = 9, then buy = 7 pieces.

On-Hand and On-Order Connection

This section shows how to measure the average on-hand and average on-order inventory for planning purposes. Consider Figure 5.1 that shows the flow of OH and OO inventory over time in relation to the OP and OL. When (OH + OO) drops to the OP level, a new replenishment quantity of size Q is ordered to bring the (OH + OO) up to the OL. In the figure, the replenish quantity is ordered at time t_1, and is received a lead time (L) later at t_2. The next replenishment of stock occurs at t_3, and is received a lead time later. The figure shows the level of stock OH as a solid line, and the level of (OH + OO) as a dotted line. In this situation, an order cycle is the time period from t_1 to t_3, the elapsed time between two orders of replenish stock. Recall, the replenish quantity is Q = M × F, where F is the average forecast per month, and M is the month's supply in Q. Thus, the average time length of the order cycle is M, which is the same as the months of forecast in the order quantity. The figure shows where the elapsed time from t_1 to t_2 is L, the lead time, and the average time from t_1 to t_3 is M. The average OH and OO quantities over the order cycle are computed as shown below:

$$\begin{aligned}\text{Average OH} &= SS + 0.5 \times Q \\ \text{Average OO} &= [L \times Q + (M - L) \times 0]/M \\ &= [L \times M \times F + 0]/M \\ &= L \times F = F_L\end{aligned}$$

Thereby, the average on-order inventory is equal to the lead time forecast.

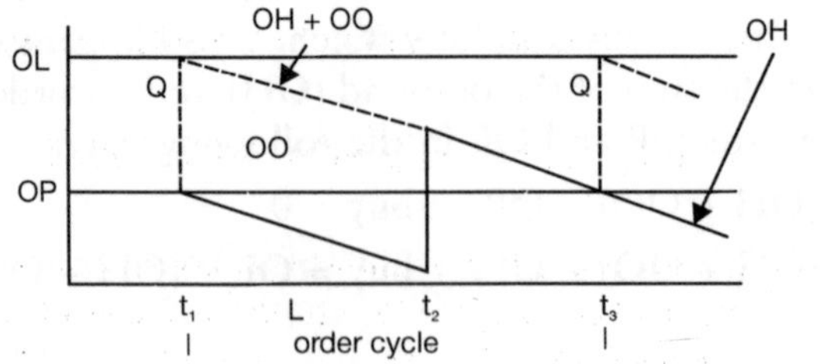

Figure 5.1: Order Point, Order Level, On-Hand and On-Order

Low Volume Items

In the event of a very low demand item, the computations for the forecasts, safety stock and order quantities are small and near zero. This causes, the order point and order level to round as OP = OL = 0. Using the rule given earlier, OP = –1 and OL = 0. This combination of OP and OL signifies that no inventory is needed for the part; and even when (OH + OO) = 0, no new buy is needed. A new order is placed only when a new customer demand comes in and causes a back order. For example, if the unfilled demand is for d pieces, the on-hand goes negative (OH = –d) and thereby, a buy for d pieces is called to bring (OH + OO) back up to zero, since OL = 0.

12 Month Replenishments

The examples below illustrate various situations where a part is stocked in one location, and cover a time horizon of the future 12 months. The time line goes from t = 0 to t = 12, where t = 0 identifies the current time. If a buy is needed at t = 0, the quantity is placed on a purchase order and sent from the stocking facility to the supplier. A lead time later, the supplier ships the quantity to the stocking facility. Any buy quantity needed after t = 0, on the time line, is projected for a future date and is called a planned replenish quantity. The projected replenishments for the future months are for planning purposes only at the stocking facility. They are, however, very useful to the supplier, serving as forecasts for their schedule activities over the future production horizon.

Below are three replenishment examples. A worksheet is provided with each and illustrates how the data is used to determine the current buy. As stated above, the current buy is the only buy that is needed now; all other buys are projected buys for the remaining months out through month 12. The worksheet shows how the forecasts, safety stock, order level, order point, buy quantities, on-hand, and on-order inventory quantities are related, and how they are changing along the time horizon.

Example 5.1. Consider the example below where the forecast is F = 10 pieces per month, the safety stock is SS = 5 pieces, the lead time is L = 1 month, and the months-in-buy is M = 2 months. Also, the opening on-hand and on-order quantities are OH = 20 and OO = 0, respectively. The above data yields the lead time forecast, FL = L × F = 10, order quantity, Q = M × F = 20, order point, OP = FL + SS = 15, and order level, OL = OP + Q = 35.

The worksheet below shows how the on-hand, on-order and replenish quantities are projected for the months t = 0 to 12. Since the opening OH + OO is larger than the OP, no replenish order is needed at the outset, t = 0. The first replenishment is projected at t = 0.5 when the OH + OO reaches the order point. So the projected replenish quantity at t = 0.5 is $Q_{0.5}$ = OL – OP = 20. The worksheet shows six projected buy quantities for the planning horizon of 12 months. Note the first replenish order is at t = 0.5 and the stock arrives a lead time L later at t = 1.5.

	Current		Projected replenish schedule				
month t	0.0	0.5	2.5	4.5	6.5	8.5	10.5
OH+OO	20	15	15	15	15	15	15
buy Q		20	20	20	20	20	20
OH+OO+Q		35	35	35	35	35	35
receive t		1.5	3.5	5.5	7.5	9.5	11.5

Example 5.2. In this example, the forecast and safety stock are the same as Example 5.1. The lead time is L = 2 months, and the months-in-buy is M = 1 month. The lead time forecast is 20 pieces, and the order quantity is 10 pieces. With this data, the order point becomes OP = 25, and an order level is OL = 35 pieces. The example continues with the opening on-hand plus on-order of 30 pieces, and thereby the first projected replenishment is ordered at t = 0.5, and is received a lead time (L = 2) later at t = 2.5, with $Q_{0.5}$ = 10 pieces. The worksheet lists the flow of on-hand, on-order and replenish quantities from t = 0 to 12.

	Current		Projected replenish schedule										
month t	0.0	0.5	1.5	2.5	3.5	4.5	5.5	6.5	7.5	8.5	9.5	10.5	11.5
OH+OO	30	25	25	25	25	25	25	25	25	25	25	25	25
buy Q	0	10	10	10	10	10	10	10	10	10	10	10	10
OH+OO+Q		35	35	35	35	35	35	35	35	35	35	35	
receive t		2.5	3.5	4.5	5.5	6.5	7.5	8.5	9.5	10.5	11.5	12.5	13.5

Example 5.3. In this example, the forecast and safety stock are the same as Example 5.1. The lead time is L = 1 month, and the months-in-buy is M = 2 months. But here, the lead time forecast is 10 pieces, and the order quantity is 20 pieces. The computations show the order point is OP = 15, and the order level is OL = 35 pieces. When the opening on-hand plus on-order is 10 pieces, the first projected replenishment is at t = 0.0, whereby $Q_{0.0}$ = 25 pieces. The worksheet lists the flow of on-hand, on-order, and replenish quantities from t = 0 to 12. Note the replenish order is at t = 0.0, and the stock arrives a lead time L later at t = 1.0. In this example, the quantity of 25 pieces is ordered with the supplier. The remaining projected buy quantities are for planning purposes only, and cause no buy.

	Current		Projected replenish schedule			
month t	0.0	2.0	4.0	6.0	8.0	10.0
OH+OO	10	15	15	15	15	15
buy Q	25	20	20	20	20	20
OH+OO+Q	35	35	35	35	35	35
receive t	1.0	3.0	5.0	7.0	9.0	11.0

Regional Order Point and Order Level

The following examples show how the order point and order level are generated for a part that is stocked in a multiple number of locations. In the example, it is assumed that each location monitors their individual stock status (OH + OO) daily, and calls for a replenish quantity to their location when new stock is needed. The examples show how to determine the order point and order level by location. For comparison sake, the example also determines the same measures for the total part when all the inventory is in one location.

Example 5.4. Assume the part data are the following: D12 = 960 (prior 12 month demand), F1 = D12/12 = 80 (average one month forecast), σ = 24 (one month standard deviation of forecast error), L = 2 months (lead time), M = 1 (months-in-buy) and SL = 0.95 (desired service level). Suppose also, the part is stocked in five locations (1, 2, 3, 4, 5), and an order point and order level are needed for each location. Also suppose, the only data available for each location is the prior 12 month demand (d12) as listed in the table below. Note D12 = Σd12 = 960, is the total demand over all locations.

Five Location Example

The computations by location are the following:

p = d12/D12 = percent of total demand for location i

f1 = p × F1 = one month forecast

q = M × f1 = order quantity

$\sigma_i^2 = p(1 - p)\,F1 + (p \times \sigma)^2$ = variance of one month forecast error for location i

$\sigma_L = \sqrt{L}\sigma_i$ = lead time standard deviation

$E(k) = (1 - SL)q/\sigma_L$ = partial expectation

From the standard normal tables, locate E(k), and find k.

k = safety factor

ss = $k\sigma_L$ = safety stock

fL = L × f1 = lead time forecast

op = fL + ss = order point

ol = op + q = order level

ts = q/2 + ss = average total stock

The worksheet below lists the location results from the above computations. Note the sum of the total stock from all locations is Σts = 79.1 pieces.

For comparison sake, the worksheet also shows the counterpart results when only one location is in use. The same equations are used to find the order quantity, safety stock, order point, and order level assuming all the stock is held in one location. In this scenario, the safety stock = SS = 27.5, and the average total stock is TS = 67.5 pieces. Note, less safety stock is needed when one location carries all the stock (27.5), than when the five individual locations each carry safety stock (39.1).

Table 5.1: Worksheet for the Five Location Example

F1	σ	L	M	SL
80	24.0	2.00	1.00	0.95

Location	d12	p	f1	σ	ss	fL	q	op	ol	sl	ts
1	60	0.0625	5.0	2.6	4.1	10.0	5	14	19	0.95	6.6
2	120	0.1250	10.0	4.2	5.9	20.0	10	26	36	0.95	10.9
3	180	0.1875	15.0	5.7	7.6	30.0	15	38	53	0.95	15.1
4	240	0.2500	20.0	7.1	9.2	40.0	20	49	69	0.95	19.2
5	360	0.3750	30.0	10.0	12.3	60.0	30	72	102	0.95	27.3
5 loc sum	960	1.0000	80.0		39.1	160.0	80	199	279	0.95	79.1
1 loc	960	1.0000	80.0	24.0	27.5	160.0	80	188	268	0.95	67.5

Five Size Example

Example 5.5. A sweater comes in five sizes (small, medium, large, extra-large, extra-extra-large). Suppose the sweater data (all sizes) are the following: D12 = 150 (prior 12 month demand), F1 = D12/12 = 12.5 (average one month forecast), σ = 6.3 (one month standard deviation of forecast error), L = 2 months (lead time), M = 0.5 (months in buy), and SL = 0.95 (desired service level). The worksheet below lists the measures for each size and the total for all sizes. Note the safety stock for the five sizes is 18.9 pieces, and the total stock is 23.4 pieces.

Table 5.2: Worksheet for the Five Size Example

F1	σ	L	M	SL
13	6.3	2.00	0.50	0.95

Size	d12	p	f1	σ	ss	fL	q	op	ol	sl	ts
s	10	0.067	0.8	1.0	1.9	1.7	1	4	5	0.95	2.4
m	50	0.333	4.2	2.7	5.1	8.3	3	13	16	0.95	6.6
l	40	0.267	3.3	2.3	4.8	6.7	2	11	13	0.95	5.8
xl	30	0.200	2.5	1.9	3.7	5.0	2	9	11	0.95	4.7
xxl	20	0.133	1.7	1.5	3.3	3.3	1	7	8	0.95	3.8
Sum	150	1.000	12.5		18.9	25.0	9	44	53	0.95	23.4

Summary

The order point (OP) and order level (OL) are computed for each part and location (sku) typically once a month. The computations coincide with each new monthly demand entry, and trigger the need for a new forecast that calls for a subsequent set of replenish computations. In essence, the order point and order level, for a part and location, are refreshed whenever the forecast is revised, and also whenever any change happens in the supplier contract terms, like cost per unit, multiple quantity or lead time. Everyday, the current on-hand plus on-order inventory (OH + OO) is monitored, and when the sum falls at or below the order point, a buy quantity is ordered with the supplier to bring the OH + OO back up to the order level.

References

Minner, Stephan, *Strategic Safety Stocks in Supply Chains*, Springer Verlag, 2000.

Thomopoulos, Nick T., *Strategic Inventory Management and Planning*, Hitchcock Publishing Co., Carol Stream, Il. 1990.

Vollman, Thomas E., William L. Berry and D. Clay Whybark, *Manufacturing Planning and Control*, McGraw Hill, 1997.

6

Low Demand Items

In this chapter, the reader will learn how the Poisson distribution is used instead of the normal distribution for low demand items for inventory control applications. As in the higher demand items, the inventory status on each part is monitored everyday and compared to an order point and order level to determine when and how much to order. The chapter shows how to compute the order point and the order level to achieve the service level as called by the management. The methods pertain to both the lost sales case (like retail items), and also the backorder case (like service parts). Examples are presented to guide the reader on how to use the tables of the chapter.

Introduction

This chapter concerns low demand items and shows how to determine the order point and order level to satisfy the desired service level specified by the management. The model pertains to scenarios of lost sales and backorders. In retail stores, as in the sale of shoes (with various sizes), sweaters, shirts, coats, so forth, most of the items have low demands. In service parts facilities (like automobiles, appliances), parts are held in stock awaiting any maintenance or repair needs on the finished good items. Some of the parts have high to moderate demands, but most have low demands.

In the discussion, the symbol d will represent the expected demand per month for an item, and L the lead time in months. The expected demand for the lead time duration becomes: $m = d \times L$. Now let x represent the demand over the lead time duration, and since the demands are low, x is assumed to follow a Poisson probability distribution with expected value of E(x) = m = d × L.

An order cycle (OC) is defined as the time interval between two receipts of stock on a part. For notation, OP = order point and OL = order level. At the beginning of the order cycle, the on-hand plus on-order (OH + OO) inventory is set to OL. When (OH + OO) drops to OP, an order quantity Q is called to bring the (OH + OO) back up to OL. The inventory will arrive a lead time, L, after the order is placed. The end of the order cycle is when the replenish quantity arrives.

When a demand occurs and stock is available to fill the demand, the OH is decreased by the amount of the demand. When a demand occurs and the stock is not available to fill the demand, the OH is measured differently for the lost sales and backorder cases. In the lost sales case, the on-hand remains at zero, even when demands are not filled; in the backorder case, the on-hand drops below zero signifying demand waiting to be filled as soon as new stock becomes available.

When a new quantity, Q, of stock is ordered, the replenish quantity becomes Q = OL – (OH + OO). In the backorder case, OH could be a negative value, but in the lost sales case, OH never falls below zero.

Lost Sales

In the lost sales situation, the expected service level is defined as E(SL) = E(sales/demand). When a demand occurs and the stock is available, a sale occurs. But when the stock is not available, the sale is lost.

For convenience, the service level (SL) is measured from the start to the end of the order cycle (OC), and thereby, the relation is SL = E(sales in OC)/E(demand in OC). The expected demand over the order cycle is obtained by splitting the order cycle into two time periods. The first time period is when the on-hand plus on-order (OH + OO), falls from OL to OP, and the expected demand here is (OL – OP). The second time period occurs while the inventory is replenished. The lead time is L and the expected demand is m. Thereby the expected demand over the order cycle is computed by E(demand in OC) = (OL – OP + m).

To find the expected sales over the order cycle, the order cycle is again split into the same two time periods described above. The expected sales for the time period when the inventory drops from OL to OP is (OL – OP). To compute the expected sales for the lead time duration, we let the symbol s represent the sales during the lead time. Because x is the demand for the lead time duration, the expected sales for the lead time is $E(s) = \sum_{x=0}^{OP} xp(x) + OP \sum_{x>OP} p(x)$. So now the expected sales over the entire order cycle becomes E(sales in OC) = [OL – OP + E(s)]. Finally, SL = E(sales in OC)/E(demand in OC) is computed.

Backorders

In the backorder situation, the expected service level is defined as E(SL) = E(demand filled/demand). When a demand occurs and the stock is available, a demand-filled measure is increased by the size of the demand. But when the stock is not available, the demand-filled measure is not incremented. Any unfilled demand causes the on-hand measure to become negative, awaiting to be filled by a future replenishment of stock.

The service level (SL) is measured for the time ranging from the start to the end of the order cycle (OC). The relation SL = E(demand filled in OC)/E(demand in OC) is used. The expected demand over the order cycle is the same as shown above, i.e. E(demand in OC) = (OL – OP + m).

The expected demand-filled over the order cycle is the same as described above for the expected sales over the order cycle. Hence, E(demand-filled in OC) = [OL – OP + E(s)] and thereby SL is computed.

Poisson Distribution

Table 6.1 lists the probability of variable x from the Poisson distribution when the expected value of x is m. The probability of x is the following:

$$P(x) = e^{-m}m^{x}/x! \quad x = 0, 1, 2, \ldots$$

This table also represents the distribution of the lead time demand for a low demand item. Recall, for low demand items,

x = demand over the lead time

m = E(demand for the lead time)

Suppose the average demand for an item is one per month and the lead time is two weeks, thereby, L = 0.5 months. So the average demand for the lead time is m = 1.0 × L = 0.50. Table 6.1 shows when m = 0.50, the probability of zero demands in the lead time is 0.607, the probability of one unit of demand is 0.303, and so forth.

It is noted, for the Poisson distribution, the variance of x is the same as the mean, i.e. $\sigma^2 = m$. Further, (for the Poisson distribution) as the mean m gets large, ($m \geq 10$), the distribution looks much like the normal distribution. So when m is 10 or larger, the variable x can be approximated by the normal distribution and thereby, the order point and order level can be obtained as shown in Chapter 5.

Order Point, Order Level and Service Level

Tables 6.2 to 6.5 list the OP and OL needs by d = E(demand per month), service level SL (0.85, 0.90, 0.95, 0.99) and the lead time L (0.25, 0.50, 0.75, 1.00) in months. Five examples on the use of the tables are given below.

Example 6.1. Suppose a sporting goods store stocks a rubber life boat with a lead time of two weeks. During the warm weather season, the demand for the boat is estimated as 2 per month, (d = 2.0). The store manager would like the service level (sales/demand) to be 0.95. Table 6.3 shows when d = 2.0, L = 0.50 and SL = 0.95, the minimum order point and order level are OP = 2 and OL = 4. So when the on-hand plus on-order falls to 2 pieces, an order for Q = 2 pieces should be placed with the supplier.

Example 6.2. Consider the life boat from above and now suppose the lead time is lowered to one week. How does this affect the stocking policy? When d = 2.0 and L = 0.25, Table 6.2 shows (OP, OL) = (1, 3) will yield a service level of SL = 0.95.

Example 6.3. Using the Poisson probability tables, verify the results found in Example 6.1 where OP = 2, OL = 4 are obtained when d = 2 per month and L = 0.5 months.

Note Table 6.1 (where the average is denoted as m) lists the Poisson probabilities for the average lead time demand. When the expected monthly demand is d = 2.0 and the lead time is L = 0.50 months, the expected demand over the lead time is $m = d \times L = 2 \times 0.5 = 1.00$. When OP = 2 and OL = 4, the expected demand over the order cycle is:

$$\begin{aligned}E(\text{demand for the order cycle}) &= OL - OP + m \\ &= (4 - 2 + 1) = 3\end{aligned}$$

The expected sales over the lead time are computed in the following way where m = 1.0. Let x represent the sales over the lead time and p(x) the probability of x. So the expected sales over the lead time, denoted by E(s), are as follows:

$$\begin{aligned}E(s) &= 0p(x{=}0) + 1p(x{=}1) + 2p(x{=}2) + 2p(x{>}2) \\ &= 0 \times 0.368 + 1 \times 0.368 + 2 \times 0.184 + 2 \times (0.061 + 0.015 + 0.003) \\ &= 0.894.\end{aligned}$$

Thereby,

$$\begin{aligned}E(\text{sales for the order cycle}) &= OL - OP + E(s) \\ &= (4 - 2 + 0.894) = 2.894\end{aligned}$$

The service level, (sales/demand), becomes SL = 2.894/3.000 = 0.965, which is just over 0.95 as specified.

Example 6.4. Consider a clothing store that stocks a particular men's suit in 8 sizes. Assume the average demand for the suit is 40 units per month and the lead time is 3 weeks. Suppose further that size 40-short receives 10 percent of the demand for this suit. What setting of the order point and order level is needed to maintain a service level of 90 percent?

Note the average monthly demand for size 40-short is $d = 0.10 \times 40 = 4.00$. So now, Table 6.4 is searched with d = 4.0, L = 0.75 and SL = 0.90 to find the pair (OP, OL). The service level is achieved when (OP, OL) = (4, 5).

Example 6.5. Suppose a dealer holds stock for a service part with a forecast of 0.2 units per month. The replenish lead time is one week and the desired service level is 0.95. How much stock should be held for this part at the dealer? Table 6.2 shows when the average monthly demand is d = 0.2, the lead time is L = 0.25 months and the desired service level is 0.95, (OP, OL) = (0, 1).

Table 6.1: The Poisson Probability Distribution for Random Variable x and Parameters 0.1 to 10.0

x | m	0.1	0.2	0.3	0.4	0.5	0.6	0.7	0.8	0.9	1.0
0	.905	.819	.741	.670	.607	.549	.497	.449	.407	.368
1	.090	.164	.222	.268	.303	.329	.348	.359	.366	.368
2	.005	.016	.033	.054	.076	.099	.122	.144	.165	.184
3	.000	.001	.003	.007	.013	.020	.028	.038	.049	.061
4	.000	.000	.000	.001	.002	.003	.005	.008	.011	.015
5	.000	.000	.000	.000	.000	.000	.001	.001	.002	.003
6	.000	.000	.000	.000	.000	.000	.000	.000	.000	.000

x | m	1.1	1.2	1.3	1.4	1.5	1.6	1.7	1.8	1.9	2.0
0	.333	.301	.273	.247	.223	.202	.183	.165	.150	.135
1	.366	.361	.354	.345	.335	.323	.311	.298	.284	.271
2	.201	.217	.230	.242	.251	.258	.264	.268	.270	.271
3	.074	.087	.100	.113	.126	.138	.150	.161	.171	.180
4	.020	.026	.032	.039	.047	.055	.064	.072	.081	.090
5	.004	.006	.008	.011	.014	.018	.022	.026	.031	.036
6	.001	.001	.002	.003	.004	.005	.006	.008	.010	.012
7	.000	.000	.000	.001	.001	.001	.001	.002	.003	.003
8	.000	.000	.000	.000	.000	.000	.000	.000	.001	.001

x | m	2.1	2.2	2.3	2.4	2.5	2.6	2.7	2.8	2.9	3.0
0	.122	.111	.100	.091	.082	.074	.067	.061	.055	.050
1	.257	.244	.231	.218	.205	.193	.181	.170	.160	.149
2	.270	.268	.265	.261	.257	.251	.245	.238	.231	.224
3	.189	.197	.203	.209	.214	.218	.220	.222	.224	.224
4	.099	.108	.117	.125	.134	.141	.149	.156	.162	.168
5	.042	.048	.054	.060	.067	.074	.080	.087	.094	.101
6	.015	.017	.021	.024	.028	.032	.036	.041	.045	.050
7	.004	.005	.007	.008	.010	.012	.014	.016	.019	.022

8	.001	.002	.002	.002	.003	.004	.005	.006	.007	.008
9	.000	.000	.000	.001	.001	.001	.001	.002	.002	.003
10	.000	.000	.000	.000	.000	.000	.000	.000	.001	.001

x	m 3.1	3.2	3.3	3.4	3.5	3.6	3.7	3.8	3.9	4.0
0	.045	.041	.037	.033	.030	.027	.025	.022	.020	.018
1	.140	.130	.122	.113	.106	.098	.091	.085	.079	.073
2	.216	.209	.201	.193	.185	.177	.169	.162	.154	.147
3	.224	.223	.221	.219	.216	.212	.209	.205	.200	.195
4	.173	.178	.182	.186	.189	.191	.193	.194	.195	.195
5	.107	.114	.120	.126	.132	.138	.143	.148	.152	.156
6	.056	.061	.066	.072	.077	.083	.088	.094	.099	.104
7	.025	.028	.031	.035	.039	.042	.047	.051	.055	.060
8	.010	.011	.013	.015	.017	.019	.022	.024	.027	.030
9	.003	.004	.005	.006	.007	.008	.009	.010	.012	.013
10	.001	.001	.002	.002	.002	.003	.003	.004	.005	.005
11	.000	.000	.000	.001	.001	.001	.001	.001	.002	.002
12	.000	.000	.000	.000	.000	.000	.000	.000	.001	.001

x	m 4.1	4.2	4.3	4.4	4.5	4.6	4.7	4.8	4.9	5.0
0	.017	.015	.014	.012	.011	.010	.009	.008	.007	.007
1	.068	.063	.058	.054	.050	.046	.043	.040	.036	.034
2	.139	.132	.125	.119	.112	.106	.100	.095	.089	.084
3	.190	.185	.180	.174	.169	.163	.157	.152	.146	.140
4	.195	.194	.193	.192	.190	.188	.185	.182	.179	.175
5	.160	.163	.166	.169	.171	.173	.174	.175	.175	.175
6	.109	.114	.119	.124	.128	.132	.136	.140	.143	.146
7	.064	.069	.073	.078	.082	.087	.091	.096	.100	.104
8	.033	.036	.039	.043	.046	.050	.054	.058	.061	.065
9	.015	.017	.019	.021	.023	.026	.028	.031	.033	.036
10	.006	.007	.008	.009	.010	.012	.013	.015	.016	.018
11	.002	.003	.003	.004	.004	.005	.006	.006	.007	.008
12	.001	.001	.001	.001	.002	.002	.002	.003	.003	.003
13	.000	.000	.000	.000	.001	.001	.001	.001	.001	.001
14	.000	.000	.000	.000	.000	.000	.000	.000	.000	.000

x	m 5.1	5.2	5.3	5.4	5.5	5.6	5.7	5.8	5.9	6.0
0	.006	.006	.005	.005	.004	.004	.003	.003	.003	.002
1	.031	.029	.026	.024	.022	.021	.019	.018	.016	.015
2	.079	.075	.070	.066	.062	.058	.054	.051	.048	.045
3	.135	.129	.124	.119	.113	.108	.103	.098	.094	.089
4	.172	.168	.164	.160	.156	.152	.147	.143	.138	.134
5	.175	.175	.174	.173	.171	.170	.168	.166	.163	.161
6	.149	.151	.154	.156	.157	.158	.159	.160	.160	.161
7	.109	.113	.116	.120	.123	.127	.130	.133	.135	.138
8	.069	.073	.077	.081	.085	.089	.092	.096	.100	.103
9	.039	.042	.045	.049	.052	.055	.059	.062	.065	.069
10	.020	.022	.024	.026	.029	.031	.033	.036	.039	.041
11	.009	.010	.012	.013	.014	.016	.017	.019	.021	.023
12	.004	.005	.005	.006	.007	.007	.008	.009	.010	.011
13	.002	.002	.002	.002	.003	.003	.004	.004	.005	.005
14	.001	.001	.001	.001	.001	.001	.001	.002	.002	.002
15	.000	.000	.000	.000	.000	.000	.001	.001	.001	.001
16	.000	.000	.000	.000	.000	.000	.000	.000	.000	.000

x	m 6.1	6.2	6.3	6.4	6.5	6.6	6.7	6.8	6.9	7.0
0	.002	.002	.002	.002	.002	.001	.001	.001	.001	.001
1	.014	.013	.012	.011	.010	.009	.008	.008	.007	.006
2	.042	.039	.036	.034	.032	.030	.028	.026	.024	.022
3	.085	.081	.077	.073	.069	.065	.062	.058	.055	.052
4	.129	.125	.121	.116	.112	.108	.103	.099	.095	.091
5	.158	.155	.152	.149	.145	.142	.138	.135	.131	.128
6	.160	.160	.159	.159	.157	.156	.155	.153	.151	.149
7	.140	.142	.144	.145	.146	.147	.148	.149	.149	.149
8	.107	.110	.113	.116	.119	.121	.124	.126	.128	.130
9	.072	.076	.079	.082	.086	.089	.092	.095	.098	.101
10	.044	.047	.050	.053	.056	.059	.062	.065	.068	.071
11	.024	.026	.029	.031	.033	.035	.038	.040	.043	.045
12	.012	.014	.015	.016	.018	.019	.021	.023	.025	.026
13	.006	.007	.007	.008	.009	.010	.011	.012	.013	.014
14	.003	.003	.003	.004	.004	.005	.005	.006	.006	.007

15	.001	.001	.001	.002	.002	.002	.002	.003	.003	.003
16	.000	.000	.001	.001	.001	.001	.001	.001	.001	.001
17	.000	.000	.000	.000	.000	.000	.000	.000	.001	.001
18	.000	.000	.000	.000	.000	.000	.000	.000	.000	.000

x	m 7.1	7.2	7.3	7.4	7.5	7.6	7.7	7.8	7.9	8.0
0	.001	.001	.001	.001	.001	.001	.000	.000	.000	.000
1	.006	.005	.005	.005	.004	.004	.003	.003	.003	.003
2	.021	.019	.018	.017	.016	.014	.013	.012	.012	.011
3	.049	.046	.044	.041	.039	.037	.034	.032	.030	.029
4	.087	.084	.080	.076	.073	.070	.066	.063	.060	.057
5	.124	.120	.117	.113	.109	.106	.102	.099	.095	.092
6	.147	.144	.142	.139	.137	.134	.131	.128	.125	.122
7	.149	.149	.148	.147	.146	.145	.144	.143	.141	.140
8	.132	.134	.135	.136	.137	.138	.139	.139	.139	.140
9	.104	.107	.110	.112	.114	.117	.119	.121	.122	.124
10	.074	.077	.080	.083	.086	.089	.091	.094	.097	.099
11	.048	.050	.053	.056	.059	.061	.064	.067	.069	.072
12	.028	.030	.032	.034	.037	.039	.041	.043	.046	.048
13	.015	.017	.018	.020	.021	.023	.024	.026	.028	.030
14	.008	.009	.009	.010	.011	.012	.013	.015	.016	.017
15	.004	.004	.005	.005	.006	.006	.007	.008	.008	.009
16	.002	.002	.002	.002	.003	.003	.003	.004	.004	.005
17	.001	.001	.001	.001	.001	.001	.001	.002	.002	.002
18	.000	.000	.000	.000	.000	.001	.001	.001	.001	.001

x	m 8.1	8.2	8.3	8.4	8.5	8.6	8.7	8.8	8.9	9.0
0	.000	.000	.000	.000	.000	.000	.000	.000	.000	.000
1	.002	.002	.002	.002	.002	.002	.001	.001	.001	.001
2	.010	.009	.009	.008	.007	.007	.006	.006	.005	.005
3	.027	.025	.024	.022	.021	.020	.018	.017	.016	.015
4	.054	.052	.049	.047	.044	.042	.040	.038	.036	.034
5	.088	.085	.082	.078	.075	.072	.069	.066	.063	.061
6	.119	.116	.113	.110	.107	.103	.100	.097	.094	.091
7	.138	.136	.134	.132	.129	.127	.125	.122	.120	.117
8	.140	.139	.139	.138	.138	.137	.136	.134	.133	.132

9	.126	.127	.128	.129	.130	.131	.131	.131	.132	.132
10	.102	.104	.106	.108	.110	.112	.114	.116	.117	.119
11	.075	.078	.080	.083	.085	.088	.090	.093	.095	.097
12	.051	.053	.055	.058	.060	.063	.065	.068	.070	.073
13	.031	.033	.035	.037	.040	.042	.044	.046	.048	.050
14	.018	.020	.021	.022	.024	.026	.027	.029	.031	.032
15	.010	.011	.012	.013	.014	.015	.016	.017	.018	.019
16	.005	.005	.006	.007	.007	.008	.009	.009	.010	.011
17	.002	.003	.003	.003	.004	.004	.004	.005	.005	.006
18	.001	.001	.001	.002	.002	.002	.002	.002	.003	.003
19	.000	.001	.001	.001	.001	.001	.001	.001	.001	.001
20	.000	.000	.000	.000	.000	.000	.000	.000	.001	.001

x	m 9.1	9.2	9.3	9.4	9.5	9.6	9.7	9.8	9.9	10.0
0	.000	.000	.000	.000	.000	.000	.000	.000	.000	.000
1	.001	.001	.001	.001	.001	.001	.001	.001	.000	.000
2	.005	.004	.004	.004	.003	.003	.003	.003	.002	.002
3	.014	.013	.012	.011	.011	.010	.009	.009	.008	.008
4	.032	.030	.028	.027	.025	.024	.023	.021	.020	.019
5	.058	.055	.053	.051	.048	.046	.044	.042	.040	.038
6	.088	.085	.082	.079	.076	.074	.071	.068	.066	.063
7	.114	.112	.109	.106	.104	.101	.098	.096	.093	.090
8	.130	.129	.127	.125	.123	.121	.119	.117	.115	.113
9	.132	.131	.131	.131	.130	.129	.128	.127	.126	.125
10	.120	.121	.122	.123	.124	.124	.125	.125	.125	.125
11	.099	.101	.103	.105	.107	.108	.110	.111	.113	.114
12	.075	.078	.080	.082	.084	.087	.089	.091	.093	.095
13	.053	.055	.057	.059	.062	.064	.066	.068	.071	.073
14	.034	.036	.038	.040	.042	.044	.046	.048	.050	.052
15	.021	.022	.024	.025	.027	.028	.030	.031	.033	.035
16	.012	.013	.014	.015	.016	.017	.018	.019	.020	.022
17	.006	.007	.007	.008	.009	.010	.010	.011	.012	.013
18	.003	.004	.004	.004	.005	.005	.006	.006	.007	.007
19	.002	.002	.002	.002	.002	.003	.003	.003	.003	.004
20	.001	.001	.001	.001	.001	.001	.001	.002	.002	.002
21	.000	.000	.000	.000	.000	.001	.001	.001	.001	.001

Table 6.2: Order Point and Order Level for Low Demand Items When Monthly Demands d, Service Level (SL) and Lead Time = 0.25 Months

	SL							
	.85		.90		.95		.99	
d	OP	OL	OP	OL	OP	OL	OP	OL
0.1	0	1	0	1	0	1	1	2
0.2	0	1	0	1	0	1	1	2
0.3	0	1	0	1	0	2	1	2
0.4	0	1	0	1	0	2	1	2
0.5	0	1	0	2	1	2	1	2
0.6	0	1	0	2	1	2	1	2
0.7	0	1	0	2	1	2	1	3
0.8	0	2	0	2	1	2	1	3
0.9	0	2	1	2	1	2	2	3
1.0	0	2	1	2	1	2	2	3
1.1	0	2	1	2	1	2	2	3
1.2	0	2	1	2	1	2	2	3
1.3	0	2	1	2	1	2	2	3
1.4	0	2	1	2	1	2	2	3
1.5	1	2	1	2	1	2	2	3
1.6	1	2	1	2	1	3	2	3
1.7	1	2	1	2	1	3	2	3
1.8	1	2	1	2	1	3	2	3
1.9	1	2	1	2	1	3	2	3
2.0	1	2	1	2	1	3	2	4
2.1	1	2	1	3	2	3	3	4
2.2	1	2	1	3	2	3	3	4
2.3	1	2	1	3	2	3	3	4
2.4	1	2	1	3	2	3	3	4
2.5	1	2	1	3	2	3	3	4
2.6	1	2	1	3	2	3	3	4
2.7	1	2	1	3	2	3	3	4

2.8	1	2	1	3	2	3	3	4
2.9	1	2	1	3	2	3	3	4
3.0	1	2	1	3	2	3	3	4
3.1	1	2	1	3	2	3	3	4
3.2	1	2	1	3	2	3	3	4
3.3	1	2	1	3	2	3	3	4
3.4	1	2	1	3	2	3	3	4
3.5	1	3	2	3	2	3	3	4
3.6	1	3	2	3	2	3	3	4
3.7	1	3	2	3	2	3	3	4
3.8	1	3	2	3	2	3	3	5
3.9	1	3	2	3	2	3	3	5
4.0	1	3	2	3	2	4	3	5
4.1	1	3	2	3	2	4	3	5
4.2	1	3	2	3	2	4	3	5
4.3	1	3	2	3	2	4	3	5
4.4	1	3	2	3	2	4	4	5
4.5	1	3	2	3	2	4	4	5
4.6	1	3	2	3	2	4	4	5
4.7	2	3	2	3	2	4	4	5
4.8	2	3	2	3	3	4	4	5
4.9	2	3	2	3	3	4	4	5
5.0	2	3	2	3	3	4	4	5

Table 6.3: Order Point and Order Level for Low Demand Items When Monthly Demands d, Service Level (SL) and Lead Time = 0.50 Months

	SL							
	.85		.90		.95		.99	
d	OP	OL	OP	OL	OP	OL	OP	OL
0.1	0	1	0	1	0	1	1	2
0.2	0	1	0	1	0	2	1	2
0.3	0	1	0	2	1	2	1	2

0.4	0	2	0	2	1	2	1	3
0.5	0	2	1	2	1	2	2	3
0.6	0	2	1	2	1	2	2	3
0.7	0	2	1	2	1	2	2	3
0.8	1	2	1	2	1	3	2	3
0.9	1	2	1	2	1	3	2	3
1.0	1	2	1	2	1	3	2	4
1.1	1	2	1	2	1	3	2	4
1.2	1	2	1	2	2	3	3	4
1.3	1	2	1	3	2	3	3	4
1.4	1	2	1	3	2	3	3	4
1.5	1	2	1	3	2	3	3	4
1.6	1	2	1	3	2	3	3	4
1.7	1	2	1	3	2	3	3	4
1.8	1	3	2	3	2	3	3	4
1.9	1	3	2	3	2	3	3	5
2.0	1	3	2	3	2	4	3	5
2.1	1	3	2	3	2	4	3	5
2.2	1	3	2	3	2	4	4	5
2.3	1	3	2	3	2	4	4	5
2.4	2	3	2	3	3	4	4	5
2.5	2	3	2	3	3	4	4	5
2.6	2	3	2	3	3	4	4	5
2.7	2	3	2	3	3	4	4	5
2.8	2	3	2	3	3	4	4	5
2.9	2	3	2	4	3	4	4	5
3.0	2	3	2	4	3	4	4	5
3.1	2	3	2	4	3	4	4	6
3.2	2	3	2	4	3	4	4	6
3.3	2	3	2	4	3	4	4	6
3.4	2	3	3	4	3	4	5	6

3.5	2	3	3	4	3	5	5	6
3.6	2	4	3	4	3	5	5	6
3.7	2	4	3	4	3	5	5	6
3.8	2	4	3	4	3	5	5	6
3.9	2	4	3	4	4	5	5	6
4.0	2	4	3	4	4	5	5	6
4.1	2	4	3	4	4	5	5	6
4.2	2	4	3	4	4	5	5	6
4.3	3	4	3	4	4	5	5	6
4.4	3	4	3	4	4	5	5	7
4.5	3	4	3	4	4	5	5	7
4.6	3	4	3	4	4	5	5	7
4.7	3	4	3	5	4	5	6	7
4.8	3	4	3	5	4	5	6	7
4.9	3	4	3	5	4	5	6	7
5.0	3	4	3	5	4	5	6	7

Table 6.4: Order Point and Order Level for Low Demand Items When Monthly Demands d, Service Level (SL) and Lead Time = 0.75 Months

	SL							
	.85		.90		.95		.99	
d	OP	OL	OP	OL	OP	OL	OP	OL
0.1	0	1	0	1	0	2	1	2
0.2	0	1	0	2	1	2	1	2
0.3	0	2	1	2	1	2	2	3
0.4	0	2	1	2	1	2	2	3
0.5	1	2	1	2	1	2	2	3
0.6	1	2	1	2	1	3	2	3
0.7	1	2	1	2	1	3	2	4
0.8	1	2	1	2	2	3	3	4
0.9	1	2	1	3	2	3	3	4

1.0	1	2	1	3	2	3	3	4
1.1	1	2	1	3	2	3	3	4
1.2	1	3	2	3	2	3	3	4
1.3	1	3	2	3	2	3	3	5
1.4	1	3	2	3	2	4	3	5
1.5	1	3	2	3	2	4	4	5
1.6	2	3	2	3	3	4	4	5
1.7	2	3	2	3	3	4	4	5
1.8	2	3	2	3	3	4	4	5
1.9	2	3	2	4	3	4	4	5
2.0	2	3	2	4	3	4	4	5
2.1	2	3	2	4	3	4	4	6
2.2	2	3	2	4	3	4	4	6
2.3	2	3	3	4	3	5	5	6
2.4	2	4	3	4	3	5	5	6
2.5	2	4	3	4	3	5	5	6
2.6	2	4	3	4	4	5	5	6
2.7	2	4	3	4	4	5	5	6
2.8	2	4	3	4	4	5	5	6
2.9	3	4	3	4	4	5	5	7
3.0	3	4	3	4	4	5	5	7
3.1	3	4	3	5	4	5	6	7
3.2	3	4	3	5	4	5	6	7
3.3	3	4	3	5	4	5	6	7
3.4	3	4	3	5	4	6	6	7
3.5	3	4	4	5	4	6	6	7
3.6	3	4	4	5	4	6	6	7
3.7	3	4	4	5	5	6	6	7
3.8	3	5	4	5	5	6	6	8
3.9	3	5	4	5	5	6	6	8
4.0	3	5	4	5	5	6	7	8

4.1	3	5	4	5	5	6	7	8
4.2	3	5	4	5	5	6	7	8
4.3	4	5	4	5	5	6	7	8
4.4	4	5	4	6	5	6	7	8
4.5	4	5	4	6	5	6	7	8
4.6	4	5	4	6	5	7	7	8
4.7	4	5	4	6	5	7	7	8
4.8	4	5	5	6	5	7	7	9
4.9	4	5	5	6	6	7	7	9
5.0	4	5	5	6	6	7	8	9

Table 6.5: Order Point and Order Level for Low Demand Items When Monthly Demands d, Service Level (SL) and Lead Time = 1.00 Months

	SL							
	.85		.90		.95		.99	
d	OP	OL	OP	OL	OP	OL	OP	OL
0.1	0	1	0	1	0	2	1	2
0.2	0	2	0	2	1	2	1	3
0.3	0	2	1	2	1	2	2	3
0.4	1	2	1	2	1	3	2	3
0.5	1	2	1	2	1	3	2	4
0.6	1	2	1	2	2	3	3	4
0.7	1	2	1	3	2	3	3	4
0.8	1	2	1	3	2	3	3	4
0.9	1	3	2	3	2	3	3	4
1.0	1	3	2	3	2	4	3	5
1.1	1	3	2	3	2	4	4	5
1.2	2	3	2	3	3	4	4	5
1.3	2	3	2	3	3	4	4	5
1.4	2	3	2	3	3	4	4	5
1.5	2	3	2	4	3	4	4	5

1.6	2	3	2	4	3	4	4	6
1.7	2	3	2	4	3	4	4	6
1.8	2	3	2	4	3	4	4	6
1.9	2	3	2	4	3	4	4	6
2.0	2	4	3	4	4	5	5	6
2.1	2	4	3	4	4	5	5	6
2.2	3	4	3	4	4	5	5	7
2.3	3	4	3	4	4	5	5	7
2.4	3	4	3	5	4	5	6	7
2.5	3	4	3	5	4	5	6	7
2.6	3	4	4	5	4	6	6	7
2.7	3	4	4	5	4	6	6	7
2.8	3	4	4	5	5	6	6	7
2.9	3	5	4	5	5	6	6	8
3.0	3	5	4	5	5	6	7	8
3.1	3	5	4	5	5	6	7	8
3.2	4	5	4	5	5	6	7	8
3.3	4	5	4	6	5	6	7	8
3.4	4	5	4	6	5	7	7	8
3.5	4	5	4	6	5	7	7	8
3.6	4	5	5	6	5	7	7	9
3.7	4	5	5	6	6	7	7	9
3.8	4	5	5	6	6	7	8	9
3.9	4	5	5	6	6	7	8	9
4.0	4	6	5	6	6	7	8	9
4.1	4	6	5	6	6	7	8	9
4.2	4	6	5	6	6	7	8	9
4.3	5	6	5	7	6	8	8	9
4.4	5	6	5	7	6	8	8	10
4.5	5	6	5	7	6	8	9	10
4.6	5	6	6	7	7	8	9	10

4.7	5	6	6	7	7	8	9	10
4.8	5	6	6	7	7	8	9	10
4.9	5	6	6	7	7	8	9	10
5.0	5	6	6	7	7	8	9	10

Summary

In many stocking facilities, like dealers, stores, retailers, the monthly demands are low for most or all of the items in the inventory. Low volume items are particularly common in retail entities where the items are available in a large variety of models, colors and sizes. In the service parts industry, many parts also have low demands. The Poisson distribution applies for these low volume items. This chapter shows how to determine the order point and order level to satisfy the service level specified by management.

Reference

Thomopoulos, Nick T., *Strategic Inventory Management and Planning*, Hitchcock Publishing Company, Carol Stream, Il, 1990.

7

Multi-Locations

This chapter describes the methods used to control the inventory for parts stocked in multi-locations. In the typical situation, each location is assigned to a region (territory) with the goal to fill the local customer demands. On high volume parts, all the locations have some inventory; and for parts with low demands, not all locations will stock the part. For the discussion here, each location and part combination is labeled by stocking type in the following way: master location, stocking branch location, non-stocking branch location, and 2-level-service location. The chapter describes a way to assign the stocking type to each location; how each location is replenished with new stock, and how the demands of their customers are filled. The reader will learn how new stock from the supplier is allotted to the locations. The chapter also shows how to detect if one of the locations is dangerously low in stock and whether another location has adequate stock to send in transfer. The chapter also describes the concept of the supplier lead time, the transfer lead time, the supplier multiple quantity and the transfer multiple quantity.

Introduction

In the typical distribution system with two or more locations, each location is assigned a region and is charged with filling the demands from the customers in the region. Often, one location is designated as the master location, and holds inventory on all parts, and may also serve as the source to all locations. The other locations hold inventory just sufficient to satisfy the regional demands. The goal is to achieve a high service level and maintain the minimum overall investment in inventory for the total system. In this multi-location system, management is confronted with added inventory decisions. Some of the decisions are described in this chapter. A short review is below.

Network Design is the task of deciding how many locations to have, where they should be located and how large they should be. This is a classic logistics problem and much care is needed to achieve a smooth flow of the inventory, and also accomplish the minimum transportation and warehousing costs.

Network Replenishment is the manner of replenishing stock to the locations in the network. One location is designated as the master location on all parts. On low demand parts, some locations are non-stocking branch locations, and their customer demands are filled by the master location. On other parts, the locations may be stocking branch locations, and are replenished by the supplier. If the location is small in space and/or budget, the location may be replenished in a 2-level-service manner from the master location.

Part Location Assignment establishes the locations that stock a part. A part with low demands is stocked in only the master location; parts with higher demands are stocked in two or more locations.

Allocation is called when a new replenish quantity arrives from the supplier and is to be shared by all the stocking locations. This happens when the replenish needs are lumped into one purchase order with the supplier. A lead time later, when the stock is ready from the supplier, a decision is called on how to allot the quantity to each location.

Transfer is called when one location is dangerously low in inventory and another location is found to have extra stock. Stock is sent between the locations to avoid mal-distribution of inventory. Applying transfer in this way can reduce the number of buys needed from the supplier.

Network Design

Suppose a system where parts are housed in multi-locations, with one location designated as the master location. When a new replenishment is needed at the network, the master buys from the supplier of the part. The inventory is shared among the locations in a way that minimizes the total investment in inventory and achieves a high service level with the customer demands. Each location is assigned to a region, and the typical customer will buy from the location in the region.

A critical function of the management occurs at the outset in the design stage of the inventory system. The design of the total network is complex, and decisions are needed on how many locations to have, where to locate the master location as well as the other locations, and how large should the location facilities be. This is a logistics problem that seeks to find the network of locations that minimizes the overall flow of inventory from suppliers to distribution centers to customers. The network that accomplishes all of the goals and yet has a minimum number of locations is desired.

Location centers are often used to identify where each facility lies on a map. A finite number of known location centers are included in the analysis; and the distance from one location center to another is known and is included in the database tables. The facilities of interest pertain to the suppliers, the stocking locations and the customers. Each facility is assigned a location center that is closest.

Parameters are values assigned by the management and are used to steer the calculations on each option. These are especially essential for the inventory computations. The parameters 'hold rate' and 'cost per order' are needed in the computations to determine the order size for each part and location. The parameter 'service level' is needed to determine the amount of safety stock to have. The order size and the safety stock are used to measure the number of receives (from the supplier) in a year and the average on-hand inventory by location.

A series of computer routines are needed to analyze the various network-options. Each option is run—one at a time—and becomes a candidate for the final distribution network to use. The option consists of a master location and an accompanying set of stock locations. With each option, the routine determines, for each part, how much inventory is needed, where is it stocked, how often is it ordered and so forth. The compilation over all of the parts yields the reports that allow the management to estimate the total cost when applying the option. The computations tally the costs of inventory, receiving, shipping, transportation and warehouse by location and in total. The option with the minimum total cost is favored as the distribution network to use.

Network Replenishments

Consider a network where parts (products) are stored in more than one location. Could be an OEM with a series of distribution centers, a dealership with two or more locations, or possibly a retailer with a string of stores. In essence, this is a multi-location stocking network with N locations where stock is held in each location to fill the demands from the local customers. The network consists of one master location (ML) and N-1 branch locations (BL). Not all parts are housed at every branch. The slow moving parts might be stocked only at the master location.

There are essentially four stocking types (ST) of locations in the network. For convenience, they are labeled as below:

Master location (ML)

Stocking branch location (SBL)

Non-stocking branch location (NSBL)

2-level-service location (2LS)

The master location is the same location for all parts, and in this way, there is only one master location. Typically, a location delegated as 2-level-service for one part, is also a 2-level-service location for all parts. But the stocking and non-stocking branch locations can be different for each part. That is, location A could be a stocking location for part 111 and a non-stocking location for part 222, and so forth. A description on each of the stocking type follows.

Master Location (ML)

The master location is also a branch location. It serves as the leader to all the locations, it is centrally located and often has more storage space than the other locations. It also has its own customers and holds inventory to fill its customer demands. The master also holds extra stock so that it can fill the demands for any non-stocking location. Further, the master location will hold extra stock should it serve as the supplier to any 2-level-service location.

Stocking Branch Location (SBL)

This is a location with sufficient demand on a part where the location is deemed efficient to hold stock and shares any new stock that comes in from the supplier. Recall, the master location is always included as a stocking branch location. The demand history is from the location's regional customers.

In the event the SBL is the ML, the demand history fields hold the sum of monthly (or weekly) local demands at the ML and also the demands from the NSBL and 2LS locations. This added demand is included when forecasting, since the ML is charged with holding stock for these locations.

Non-Stocking Branch Location (NSBL)

This is a location with low demand on a part and stock is not held. Any demands from the local customers on this part are directed to the master location that fills the order. The demand history from this location is included in the aggregate demand history at the ML. The forecast for this location is set to zero.

Although this is a non-stocking location, the location might have some inventory left-over from a prior period when it held stock. Such inventory can be used, as needed, at a subsequent time to transfer stock from one location to another. The history demands should remain on the database record for the location.

2-Level-Service Location (2LS)

This type of location has limited space and cannot hold much inventory. The location may have sufficient demand on a part where it is deemed efficient to holds stock, but this location does not directly receive any new stock from the supplier. Instead, the ML is the source for this location. When new stock is needed here, the 2LS location sends a buy order to the ML who is obliged to ship the replenishment stock in return. The demand history from this location is included in the aggregate demand history at the ML. This location uses the transfer lead time, Lt, and the transfer multiple quantity, Mt, in the computations to find the order point and order level on the part. The transfer lead time is typically much smaller than the supplier lead time, and the transfer multiple quantity is often smaller than the supplier multiple quantity.

Network Configuration

There are many ways to configure the locations in a network. One arrangement is where all the locations stock the parts, one location is the ML and the others are stocking locations. Another arrangement is where the ML receives all the stock from the supplier, and the ML serves as the source to all other locations in a 2LS way.

Replenish Quantity for Each Location

To illustrate, consider a part with the following lead time and multiple quantity data:

Supplier lead time = Ls

Suppler multiple quantity = Ms

Transfer lead time = Lt

Transfer multiple quantity = Mt

The supplier entries above pertain to stock coming from the supplier, and the transfer entries are when stock is coming from another location.

Assume the network has four locations and are labeled as: (1, 2, 3, 4). Suppose a part, where the stocking type (ST) by locations are assigned: ML, SBL, NSBL, 2LS, respectively, for locations 1, 2, 3, 4. The part-location record on the database for these locations would include data fields as below:

Fields	Records			
Location	1	2	3	4
ST	ML	SBL	NSBL	2LS
d(t)	d1(t)	d2(t)	d3(t)	d4(t)
oh	oh1	oh2	oh3	oh4

oo	oo1	oo2	oo3	oo4
de(t)	d1(t)+ d3(t)+ d4(t)	d2(t)	0	d4(t)

Note the demands d(t) are for history months t = 1 to T. The demand history d(t) are not changed and remain on the part-location record, regardless of the stocking type (ST). The demand history that is used to generate the forecasts is also listed and is called the effective demand, de(t). The effective demand at location 1 is the sum of demands from locations 1, 3 and 4. This is because, location 1 is charged with filling the demands from locations 1, 3 and 4. The effective demands at location 3 are set to zero since it is a non-stocking location. The forecasts are needed to compute the order point (op) and order level (ol) for each part. In the computations, the lead time used is Ls for locations 1, 2, 3, and Lt for location 4. The multiple quantity is Ms for locations 1, 2, 3, and Mt for location 4.

Replenish at ML and SBL

These locations are replenished in either of two ways as described here: First is when each location independently orders replenish stock from the supplier. This happens when the on-hand plus on-order (oh + oo) inventory at the location is at the order point or below. The location orders q = [ol – (oh + oo)] and this quantity is adjusted to comply with the supplier multiple quantity, Ms. Second is when the network orders stock for all the stocking locations. The network data is needed here. If the network on-hand plus on-order is less than the order point, a replenish quantity of Q = [OL – (OH + OO)], adjusted for Ms, is ordered. When this stock comes in, an allocate routine is run to determine how to split the stock to the locations, as described later in the Allocate section.

Replenish at NSBL

Since this location is a non-stocking location, the NSBL location receives no replenish stock.

Replenish at 2LS

Everyday, the on-hand (oh) plus on-order (oo) inventory at each 2LS location is compared to the order point (op) and order level (ol), and if (oh + oo) $\leq$ op, a replenish buy to the ML is called for the quantity q = ol – (oh + oo). The quantity is adjusted so that q is compliant with the transfer multiple quantity, Mt.

Replenish Quantity for the Network

The associated record for the part would have data as below:

Fields	Record
Location	Part
ST	NW
d(t)	d1(t) + d2(t) + d3(t) + d4(t)
oh	oh1 + oh2 + oh3
oo	oo1

The part record for the NW (network) is used to generate the forecasts on the part. The supplier data Ls and Ms are used with the forecasts to compute the order point (op) and order level (ol) for the part. Each day the current on-hand (oh) and on-order (oo) inventory is compared to op to determine if new stock is needed from the supplier. If (oh + oo) $\leq$ op, the replenish quantity is Q = ol – (oh + oo). This quantity is adjusted to be compliant with Ms.

Part Location Assignment

This section shows a way to decide which locations should stock the part. The method assumes the part is always stocked at the master location, ML. Also, the master location is charged with filling all demands from any non-stock location, and this process is called sourcing. Sourcing is the term used when one location fills the demands of another location.

To carry out this method, the part data used are as follows:

part data: F12 = 12 month forecast

ppo = average pieces per order

location i data: p(i) = portion of total demand

parameters: n12Min = min 12 month lines to stock

k-month-rule = successive months to change (defined below)

computations per location:

$$n12(i) = F12 \times p(i)/ppo = \text{forecast of 12 month lines}$$

Note, n12 is the forecast of lines at location i for the next 12 months, i.e. the number of customer orders at location i. The decision on whether to stock the part in location i is as follows:

if $n12(i) \geq n12Min$, stock the part in location i

if $n12(i) < n12Min$, do not stock the part in location i

Two worksheets below illustrate the methods for a network of four locations (1, 2, 3, 4) with location 1 as the master location. The examples also follow two parts (A, B) where F12 = 100 for part A, and F12 = 20 for part B. The examples assume the average pieces per order are ppo = 2.00 for both parts A and B. The worksheets list the computations of 12 month lines, n12, and the stocking decision for each location. The examples assume the parameter on the 12 month minimum lines is n12Min = 3.00 lines.

Table 7.1: Worksheet for Part A
(F12 = 100, ppo = 2.00 and n12Min = 3)

Location	p	f12	n12	Decision
1	0.4	40	20	stock
2	0.3	30	15	stock
3	0.2	20	10	stock
4	0.1	10	5	stock

Table 7.2: Worksheet for Part B
(F12 = 20, ppo = 2.00 and n12Min = 3)

Location	p	f12	n12	Decision
1	0.4	8	4	stock
2	0.3	6	3	stock
3	0.2	4	2	non-stock
4	0.1	2	1	non-stock

So for part A, with a higher 12 month forecast than part B, all of the locations will stock the part.

For part B, only locations 1 and 2 will stock the part.

K-Month-Rule

For part-locations (skus) that are on the border of stock and non-stock, a 'k-month-rule' may be used. As an example, the parameter for the k-month-rule is set at 3 months. If a part is currently stocked, and the monthly computations point to non-stock on k successive months, then the part should be switched to non-stock. On the other hand, if the part is now non-stocked and the monthly computations call for stocking the part on k successive months, then the part is changed to stock.

2-Level-Service (2LS)

If the location has sufficient demand on a part, but the location has limited space to stock the part, the location may be assigned as a 2-level-service location (2LS), rather than as a stocking branch location (SBL). This way, the location can cover its customer demands and requires less storage space.

Allocate

An Allocate routine is run when new replenish stock arrives from the supplier and more than one location is designated to share the new stock. The only locations who can receive stock are the locations with stocking type SBL. This routine determines how to apportion the stock to the locations in a fair share way.

The locations that share the new replenish stock are the master location and all other SBLs. Three allocation scenarios are as below:

1. If the only location to stock the part is the master location, then all the new replenish stock goes to the master location.
2. Some suppliers will only ship to one location, say location A, typically the ML. When new stock arrives at location A, an allocate routine is called to determine how to split the new stock to the stocking locations; whereby location A ships to the locations, accordingly.

3. When a supplier will ship the new replenish stock directly to all locations, the allocate routine is run in advance of shipment date to notify the supplier how to apportion the stock for direct shipment to each of the locations.

Allocate is needed when a new replenish quantity from the supplier becomes available to the network and this new stock is to be shared by one or more of the locations. A first priority is to send stock to fill any backorder demands. After the backorders are filled, the allocation of the remaining replenish stock is determined in a fair share way, whereby the inventory status of the locations are balanced with the future forecasts at the locations. A quantity called the months-supply (MS) is computed for each location and is a measure on how far out in the future the net on-hand inventory will last. The goal is to split the new stock to maximize the MS. In this section, the inventory status is denoted as the net on-hand inventory (OH′) where OH′ = (OH + IT – SS), and OH = on-hand inventory, IT = in-transit inventory (stock coming from another location in the network), and SS = safety stock at the location. OH′ is compared to the future monthly forecasts F(t) (t = 1, 2, ...) to determine how far into the future the stock will last.

Allocation Method: The first step is to compute the ratio ms′ = [Σ(OH′(i) + Q]/[F(ms)] with all the locations (i) included. The ratio, ms' represents the aggregate months-supply after including the allocate quantity Q. The numerator is the sum of (net inventory plus allocate quantity); and the denominator is the average monthly forecast for ms months. The second step is to find the month's supply by location using the net inventory quantity, labeled as MS(i). If any location i has a MS(i) greater than ms′, then that location (say i_0) is dropped in the allocate computations, and the ratio of ms′ is re-computed. The third step is to find the raw allocate quantity for all locations (not including i_0) using the relation: Q(i) = [F(i, ms′) – OH(i)′], where F(i, ms′) is the cumulative forecast at location i for ms′ months. Note ms′ represents the maximum months supply for the locations in the network.

To illustrate, assume a part with four stocking locations (1, 2, 3, 4) and worksheet (Table 7.3) data as below. Suppose the supplier ships a replenish quantity of Q = 48 pieces and the supplier multiple quantity is Ms = 6 pieces. A decision on how to split the replenish quantity to the locations is needed.

Table 7.3: Worksheet with Allocate Location Data

Locations (i)	OH	IT	SS	F(1)	F(2)	F(3)	F(4)
1	10	0	6	12	12	12	12
2	5	0	3	6	6	6	6
3	25	0	4	8	8	8	8
4	20	0	8	16	16	16	16

The net on-hand (OH′ = OH + IT – SS) is listed for each location in the worksheet (Table 7.4) below. These are compared to the monthly forecasts to give the pre-month-supply measures. The allocate quantities (raw allot) in the worksheet represent the fair share way to split the 48 pieces (without regard to Ms). The raw allot yields the raw MS measures as listed.

But the allocation mix is constrained by the supplier multiple quantity, Ms, since each allocation quantity must be in multiples of Ms. Also, one or more locations may already have excess stock to begin. In the worksheet below, the post allot mix is (18, 12, 0, 18) to locations (1, 2, 3, 4), respectively. This allocation is compliant with Ms and Q and maximizes the MS for each location. The worksheet lists pre-MS, the months-supply before allocation, and the post-MS, the months-supply after allocation. The post allot is the final allocation mix to use.

In this example, ms′ = [39 + 48]/[42] = 2.07. In the worksheet below, this quantity, 2.07, is compared to each location's MS(i) and since, MS(3) is larger than ms′, location 3 is dropped from the computations and ms′ is re-computed. The revised ms′ becomes ms′ = [18 + 48]/[34] = 1.94. So now, the raw allocate quantity for location i becomes Q(i) = F(i, 1.94) – OH′. The raw allocate (allot) quantities are listed in the worksheet.

Table 7.4: Worksheet with Allocate Part and Location Data

Locations (i)	pre OH′	pre MS	raw Allot	raw MS	post Allot	post MS
1	4	0.33	19.28	1.94	18	1.83
2	2	0.33	9.64	1.94	12	2.33
3	21	2.62	0	2.62	0	2.62
4	12	0.75	19.04	1.94	18	1.87
sum			48		48	

Notes: Q = 48 = new replenish quantity
Ms = 6 = supplier multiple quantity

Transfer

This routine is run for all parts that are stocked in two or more locations. The locations that can receive stock are those with stocking type ML and SBL, and the locations that can send stock are the ones with stocking type ML, SBL and NSBL. This routine is run (periodically) to balance the mix of stock between the locations striving to avoid mal-distribution on inventory. One part at-a-time is scanned seeking if any location is dangerously low in stock and if another location has excess stock to send. When a combination is found, a transfer order is submitted with information on the part, the send location, receive location and the quantity to transfer. An example is shown below.

Suppose a part that is stocked in four locations (1, 2, 3, 4) with data as listed below.

Table 7.5: Worksheet with Transfer Part and Location Data

Locations	OH	IT	SS	F1	F2	F3	F4
1	34	0	4	8	8	9	9
2	25	0	6	12	12	12	13
3	9	0	5	10	10	10	11
4	30	0	7	14	14	15	15
sum	98		22	44	44	46	48

Notes: OO = 0 (on-order quantity)
Mt = 5 (transfer multiple quantity)

Prior to seeking a transfer, if the on-order (OO) is a positive quantity, transfer may be bypassed since new stock is soon coming from the supplier and allocation will distribute the stock to the locations in a fair share manner.

A first step is to compute the net-on-hand inventory at each location (OH′ = OH + IT – SS). Using this OH′, a second step is to compute the month-supply (MS) for each location. For location 1, OH′ = 30 pieces is projected to last for 3.55 months (F1 + F2 + F3 + 0.55F4) = 30. In the same way, the months-supply for the other locations are found. The worksheet below shows location 3 is dangerously low (MS = 0.40) and is a potential receiver location. A transfer can only take place if another location has excess stock to send. Note where location 1 has MS = 3.55 months of stock and thereby is a potential sender location. Because the transfer multiple quantity is Mt = 5 pieces, the amount to send must be in multiples of 5 pieces for this part.

Table 7.6: Worksheet with Transfer Months Supply

Locations	OH′	F1	F2	F3	F4	MS
1	30	8	8	9	9	3.55
2	19	12	12	12	13	1.58
3	4	10	10	10	11	0.40
4	23	14	14	15	15	1.64

An adequate transfer quantity exists when 10 pieces are shipped from location 1 to 3. The worksheet below shows the pre and post transfer month-supply for the four locations. Note the month-supply for location 1 goes from 3.55 to 2.44, and for location 3, it changes from 0.40 to 1.40.

Table 7.7: Worksheet with Transfer Results

Locations	pre MS	send	receive	OH′	post MS
1	3.55	10		20	2.44
2	1.58			19	1.58
3	0.40		10	14	1.40
4	1.64			23	1.64

Summary

When parts are stocked in a multiple number of locations, the stocking of the parts requires careful planning and some distribution unique methods. The chapter describes some of the problems encountered and the methods needed in network design, network replenishments, part-location assignment, allocation and transfer.

References

Minner, Stephan, *Strategic Safety Stocks in Supply Chains*, Springer-Verlag, 2000.

Thomopoulos, Nick T., *Strategic Inventory Management and Planning*, Hitchcock Publishing Co., Carol Stream, II. 1990.

8

Production

This chapter describes the way a typical manufacturing plant is run. The goal is to use the minimum production resources that are needed to produce and meet the customer order quantities and promise delivery dates. The resources are the inventory (raw materials, parts, end-items), employees and machinery. At the beginning, the management determines a production plan that specifies the output levels to achieve for the near time horizon. The production plan depends on whether the finished items are of the type: make-to-order, make-to-stock or a combination of the two. To run the plant in a systematic way, each finished good item is processed through a master production scheduling system to determine when to produce the items and how much. To ensure the schedules are feasible, the results are passed through a rough-cut-capacity-planning system. Adjustments to the schedules may be needed when the schedule does not conform to the capacity. All of the end-items and sub-assemblies are documented with a bill-of-material (BOM) that itemizes all the parts and components needed to build one unit of product. The BOM is essential in material requirements planning to schedule the inflow and production on all the items (named in the BOM) to meet the production requirements on each end-item. Indeed, to run an efficient and smooth manufacturing operation, requires systematic planning and control and the tasks are very challenging.

Introduction

Production takes place at the part and component suppliers, and at the OEMs that produce the finished goods. The production planning and scheduling of the operations is a complicated process and requires careful coordination between materials, labor, machines and facilities. This chapter describes some of the main methods used in the production process. These include the production plan, the master production schedule, rough cut capacity planning, bill of materials and material requirements planning.

Production Plan

The production plan is a function of the top management in a manufacturing firm and covers production, finance, marketing and accounting. This is the schedule on the production over the near planning horizon for the plant. It is the aggregate build schedule and the plan is listed in units that pertain to the type of product. Could be dollars, tons, units or barrels, whatever is appropriate. This production plan is essentially a management directive on what to produce. Upon completion of the plan by the upper management, the plant management is responsible to meet the plan. The units produced by the plant should meet the production plan and not deviate higher or lower. The production plan is typically reviewed and revised each month.

The computations of the production plan depend on how customer orders are fulfilled by the company. Below shows three typical scenarios: make to stock, make to order and the combination of make to stock and make to order.

Make to Stock

This production method pertains when the items produced are placed in a plant warehouse to await future demands from the downstream customers. The demands for the items are not known and are forecast for the future time horizon. The production schedule is heavily depended on the forecast of sales over the future time period.

In the example below, t = 0 designates the current time, t = 1 is the first future month, and so forth. The data needed to determine the production plan are the forecast of sales by future months and the desired ending inventory (current and future months). Recall, the figures are aggregate type representing the total of all finished goods in the plant.

Table 8.1: Worksheet Example of Make-to-Stock Production Plan

months (t)		0	1	2	3
forecast of sales	(F)	–	350	320	342
desired ending inventory	(I)	500	520	550	490
production plan	(P)		370	350	282

$P(t) = F(t) + [I(t) - I(t - 1)]$

Make to Order

This production method pertains when the production of goods depends on the orders from the customers. It could be for big ticket items like cars and trucks. The units produced on the line each have an associated customer order with a series of features specified and a promise delivery date. The output from the plant is delivered to the customer directly or by way of a dealer from where the sales order was placed. The production schedule depends on the sales in hand (backlogs) and the forecast of sales over the future time period.

As before, t = 0 designates the current time, t = 1 is the first future month, and so forth. The data needed to determine the production plan are the forecast of sales by future months and the desired ending backlog (current and future months). Recall, the figures are aggregate type representing the total of all finished goods in the plant.

Table 8.2: Worksheet Example of Make-to-Order Production Plan

months (t)		0	1	2	3
forecast of sales	(F)	–	250	260	266
desired ending backlog	(B)	140	150	128	166
production plan	(P)		240	282	228

$P(t) = F(t) - [B(t) - B(t - 1)]$

Make to Stock and Make to Order

This production plan is a combination of the two methods described above. The production in the plant depends on the customer orders for future delivery (backlog), and also on the units to stock in the inventory awaiting the future customer orders. In the former case, the customer places an order for future delivery (by feature and options); and in the latter case, the customer needs the item now and is willing to take one of the items already available in stock. The units produced on the each line have an associated customer order with specifications and due dates. The output from the plant is delivered to the customer directly or by way of a dealer from where the sales order was placed. The production schedule depends on the projection of sales in hand (backlogs), and the forecast of sales over the horizon time period. Also needed are the current on-hand inventory and the current backlogs.

As before, t = 0 designates the current time, t = 1 is the first future month, and so forth. The data needed to determine the production plan are the forecast of sales by future months, the desired ending backlog and ending inventory (current and for future months). Recall, the figures are aggregate type representing the total of all finished goods in the plant.

Table 8.3: Worksheet Example of Make-to-Stock and Make-to-Order Production Plan

months (t)		0	1	2	3	4
forecast of sales	(F)	–	740	700	790	890
desired ending backlog	(B)	160	180	220	220	240
desired ending inventory	(I)	780	820	860	900	940
production plan	(P)		760	700	830	910

$P(t) = F(t) + [I(t) - I(t-1)] - [B(t) - B(t-1)]$

Master Production Schedule

The master production schedule (MPS) is run for each finished good item in the plant and covers the time periods over the near horizon, typically the weeks of the coming one to two months. The aggregate of the schedule should sum to the production plan. The results of the schedule are used in the subsequent runs of material requirement planning (MRP). This is where the part and component inventories are planned and scheduled to meet the MPS needs of the finished goods. The MPS can be run each week to account for the latest data available on the finished goods.

In the example below, a seven week time horizon is assumed. The quantity to schedule each week depends on the future weekly requirements on the item and also on the current inventory available. The future requirements are computed by weeks and are the sum of the forecasts of demands for both service and production, plus the actual demands already known for the future weeks.

The notation is listed below.

- t = weeks
- F = forecast of service demand
- PF = production forecast
- AD = actual demand
- R = requirements = (F + PF + AD)
- PB = projected available balance
- AP = available to promise
- MPS = master production schedule

For each item, some data is needed to carry out the computations, and they are described here. The order size (Q) is the production lot quantity determined, in advance, and the size establishes a mandatory multiple whenever a replenishment is called. The current on-hand inventory (OH), is needed, and in the table below is assigned as PB(0). The lead time (L), is the elapsed time from the schedule week to the week the quantity becomes available to fill the required demands.

Table 8.4: Worksheet Example of the Master Production Schedule

t	0	1	2	3	4	5	6	7	8
F		16	0	0	0	20	0	0	0
PF		0	0	8	0	24	0	30	0
AD		28	0	20	0	4	0	0	0
R		44	0	28	0	48	0	30	0

PB	50	6	6	58	58	10	10	60	60
AP		22		56				80	0
MPS		0	0	80	0	0	0	80	0

Note: Q = 80 order size OH = 50 on-hand
L = 0 lead time SS = 0 safety stock

Computations: Projected available balance (PB) is a measure on the inventory available at the end of each week t. The measure for each week t is as below:

$$PB(t) = [PB(t - 1) + MPS(t)] - R(t)$$

Available to promise (AP) is measured at week 1 and at each future week where a new build quantity is called in the master production schedule. This is a measure on how much inventory is not committed from all the actual demands till the next build quantity. Since, in the example, the master production schedule is set for weeks 3 and 7, the available to promise is also measured for weeks 3 and 7, as shown below.

$$AP(1) = PB(0) - [AD(1) + AD(2)]$$

$$AP(3) = MPS(3) - [AD(3) + AD(4) + AD(5) + AD(6)]$$

$$AP(7) = MPS(7) - [AD(7) + AD(8)]$$

The master production schedule is called for the week when the projected inventory will fall at or below the safety stock (zero in the example). Note PB(2) = 6 for week 2, but at the next week, PB would fall below zero; thereby a build schedule is called for week 3. When an MPS is called, it must be compliant with the multiple quantity for the end item, here Q = 80. Thereby 80 pieces are scheduled for week 3 and this quantity will last until week 7, whence another schedule is called.

$$MPS(3) = 80 \geq [R(3) + R(4) + R(5) + R(6)] - PB(2)$$

$$MPS(7) = 80 \geq [R(7) + R(8)] - PB(6)$$

In the above example, to maintain weekly inventory above zero at all week-ending time periods, schedules of 80 pieces are needed in weeks 3 and 7. With the restriction that the order size of Q = 80, the master production schedule will yield the minimum inventory for the finished good item over the seven week time horizon.

In the event the lead time (L) were one week, the MPS quantities would be moved forward by one week. If the safety stock (SS) were 10 pieces, say, the MPS would be called whenever the projected available balance (PB) fell at or below SS = 10 pieces.

Rough Cut Capacity Planning

The capacity needed to produce the MPS is measured for each of the weeks over the planning period. Rough cut capacity planning concerns the labor and machine hours on a broad basis and is usually determined by the various departments or work centers separately. With this projection, management makes intermediate decisions on the capacity to meet production needs. If the capacity is too low, then decisions are made, for example, on procuring new machines, authorizing overtime, subcontracting certain operations, and other strategies.

The following is an example worksheet that is needed for each department in the plant. The department is responsible for three end items (A, B, C) and the worksheet determines the load, capacity and variance for each of the future three months.

Table 8.5: Worksheet Example for Rough Cut Capacity Planning

End item	Resource per unit			Months 1	2	3
A	0.6	planned order release		100	90	100
		resource usage		60	54	60
B	1.0	planned order release		150	200	200
		resource usage		150	200	200
C	1.5	planned order release		120	120	90
		resource usage		180	180	135
		Load	total	390	434	395
			cumulative	390	824	1219
		Capacity	total	400	400	380
			cumulative	400	800	1180
		Variance	total	10	–34	–15
			cumulative	10	–24	–39

Result: Capacity is short in months 2 and 3.

Bill-of-Material

The bill-of-materials (BOM) is somewhat like a blueprint and lists how to build a sub-assembly or an end-item. The BOM shows all the parts and components and the quantities of each that are needed to assemble one end-item. A graphical way to display the BOM is by the tree diagram. The example below shows a bill-of-material in tree diagram form for the assembly of one unit of end-item x (fastener).

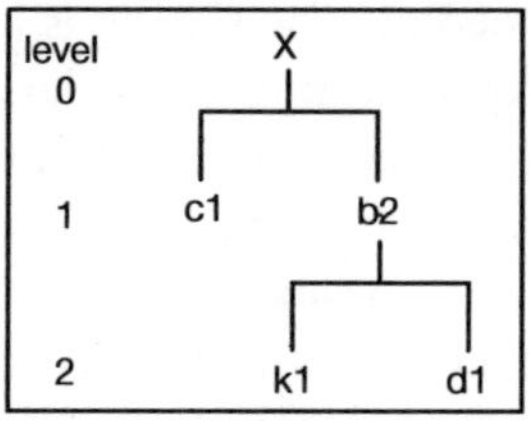

Figure 8.1: Example BOM Tree Diagram.

Note level 0 is the end-item X. To build one unit of X requires 1 unit of c and 2 units of b (level 1). One unit of b requires one unit of k and one of d (level 2).

The bill-of-material may also be listed in tabular form as in the example below. This is called the indented BOM, and includes more detail on the end-item assembly than does the tree diagram BOM. This BOM may list added data like the part description, supplier, supplier part number, make or buy, multiple quantity and quantity per unit. See the example below that shows the end-item X with some of the added detail. Note, parts k and d are obtained from an outside supplier and parts c and b are produced in the plant. Part c must be ordered in multiples of 10, b and d in multiples of 5, and k in multiples of one. Further, two units of b are needed for each unit of X.

Table 8.6: BOM Indented Form for End-Item X

Assembly part X (fastener)		Indented bill of material	
Part	Make or buy	Multiple quantity	Quantity per unit
c	make	10	1
b	make	5	2
.k	buy	1	1
.d	buy	5	1

Material Requirement Planning

With the MPS situated to accommodate the production plan and to satisfy capacity constraints, the next concern is scheduling the inflow of basic materials and also scheduling the fabrication of parts needed to fulfill the MPS. This task is accomplished by use of material requirements planning (MRP). For each end item on the MPS, the associated bill of material is "exploded" (broken down in detail) to determine timing and quantities of all parts and basic materials needed. The timing is usually associated with weekly or daily buckets (combined orders). In the calculations, lead times and routing relationships of parts and basic materials are taken into consideration, when determining the timing needs of each calculated need. Results for parts and basic materials used on more than one end item are now combined. At this time, calculated lot sizes for each component (in multiple quantities) are used along with currently available inventory to determine a schedule of order releases as well as the order receipts at the next higher stage in production.

The example below shows the table for end-item X (fastener) that requires parts and components (k, d, b, c). The plan calls for 100 pieces of X by the date 022708, (02.27.08), and shows the corresponding quantities needed by order and due dates for parts b, c, d and k.

Since X is due on 022708 and because the lead time is five working days, the units are released one week earlier, 022098 for 100 pieces. To start X on 022008, we need parts b and c. Part b is released at 020608 since its lead time is 10 working days for due date of 022008; and part c is released on 021308 (lead time = 5 days), and so forth.

Note, 100 pieces are needed on X, 100 on c, and 175 on b. The BOM on part b calls for 2 units of b for each unit of X, so altogether, 200 pieces of b are needed. But since the on-hand for b is 25, the release only requires 175 pieces. Now because one unit of k and of d are needed for each unit of b, and because 175 units of b are needed, the system calls for 165 (on-hand = 10) of k. Since part d needs 175 pieces, has 37 on-hand, and a multiple quantity of five, the release quantity becomes 140.

Table 8.7: MRP Worksheet for End-Item X

	Part number	Order by	Due date	Supplier	Release quantity	Lead time	Unit multiple	On hand
MPS	X	022008	022708		100	5	1	0
make report	k	013008	020608	plant	165	5	1	10
	d	012308	020608	plant	140	10	5	37
buy report	b	020608	022008	ABC	175	10	5	25
	c	021308	022008	Apix	100	5	10	0

The major difficulty in MRP concerns the integrity of the data used in the computations. These include the inventory, bill-of-material, the master-production-schedule and the actual lead time. Another concern occurs since MRP computes the schedules on all components without regard to the capacity on the operations to accomplish the schedules as planned.

Summary

The production of the components and finished goods is a complicated process and requires careful coordination between customer due dates, materials, labor, machines and facilities. This chapter describes the main methods used in the production process. These include the production plan, the master production schedule, rough cut capacity planning, bill of materials and material requirements planning.

References

Thomopoulos, Nick T., *Strategic Inventory Management and Planning*, Hitchcock Publishing Co., Carol Stream, II, 1990.

Vollman, Thomas E., William L. Berry and D. Clay Whybark, *Manufacturing Planning and Control*, McGraw Hill, 1997.

9

Assembly

This chapter describes single and mixed model assembly lines. In single model assembly, the reader will learn how to measure the cycle time and balance delay, and why these measures are important to determine the efficiency of the line. Also described is the precedence diagram and how it is used with line balancing to assign the work elements to the station operators. In mixed model assembly, the reader learns the two main tasks to attain an efficient line are assigning the work elements to the station operators, and sequencing the units down the line. The chapter shows how line balancing takes place in mixed model assembly. The reader will also learn how to sequence the units down the line when they are produced on a make-to-stock basis, and on a make-to-order basis. In the latter case, the customers specify the features and options that they desired on the individual units.

Introduction

To build one unit of a finished good item, all of the parts and components listed on the bill-of-materials are gathered and are inserted one-by-one until the unit is complete. This is the role of an assembly line. The full line of assembly tasks are listed and are assigned in a systematic way to the station operators along the line. The associated parts and components of the tasks are stocked at the stations where operators perform the assembly tasks. Each unit passes from one station to another and the unit is completed when it leaves the final station. Below is a discussion on some of the basic quantitative methods used in the control of an assembly line.

Single Model Lines

A copy machine manufacturer produces three models (A, B, C). The models are assigned to individual lines, and model A is placed on a line that runs on one shift of 440 productive minutes a day. The current demands for A call for 220 units a day (220 units per shift), and thereby the line should complete one unit every (440/220) 2.00 minutes. Since A is the only model on the line, the line is called a single model assembly line. One of the goals of the plant management is to assign the work elements associated with the copy machine to the station operators in a way where each operator has—as close as possible—equal time and where the number of units produced in a day is 220 units.

Single Model Assembly

Single model assembly is where one model is produced on the line. This way, the line is dedicated to the one model of the finished good item. For example, when a particular blender model is assigned for assembly to a line, the finished good item (blender) is assembled on a single model assembly line.

Cycle Time and Balance Delay

Suppose a unit to be assembled on a single model assembly line is composed of m work elements where E_i (i = 1, ..., m) represents the ith element, and t_i the associated element standard time. The total unit time needed to complete one unit of product is Σt_i.

Further, let n designate the minimum number of operators assigned to the line, T the length of the shift time, and N the number of units to be produced in a shift. To find the number of operators to assign to the line, first find $n' = N \times \Sigma t_i/T$. If n′ is an integer, set n = n′; and if not, n is the next higher integer to n′.

The time between units coming off the line is called the cycle time and is denoted as c′. For a given combination of N and T, the time between units coming off the line is $c' = T/N$.

The operation time is the time per unit assigned to the j-th operator and is here denoted as c_j (j = 1, ..., n). A line with no parallel stations requires $c' \geq \max(c_1, ..., c_n)$ since the cycle time cannot be any lower than the largest station assigned time.

The average operation time is $\bar{c} = \Sigma c_j/n = \Sigma t_i/n$. Note, the average idle time per operator per unit is $(c' - \bar{c})$, and the percent of idle time for the line, called the balance delay, is measured by $d = (c' - \bar{c})/c'$.

To illustrate some of the concepts, consider an example with $\Sigma t_i = 50$ minutes, and T = 450 minutes. The table below shows the measures: $(n', n, c', \bar{c}, d)$ for N = 85 to 95. Note, when N = 85, the balance delay is d = 0.056, and when N = 90, d = 0.000. Theoretically, it would be best to schedule the line to produce N = 90 units rather than N = 85 to gain the lower balance delay.

Table 9.1: Worksheet for Cycle Time, Balance Delay Example

N	n′	n	c′	$\bar{c}$	d
85	9.44	10	5.29	5.00	0.056
86	9.56	10	5.23	5.00	0.044
87	9.67	10	5.17	5.00	0.033
88	9.78	10	5.11	5.00	0.022
89	9.89	10	5.06	5.00	0.011
90	10.00	10	5.00	5.00	0.000
91	10.11	11	4.95	4.55	0.081
92	10.22	11	4.89	4.55	0.071
93	10.33	11	4.84	4.55	0.061
94	10.44	11	4.79	4.55	0.051
95	10.56	11	4.74	4.55	0.040

Parallel Lines

Sometimes two or more duplicate lines are in consideration, rather than one line. For convenience, suppose K lines are in use and the lines are denoted as k = 1, ..., K. The number of units produced for line k in time T would be N(k) for k = 1 to K. The sum $\Sigma N(k) = N$ gives the total number of units produced.

Consider the earlier example where Σt_i = 50 minutes is the total unit time, T = 450 minutes is the shift time and N = 90 units are needed in time T. Suppose K = 2 parallel lines will be in use and the two lines will produce the same quantity. So, N(1) = N(2) = N/2 = 45 units are the production needs per line. Since T and Σt_i are the same as earlier, the minimum number of operators needed per line are n(k) = N(k) × Σt_i/T = 45 × 50/450 = 5.00. Since n(k) is an integer, there is no need to round up. The average cycle time per line is $\bar{c}$ (k) = Σt_i/n(k) = 50/5 = 10 minutes. The minimum cycle time becomes c(k)′ = T/N(k) = 450/45 = 10 minutes. So the balance delay for each line is d(k) = (c(k)′ – $\bar{c}$ (k))/c(k)′ = (10 – 10)/10 = 0.00 or 0%.

Parallel lines allow flexibility in production to accommodate temporary changes in the demand fluctuations for the item. When the demands are steady (N = 90), the two lines remain in use. When the demand for the item slows down, then only one line can be used in the short term until the demand comes back up.

Sub-Assembly Lines

Sometimes one or more sub-assembly lines are needed. In the assembly system, these could be feeder (upstream) lines to the main line or post lines that feed off (down-stream) from the main line.

To illustrate, consider the earlier example where Σt_i = 50 minutes is the total unit time, T = 450 minutes is the shift time and N = 90 units are needed in time T. Recall further, the balance delay for this line is d = 0.00 (0%). Assume this is the main line and for notation ease it is denoted as k = 1. Now assume a feeder line (k = 2) that produces units prior to line 1. Suppose the total unit time on this sub-assembly line is Σt_i = 28 minutes and two units from line 2 are needed for one unit of line 1. So the production needs on line 2 become 2 × 90 = 180 units in a shift of T = 450 minutes.

The minimum number of operators needed for line 2 are computed by n(2) = N(2) × Σt_i/T = 180 × 28/450 = 11.2, which rounds up to 12 operators. Hence, with 12 operators, the average operation time per station is $\bar{c}(2) = \Sigma t_i / n(2) = 28/12 = 2.33$ minutes. Furthermore, the minimum cycle time becomes $c(2)' = T/N(2) = 450/180 = 2.50$ minutes. So, for line 2, the balance delay becomes $d(2) = (c(2)' - \bar{c}(2))/c(2)' = (2.50 - 2.33)/2.50 = 0.068$ or 6.8%.

Sometimes it is useful to measure the balance delay for the total assembly system (of K lines). In the above example, the total balance delay is obtained by the following:

$$d = [n(1) \times d(1) + n(2) \times d(2)]/[n(1) + n(2)] = [10 \times 0.00 + 12 \times 0.068]/[10 + 12] = 0.037 \text{ or } 3.7\%$$

Effective Cycle Time

In practice, the theoretical balance delay is not always achieved. This is because of the inability to distribute the work load evenly to the n operators assigned to the line.

Consider the earlier example where the total unit time is $\Sigma t_i = 50$ minutes, the number of operators is $n = 10$ and the average operation time is $\bar{c} = 5.00$ minutes. Suppose the assigned operation times for the ten operators are as follows: (4.8, 5.0, 5.0, 5.3, 4.9, 5.0, 5.0, 4.8, 5.1, 5.1) where the sum is 50 minutes. So using the relations above, the cycle time for the line becomes $c = 5.3$ minutes, the max operation time. The average operation time is $\bar{c} = 5.0$ minutes. Thereby, the effective balance delay for this line is $d = (c - \bar{c})/c = (5.3 - 5.0)/5.3 = 0.056$. This means there is 5.6% idle time in the line. In this example, the management should seek to even out the assigned *operation* times. The process of smoothing the work load evenly to the operators is called *line balancing*. Line balancing is described subsequently.

Precedence Diagram

The element precedence table is a list of all the work elements (E_i) needed to assemble one unit. The table also lists the associated standard work times (t_i) and the immediate assembly predecessor elements, if any. Predecessors are the elements that must be completed before the element can begin. This table is like a blueprint of the possible steps in the assembly of a product. It sets forth explicitly the logic inherent in a product's assembly.

To illustrate, consider the tasks associated with 'How to dress in the morning'. The elements are listed below along with the immediate predecessor elements. The element work times are not listed. A corresponding precedence diagram is depicted in Figure 9.1.

Elements	Immediate predecessors
left sock	
right sock	
left shoe	pants, left sock
right shoe	pants, right sock
shorts	
pants	shorts
belt	pants, shirt
under shirt	
shirt	under shirt
coat	shirt
hat	under shirt
tie	shirt

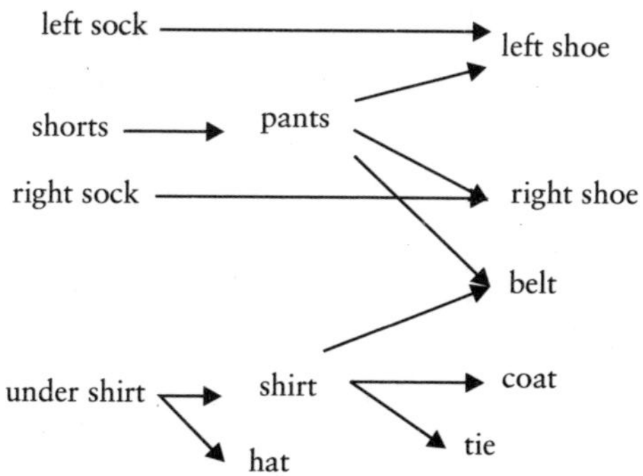

Figure 9.1: Precedence Diagram on How to Dress in the Morning

Now consider the element precedence diagram in Figure 9.2 with corresponding entries listed in Table 9.2. For simplicity, this data is called the '17 element example'. The work times are in minutes and the total unit time is 37.8 minutes.

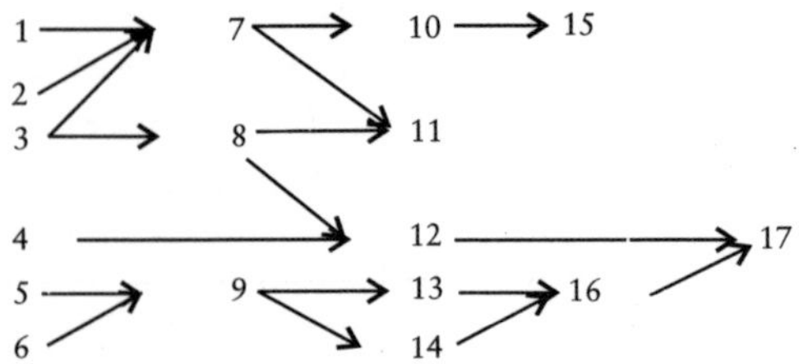

Figure 9.2: Precedence Diagram for 17 Element Example

Table 9.2: Elements for the 17 Element Example

Elements	Work time	Immediate predecessors
1	0.7	
2	2.0	
3	1.8	
4	1.0	
5	2.0	
6	1.4	
7	0.8	1, 2, 3
8	3.7	3
9	3.5	5, 6
10	3.0	7
11	3.6	7, 8
12	2.5	4, 8
13	3.1	9
14	2.6	9
15	2.8	10
16	1.9	13, 14
17	1.4	12, 16
Sum	37.8	

Line Balancing

Line balancing refers to the procedure of assigning work to the operators on the line as evenly and compactly as possible without violating any precedence or sequential restrictions. In the example, where $\Sigma t_i = 37.8$ minutes, suppose n = 3 operators are to be used. Thereby the average operation time of 37.8/3 = 12.6 minutes is desired. To accomplish, the 17 work elements should be assigned to the three station operators with equal (or near equal) operation times without violating any precedence restrictions.

The table below gives the line balance assignments by station. In this example, the elements are assigned to the three stations with equal times (12.6 minutes) and without violating any of the precedence constraints. Since the line is perfectly in balance, the balance delay is d = 0%.

Table 9.3: Line Balance Results for the 17 Element Example

Station	Elements	Work time	Station time
1	1	0.7	
	2	2.0	
	3	1.8	
	4	1.0	
	5	2.0	
	6	1.4	
	8	3.7	12.6
2	7	0.8	
	9	3.5	
	10	3.0	
	12	2.5	
	15	2.8	12.6
3	11	3.6	
	13	3.1	
	14	2.6	
	16	1.9	
	17	1.4	12.6

Mixed Model Lines

Mixed model assembly occurs when more than one model of a product is to be assembled on the same assembly line. For example, consider an automotive line that assembles three model cars that are intermixed on the line. The two main tasks to control the efficiency of the line are line balancing and sequencing. Line balancing is the process of assigning work elements to the operators. Sequencing involves selecting the order to send the units down the line.

Mixed model line balancing is similar to single model line balancing. The operators are assigned work elements in a way where no precedence violations take place, and where the workload by operator is the same over a shift time. The element times are computed as the total shift times. This is in contrary to element times that are for a single unit in single model line balancing. The element total shift time is the product of the element times and the shift schedule. The work elements are assigned to an operator on a shift basis rather than on a cycle time basis. A subsequent example will illustrate. The method assures that only one operator will perform the same element tasks on all units of all models. Hence, part stocking and learning costs, as well as confusion are reduced.

Make to Stock Mixed Model Assembly Lines

An appliance manufacturer produces clothes washing machines that come in three models. The demands are fairly steady over the year and the units are produced on a make-to-stock basis. The three models are assembled on one mixed-model assembly line that runs on one eight hour shift. The shift has 440 productive minutes and the shift schedule calls for 110 units. The average time between units coming off the line is 440/110 = 4.00 minutes. The line is mixed-model and the average demands are 50 units of model A, 40 of model B and 20 of model C. Some of the work elements are common to two or three of the models and some are unique to an individual model. When an operator is assigned a common work element in assembly, the operator is assigned this element on all three models. Two main goals to control the efficiency of the line are the following: the first is to assign the work elements to the operators on the line; and the second is to determine the order to send the units down the line. The first goal assigns the work elements in a way where the total time (per station operator) for the shift are the same. That is, each operator is assigned elements where the operator times are as close as possible to 440 minutes of total shift time. The second goal is to find the best sequence of running the units down the line. The sequence calls for sending the models down the line in a way where each model is scheduled as far away from the same model as possible. The sequence must satisfy the goal of 110 units for the shift, and where 50, 40 and 20 units of models A, B, and C, respectively, are completed. It is noted where the total number of units for the shift (110) stays fairly constant, but the mix of units to (A, B, C) may vary slightly from day-to-day.

To illustrate, consider a situation where three models (A, B, C) are to be assembled on one line, and where the daily schedule calls for 25, 15, and 10 units of A, B, C, respectively. Assume the same 17 element precedence table as given earlier.

Note the mixed model worksheet below. The total time to complete all 50 units is 1381.5 minutes. With an eight hour day (480 minutes) it is clear that three operators are needed to complete the work load. The average time per operator over the day is 1381.5/3 = 460.5 minutes.

Table 9.4: Mixed Model Worksheet (Time in Minutes)

		Number models per shift			
Elements	Unit time	A	B	C	Total time
1	0.7	25	15	10	35.0
2	2.0	25	0	10	70.0
3	1.8	25	15	10	90.0
4	1.0	25	15	10	50.0
5	2.0	0	15	10	50.0
6	1.4	25	15	10	70.0
7	0.8	0	15	10	20.0
8	3.7	25	0	10	129.5

9	3.5	25	0	10	122.5
10	3.0	25	15	10	150.0
11	3.6	0	15	10	90.0
12	2.5	0	0	10	25.0
13	3.1	25	15	10	155.0
14	2.6	25	15	0	104.0
15	2.8	25	0	10	98.0
16	1.9	25	0	10	66.5
17	1.4	25	15	0	56.0
Model time per unit		28.9	21.4	33.8	
Total shift time					1381.5

Mixed Model Line Balancing

The unit times for models (A, B, C) are 28.9, 21.4 and 33.8 minutes, respectively. Line balancing is used to assign the elements to the three stations as listed in Table 9.5. The work times for stations 1, 2 and 3 are assigned as 459.5, 461.5 and 460.5 minutes, respectively. The operation times per unit of model are also listed by station.

Table 9.5: Line Balance Results for the Mixed Model Example

Station	Elements	Work time per model A	B	C	Total time
1	2	2.0	0.0	2.0	70.0
	3	1.8	1.8	1.8	90.0
	4	1.0	1.0	1.0	50.0
	5	0.0	2.0	2.0	70.0
	6	1.4	1.4	1.4	70.0
	8	3.7	0.0	3.7	129.5
	Station time	9.9	6.2	11.9	479.5
2	1	0.7	0.7	0.7	35.0
	7	0.0	0.8	0.8	20.0

	9	3.5	0.0	3.5	122.5
	12	0.0	0.0	2.5	25.0
	13	3.1	3.1	3.1	155.0
	14	2.6	2.6	0.0	104.0
	Station time	9.9	7.2	10.6	461.5
3	10	3.0	3.0	3.0	150.0
	11	0.0	3.6	3.6	90.0
	15	2.8	0.0	2.8	98.0
	16	1.9	0.0	1.9	66.5
	17	1.4	1.4	0.0	56.0
	Station time	9.1	8.0	11.3	460.5

Mixed Model Sequencing

Let m represent the number of models on the mixed model assembly line, and let j identify the individual models, j = 1 to m. In the typical mixed model assembly operation, the number of units to produce for a shift is relatively constant from day to day. But the mix of the models in the schedule often changes each day. Suppose the schedule for the day is listed as N(j) for model j. So the sum yields the total number of units to produce for a shift. This is N = ΣN(j) where N is the number of units to produce for the shift and N(j) is the number for model j.

A way to sequence the models down the line is needed. A typical goal is to mix the station cycle times where a large cycle time is not scheduled next to another large cycle time along the sequence. You don't want a station operator to get two large cycle times together or two small ones. The sequence should seek to spread the models as far apart as possible, and in so doing, the station cycle times will also spread accordingly.

To accomplish, a sequencing algorithm is given below. The sequence index is denoted as i for i = 1 to N. The model chosen at sequence i is designated as j*. The algorithm below will sequence the models down the line in a way where they are spread as much as possible; and will fulfill the daily schedule of N(j) for j = 1 to m. The algorithm is in three steps as below:

Sequencing Algorithm for Make to Stock

Step 1. Assign a weight to each model as: w(j) = N/N(j) j = 1, ..., m.

Step 2. Let a(j, i) represent an index for model j at sequence i. At i = 1, an initial index is set to every model j in the following way: a(j, 1) = w(j)/2.

Along the sequence, j* will identify the model chosen as sequence i. Upon selecting j*, the subsequent index is revised as follows:

For all j not selected at sequence i, a(j, i + 1) = a(j, i) for i = 2 to N. For j* selected at sequence i, a(j*, i + 1) = a(j*, i) + w(j*).

Step 3. The model selected at sequence i is j* where a(j*, i) = min{a(j, i) j = 1, ..., m and i = 1, ..., N}.

An example is shown below where the three models are A, B, C and the shift schedule is N(A) = 25, N(B) = 15, N(C) = 10 and N = 50. The station cycle times by model are shown in Table 9.6. The sequence using the algorithm is listed (Table 9.7) along with the sequence index and the station cycle times at each sequence stage.

Table 9.6: Station Times by Model

Model	Station 1	Station 2	Station 3	Sum
A	9.9	9.9	9.1	28.9
B	6.2	7.2	8.0	21.4
C	11.9	10.6	11.3	33.8

Table 9.7: Worksheet to Sequence Models

	Sequence index			Station times			
Sequence (i)	a(1, i)	a(2, i)	a(3, i)	Model	t(1)	t(2)	t(3)
1	1.00	1.67	2.50	A	9.9	9.9	9.1
2	3.00	1.67	2.50	B	6.2	7.2	8.0
3	3.00	5.00	2.50	C	11.9	10.6	11.3
4	3.00	5.00	7.50	A	9.9	9.9	9.1

5	5.00	5.00	7.50	A	9.9	9.9	9.1
6	7.00	5.00	7.50	B	6.2	7.2	8.0
7	7.00	8.33	7.50	A	9.9	9.9	9.1
8	9.00	8.33	7.50	C	11.9	10.6	11.3
9	9.00	8.33	12.50	B	6.2	7.2	8.0
10	9.00	11.67	12.50	A	9.9	9.9	9.1
11	11.00	11.67	12.50	A	9.9	9.9	9.1
12	13.00	11.67	12.50	B	6.2	7.2	8.0
13	13.00	15.00	12.50	C	11.9	10.6	11.3
14	13.00	15.00	17.50	A	9.9	9.9	9.1
15	15.00	15.00	17.50	B	6.2	7.2	8.0
16	15.00	18.33	17.50	A	9.9	9.9	9.1
17	17.00	18.33	17.50	A	9.9	9.9	9.1
18	19.00	18.33	17.50	C	11.9	10.6	11.3
19	19.00	18.33	22.50	B	6.2	7.2	8.0
20	19.00	21.67	22.50	A	9.9	9.9	9.1
21	21.00	21.67	22.50	A	9.9	9.9	9.1
22	23.00	21.67	22.50	B	6.2	7.2	8.0
23	23.00	25.00	22.50	C	11.9	10.6	11.3
24	23.00	25.00	27.50	A	9.9	9.9	9.1
25	25.00	25.00	27.50	A	9.9	9.9	9.1
26	27.00	25.00	27.50	B	6.2	7.2	8.0
27	27.00	28.33	27.50	A	9.9	9.9	9.1
28	29.00	28.33	27.50	C	11.9	10.6	11.3
29	29.00	28.33	32.50	B	6.2	7.2	8.0
30	29.00	31.67	32.50	A	9.9	9.9	9.1
31	31.00	31.67	32.50	A	9.9	9.9	9.1
32	33.00	31.67	32.50	B	6.2	7.2	8.0
33	33.00	35.00	32.50	C	11.9	10.6	11.3
34	33.00	35.00	37.50	A	9.9	9.9	9.1
35	35.00	35.00	37.50	A	9.9	9.9	9.1

36	37.00	35.00	37.50	B	6.2	7.2	8.0
37	37.00	38.33	37.50	A	9.9	9.9	9.1
38	39.00	38.33	37.50	C	11.9	10.6	11.3
39	39.00	38.33	42.50	B	6.2	7.2	8.0
40	39.00	41.67	42.50	A	9.9	9.9	9.1
41	41.00	41.67	42.50	A	9.9	9.9	9.1
42	43.00	41.67	42.50	B	6.2	7.2	8.0
43	43.00	45.00	42.50	C	11.9	10.6	11.3
44	43.00	45.00	47.50	A	9.9	9.9	9.1
45	45.00	45.00	47.50	B	6.2	7.2	8.0
46	45.00	48.33	47.50	A	9.9	9.9	9.1
47	47.00	48.33	47.50	A	9.9	9.9	9.1
48	49.00	48.33	47.50	C	11.9	10.6	11.3
49	49.00	48.33	52.50	B	6.2	7.2	8.0
50	49.00	51.67	52.50	A	9.9	9.9	9.1

Make-to-Order Mixed Model Assembly Line

A manufacturer produces trucks on a make-to-order basis. The trucks come with a number of features and each feature offers a set of options. Each truck has a list of the options specified by the customer, one for each feature. So when the customer orders a truck, the truck has a list of option-features that are specified for the unit. Each such truck order is called a 'job' where the job lists the option-feature combinations. The parts and components associated with the job are gathered. The assembly takes place on a mixed-model line where each job is essentially a different model because of the wide combination of options and features. The customer is given a promise date for delivery of the truck and as much as possible, the manufacturer seeks to meet the date. The job is placed in a queue and is awaiting its turn to go down the assembly line. The job will be assigned for assembly when its turn arrives and also when all the parts and components needed on the job are available. The list of jobs to go down the line is determined about one week before the assembly date. A critical task is to determine the sequence to send the units down the line. This way, the exact parts and components by job and station will be available as the units flow from station to station. The goal is to sequence the jobs so the options needed by feature are as far apart as possible. Since some options require more assembly time (at a station) than others, this sequence method spreads the high and low work times between successive units.

Sequencing by Features and Options

Consider an assembly line where the units to assemble are make-to-order for the customers. Each unit to assemble is called a job and the units have a set of features with options available by feature. The customer chooses the combination of options by feature for the unit. In assembly, some of the feature-option combinations require more assembly time than others. Also, the customer may choose to bypass the feature and thereby no extra assembly time is required on that feature for that job. In the sequencing process, the goal is to arrange the jobs down the line in a way where the feature-options are spread as much as possible. For example, if option 1, say, is selected on 20 percent of the jobs, the ideal sequence will schedule option 1 on every fifth unit going down the line. As the number of features goes up and the variety of options increases, the sequencing process becomes more complicated. This section describes a way to arrange the jobs down the line to accomplish the goal stated.

The notation for this section is listed below:

i = sequence index

j = job index

nj = number of jobs

f = feature

nf = number of features

k = option

k(j, f) = option f of job j

n(f, k) = number of option k of feature f for the nj jobs

The sequencing algorithm is described in the six steps given below.

Sequencing Algorithm for Make-to-Order

Step 1. Perform steps 2 to 6, below, for each sequence index i where i = 1 to nj.

Step 2. Let jo = the job assigned in the prior sequence, (i – 1), and let ko represent k(jo, ko) = the option of feature f that is associated with job jo.

Step 3. Keep a measure on the last use on each feature-option as below:

x(f, k) = a measure on the last sequence assignment for option k of feature f. After each job assignment, each of the feature measures, x(f, k), are updated in the following way.

$$x(f, ko) = x(f, ko) + nj/n(f, ko) \text{ where } ko = k(jo, ko).$$

Step 4. To select the next job for sequence index i, the following measures, y(j, f), are obtained for each of the features f for every job j that is not yet assigned. This measure gives—ideally—how far in advance to place the next schedule of feature f for job j. The measure is obtained as below:

$$y(j, f) = x(f, k) + nj/n(f, k) \text{ and } k = k(j, f)$$

Step 5. For each job j that is not yet assigned, the sum of y(j, f) over all features is computed. This sum, sy(j), gives a measure on how far in advance to place the j. This measure can then be compared to all unassigned jobs in a relative way. The sum is computed as:

$$sy(j) = \Sigma_f y(j, f)$$

Step 6. With the above sums, sy(j), determined for each yet unassigned job, the best job to assign for the current sequence index i, is the job with the minimum such measure. That is, choose job jo as follows: sy(jo) = min {sy(j) for all j not yet assigned}.

A difficulty with the above algorithm concerns the initializing stage for the sequence since no prior values at i = 0 of x(f, k) are available to begin the algorithm. To overcome, and assuming the sequencing is performed each day, the measures for each feature-option, x(f, k), should be saved from the last unit of the prior days' sequence; and that last unit should give the measure for i = 0 for the next days' run. In the event the sequence data from the prior day is not available, the initial set of measures can be computed as:

$$x(f, k) = 0.5 \times nj/n(f, k)$$

To illustrate, consider the data in Table 9.8 with nj = 25 jobs and each with nf = 3 features. Feature 1 has four options, feature 2 has five options and feature 3 has two options. Note, job 1 uses option 1 of feature 1, option 1 of feature 2 and does not use feature 3.

Table 9.8: List of 25 Jobs (j) to Sequence with Three Features (f) and Associated Options (k)

		k(j, f)		
j	f	1	2	3
1		1	1	0
2		0	0	1
3		0	3	1
4		2	0	0
5		2	3	0
6		3	4	0
7		3	1	0
8		2	0	0
9		1	0	0
10		1	0	0
11		2	3	0
12		3	4	0
13		1	5	0
14		1	0	1
15		1	0	0
16		0	0	1
17		0	0	0
18		0	0	1
19		3	1	0

20	0	0	0
21	1	1	1
22	0	2	0
23	0	2	0
24	1	4	0
25	2	1	0

Table 9.9 gives the sums of options per feature for the 25 job example. Table 9.10 lists the sequence generated from the algorithm described above.

Table 9.9: Total Number of Options (k) by Feature (f)

		n(f, k)					
f	k	0	1	2	3	4	5
1		8	8	5	4		
2		11	5	2	3	3	1
3		19	6				

Table 9.10 lists the assigned sequence (i) by job (j) and associated options (k) by feature (f). Also listed is the measure sy(i) for each sequence i.

Table 9.10: Worksheet on Sequence (i) of Job (j)

			k(j, f)			
i	j	f	1	2	3	sy(i)
1	9		1	0	0	10.1
2	17		0	0	0	13.7
3	25		2	1	0	19.6
4	10		1	0	0	21.7
5	2		0	0	1	24.3
6	6		3	4	0	29.1
7	1		1	1	0	32.0
8	20		0	0	0	33.3
9	5		2	3	0	36.2
10	14		1	0	1	39.3

11	22	0	2	0	45.3
12	7	3	1	0	46.9
13	16	0	0	1	48.8
14	15	1	0	0	51.6
15	11	2	3	0	54.8
16	24	1	4	0	58.9
17	18	0	0	1	60.7
18	19	3	1	0	63.5
19	4	2	0	0	66.8
20	21	1	1	1	73.9
21	8	2	0	0	75.3
22	23	0	2	0	77.7
23	12	3	4	0	81.6
24	3	0	3	1	82.8
25	13	1	5	0	89.7

Note, the first job coming down the line is j = 9. This is followed by j = 17, and so forth.

Summary

This chapter describes some key quantitative assembly methods for single and mixed model assembly lines. The concepts of cycle time and balance delay are used to determine the number of operators (stations) to have on the line to meet the scheduled production needs. Precedence diagrams and assembly line balancing are needed to spread the work load evenly to the operators on the line. In mixed model lines, the sequencing of the units down the line is important so that the work flows smoothly along all stations over the daily schedule. Two sequencing methods are described, one is a sequence by model, and another is a sequence by job with features and options. The first applies for make-to-stock situations, and the second applies when make-to-order.

References

Chow, We-Min, *Assembly Line Design*, CRC Press, 1990.

Linhart, Robert, *The Assembly Line*, University of Massachusetts Press, 1981.

Ortiz, Chris A., *Kaizen Assembly: Designing, Constructing and Managing a Lean Assembly Line*, CRC Press, 2006.

Prenting, Ted O. and Nick T. Thomopoulos, *Humanism and Technology in Assembly Line Systems*, Hayden Book Co., 1974.

10

IOQ, EOQ and ATR

In this chapter, the reader will learn the procedure of stocking parts in service parts distribution centers. These are parts that are installed in a finished good item, one-by-one, and is thereafter a permanent component of the item. The part begins its life when an engineering change or a model change takes place on the finished good item. The part is stocked in a distribution center at the outset to fill any customer demands that come in for repair or maintenance of the finished good item. At the beginning, the first buy is needed when no demand history is known on the part. At the end, as the part is no longer installed on new finished good items in the plant, the service demand dwindles, and the supplier calls for an end of replenishments. This causes the distribution center to order one last buy that is just large enough to cover all the demands on the part that are projected for the obligation time horizon of the future.

Introduction

Consider a service parts distribution center and the three basic buy quantities on a part, IOQ, EOQ and ATR. The IOQ (initial order quantity) is the first buy on a part and is called when the part is introduced and has no prior demand history to base the forecasts. The ATR (all-time-requirement) is the last buy and is needed when the supplier will cease production on the part and calls for a final buy. In the latter buy, a forecast on all future requirements on the part is projected to determine how much to buy. The EOQ (economic order quantity) are all the buy quantities in between the IOQ and the ATR. All three of these buy quantities seek to replenish the part sufficiently to meet the oncoming demands with a high service level and with economic efficiency in the cost.

Life Cycle Curve

Consider the life cycle of a service part demand in the distribution center. At the beginning, the part is introduced in the assembly of a finished good item in the production plant. As the finished good item is sold to customers, the consumer population of the item with the part increases as time passes. This increase will stop when the part is replaced due to an engineering change or a new model. The population size of the item will eventually dampen and begin to drop as the item begins to wear and eventually is scrapped. So as time passes, the population of the finished good item, with the part, is smaller and eventually approaches zero. The life cycle of the item looks somewhat like the curve in Figure 10.1. Each part that is installed in the item has a demand history for service maintenance and repair that parallels the population of finished good items (with the part).

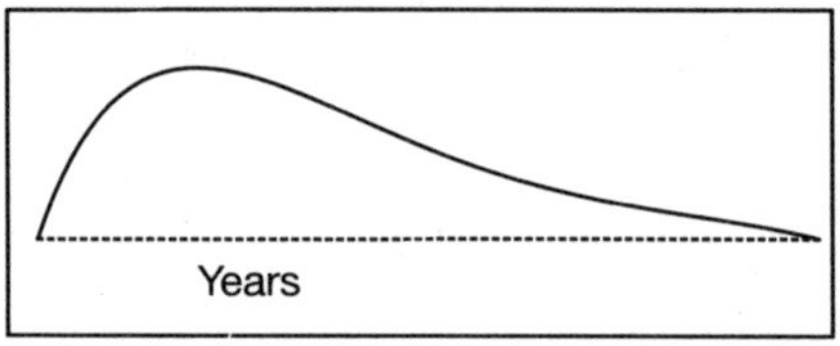

Figure 10.1: Life Cycle Curve

Buy Quantities

Figure 10.2 depicts the buying and on-hand inventory history for a typical service part at the distribution center. The history begins with the initial order quantity (IOQ), and ends with the all time requirement (ATR). In between are the economic order quantity buys (EOQ). At the outset, IOQ is meant to get the inventory off the ground, just large enough to meet the initial demands. The EOQ buys are needed to meet the steady flow of demands from the customers and yet keeping the quantity at an economic level to yield the desired service level. The ATR is needed to store enough stock to cover the demands for all the future years over the service obligation on the part.

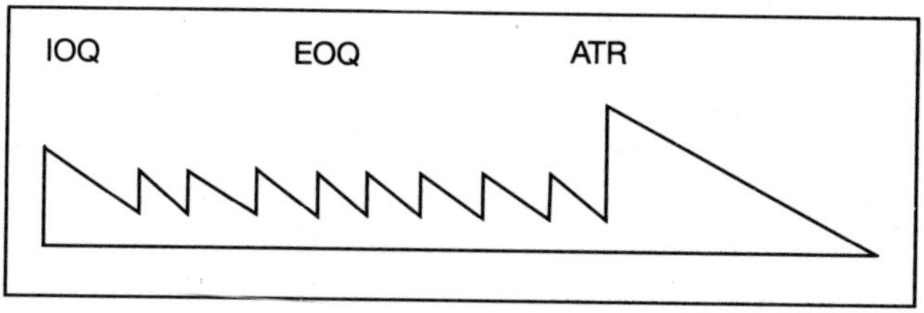

Figure 10.2: Buy Quantities and On-Hand Inventory

Initial Order Quantity

In the assembly of a finished good item, many parts and components are needed in the process. Each part has a supplier that replenishes the plant in a steady way. As time passes, the collection of parts in the assembly is ever changing due to engineering and model changes. The parts are also needed in the service parts distribution center, DC, to satisfy the demands for maintenance and repair of the finished good item. This is where the parts are stocked to fill dealer demands. When a new part is introduced in the assembly, the part must also be stocked in the DC to fill any demands for service and maintenance. A difficulty occurs, in determining how much stock to buy, since there is no demand history to base the buy decision. This first buy quantity is called the initial order quantity (IOQ). The DC management is continually getting requests to stock these new parts.

The initial order quantity (IOQ) is needed when a buy of stock is called for a new service part with no prior demand history. The part may be a stand-alone item or it may be associated with a new finished good item or associated with an engineering change on the finished good item. Regardless, the part has not been in use before. This situation is common for service parts where the parts are stored in a distribution center awaiting the demands from customers. The stocking location is confronted with determining how much to buy and store on each new part of this type.

The problem on how much to stock is indeed very elusive and difficult since there is no data to base the stocking decision.

Often the decision on the amount to stock is assigned to experts who review each new part and determine the quantity to buy. The experts have little if any data to back their decisions and rely mainly on their experience.

A cost model is described for each new part and the quantity to initially buy is selected to minimize the cost from this model. The model estimates the annual cost of each new part based on four components: the annual order cost, the annual holding cost, the annual goodwill cost and the annual excess cost. The quantity associated with the minimum annual cost is selected as the IOQ for the part.

The notions of new-parts-of-the-past and new-parts-of-the-future are introduced. The new-parts-of-the-future are the parts where a decision on the quantity to stock is needed now. This quantity is called the initial-order-quantity (IOQ). The new-parts-of-the-past are parts where the introduction phase on the part has already occurred and where demand data is still available (on the database) for the initial year of this introduction.

To carry out the cost model, some data searching from the new-parts-of-the-past is needed. The new-parts-of-the-past are gathered and data from their first year of demands are obtained. Also the cost-per-unit of each new-part-of-the-past is saved when available.

A key need is to recognize a set of attributes associated with each new-part-of-the-past. When possible, the attribute should identify the type of part, where it is used and so forth. The collection of attributes depends on the type of data available on the database for the parts. The attribute (denoted as A) is needed to form a link for the new-parts-of-the-past with the new-parts-of-the-future. This way, when a new-part-of-the-future is in need of an initial buy quantity, the data from the corresponding new-parts-of-the-past are used to help determine the quantity to stock.

New-Parts-of-the-Past

For each new-part-of-the-past, the average 1-month demand from the initial 12 months of demands D_t ($t = 1, \ldots, 12$) is obtained and this is denoted as d. Hence, $d = \Sigma D_t / 12$ ($t = 1$ to 12).

From all the parts of the past, n will represent the number of parts with a common attribute A. These n parts represent a sample of the parts of the past with the attribute A. The average 1-month demands are gathered and labeled as $d_1, ..., d_n$. This set of demands now allow computing the mean and standard deviation for the 1-month average demand for the attribute and these are here denoted as μ_d and σ_d. From the authors experience, the spread of the d entries is often skewed far to the right since there are many low values and one or a few high values. This suggests the shape is more like the lognormal distribution than as the normal distribution. For this reason, the lognormal distribution is assumed in the cost model.

Cost Per Unit. From the n sample parts with attribute A, the cost per unit is listed as $cu_1, ..., cu_n$, and the average cost per unit is computed and here denoted as c.

Attribute Data. The data known on each attribute A consists of the mean and standard deviation of average 1-month demands (μ_d, σ_d) and also the average cost per unit (c).

Probability Points. For subsequent computations, ten equally spaced probability points are selected. These are denoted as $\alpha(i)$ and are equally spaced probabilities: (.05, .15, .25, .35, .45, .55, .65, .75, .85, .95).

Ten Demand Points. The lognormal distribution is assumed for the average 1-month demands (d) of each attribute A. Of interest now is to select ten representative values of d and they are identified as d(i) (i = 1 to 10). For convenience, the values are called demand points and they are determined in a way where $P(d < d(i)) = \alpha(i)$ for i = 1 to 10. Now the four steps below are followed.

1. Find μ_y, σ_y (from μ_d and σ_d) where y is the counterpart normal distributed variable that is associated with the lognormal distributed variable of d. These are computed from the relations below that use the natural logarithm, (ln):

$$\mu_y = \ln\left(\mu_d^2 / \sqrt{\sigma_d^2 + \mu_d^2}\right)$$

$$\sigma_y^2 = \ln((\sigma_d^2 + \mu_d^2)/\mu_d^2)$$

2. Find z(i) from the standard normal distribution where $P(z < z(i)) = \alpha(i)$.
3. Find $y(i) = \mu_y + z(i)\sigma_y$.
4. Now $d(i) = \exp(y(i))$.

The results yield d(i) where $P(d < d(i)) = \alpha(i)$. Note, for attribute A, the ten demand points here represent ten equally likely values of the average 1-month demands. These will be used subsequently.

New-Parts-of-the-Future

Suppose a new part is now under review. The part has no demand history. But also assume, the data known on the part is the attribute A and also the lead time L. The lead time represents the time to procure the part from the supplier. This is the limited data that is available to determine the initial buy quantity.

The attribute, A, for the new part allows the mean and standard deviation μ_d and σ_d to be retrieved. Of need here is now to find the corresponding statistical measures associated with the average lead time demand of the attribute, denoted as d_L. Because the average 1-month demand is assumed to follow a lognormal distribution, the average L-month demand also follows a lognormal distribution. For d_L, the mean becomes $\mu_{dL} = L\mu_d$ and the standard deviation is $\sigma_{dL} = \sqrt{L}\sigma_d$.

Ten Demand Points. Ten representative values of the lead time demand are now obtained and are labeled as $d_L(i)$ where $P(d_L < d_L(i)) = \alpha(i)$ for i = 1 to 10. The values of $d_L(i)$ are found in the same way as described above for d(i). The counterpart normal variable y is now associated with the lognormal variable d_L. Note, the ten demand points here represent ten equally likely values of the average L-month demand.

Ten IOQ Points. Ten candidate values of the IOQ are now obtained. These are denoted as q(i) where $q(i) = d_L(i)$ for i = 1 to 10. In this way, the IOQ for the part will be selected from one of the ten IOQ points and these points are spread along the distribution of the average lead time demand. Recall the lead time demand is assumed to follow a lognormal distribution.

Data Summary. Consider the data that is gathered and calculated for a new part. The new part has an attribute A and also a lead time L. The attribute is linked to the new-parts-of-the-past that also has an attribute A. The data now available for the new part is the following:

A = attribute

L = lead time

c = cost per unit

d(i) = ten demand points i = 1 to 10

q(i) = ten candidate IOQ points i = 1 to 10.

Annual Cost Model

To determine an economic quantity for the IOQ, a cost model is constructed. The ten possible IOQ values determined above are assumed, and the final choice will come from one of these ten values. The purpose is to estimate the annual cost of the new part with each candidate IOQ value. The IOQ associated with the minimum cost is selected as the economic IOQ to use.

Let K(q, d) = annual cost when the IOQ is q and the average 1-month demand is d. In the model, K(q, d) is composed of four components as follows: K(q, d) = K(order) + K(hold) + K(goodwill) + K(excess). The annual costs for each of the components are computed as below.

The cost model uses the following five parameters:

h = annual holding rate.

Co = cost per order.

gw = goodwill rate, whereby the lost customers are estimated as gw × (out-of-stock demands).

mu = markup rate, whereby the selling price per unit is estimated as pu = mu × c.

sr = scrap rate, whereby any IOQ stock held over one year is scrapped by this rate.

Some initial computations are carried out prior to finding the cost for each of the components. These are below.

d_{12} = 12 × d = average 12 month demand.

$qe = \sqrt{2d_{12}\,Co/ch}$ = the economic order quantity.

$t1 = q/d$ = the number of months till q is consumed. If $t1 > 12$, then set $t1 = 12$.

$t2 = qe/d$ = the number of months till qe is consumed.

$d_L = L \times d$ = average lead time demand.

$pu = mu \times c$ = the selling price per unit.

The cost model assumes q will be used initially; and qe will be used subsequently as needed, for the remainder of the first year, as the buy quantity.

$$K(\text{order}) = \begin{cases} Co(1 + (12 - t1)/t2) & \text{if } q \le d_{12} \\ Co & \text{if } q > d_{12} \end{cases}$$

= the annual cost of ordering.

$$K(\text{hold}) = \begin{cases} c \times h/12\,(q/2 \times t1 + qe/2 \times (12 - t1) & \text{if } q \le d_{12} \\ c \times h(d_{12}/2 + (q - d_{12})) & \text{if } q > d_{12} \end{cases}$$

= the annual holding cost.

$$K(\text{goodwill}) = \begin{cases} 0 & \text{if } d_L \le q \\ (d_L - q) \times pu \times gw & \text{if } d_L > q \end{cases}$$

= the cost when the q is short of the lead time demand.

$$K(\text{excess}) = \begin{cases} 0 & \text{if } q \le d_{12} \\ (q - d_{12}) \times c \times sr & \text{if } q > d_{12} \end{cases}$$

= the cost of holding stock in excess of one year demand.

K(q, d) = K(order) + K(hold) + K(goodwill) + K(excess). K(q, d) is the annual cost when the IOQ is q and the average 1-month demand d is computed using the parameters, computations and equations listed above.

$K(q) = \Sigma_i(K(q, d(i)) \times 0.1$ = the expected annual cost when the IOQ = q.

It is the average expected cost regardless of the average 1-month demand.

Recall above where ten candidate points of q have been selected. For convenience here, these are labeled as q(j) where j = 1 to 10. With the ten candidate IOQ points, it is now possible to determine the IOQ that is associated with the minimum annual cost. This is q′ where K(q′) = min{K(q(j)) j = 1 to 10}. And so, the economic IOQ to use for the new part is IOQ = q′.

Example 10.1. An example is presented to illustrate how the economic IOQ is found. The example considers a new-part-of-the-future with an attribute A, lead time L = 2 months and cost per unit cu = \$1356. Suppose also, six new-parts-of-the-past are found with the same attribute A. The average (first year) monthly demands for these six parts are: (d_1, ..., d_6) = (8.58, 1.00, 1.25, 1.33, 1.50, 1.08). The average and standard deviation from the six demands are computed and are denoted as $\mu_d = 2.45$ and $\sigma_d = 3.01$. Since the demands (d) are assumed to follow a lognormal distribution, the relations given earlier to find the statistics for the counterpart normal distribution (y) are now used; and yield $\mu_y = 0.442$ and $\sigma_y = 0.956$.

So now the ten demand points of d are found as described here. To accomplish, we use the ten probabilities α(i), i = 1 to 10 and the corresponding ten standard normal measures z(i), i = 1 to 10. Then the ten measures of y are obtained by: $y(i) = \mu_y + z(i)\,\sigma_y$ for i = 1 to 10. Finally, the ten demand points from the lognormal distribution are obtained by d(i) = exp(y(i)) for i = 1 to 10. See the list below.

Table 10.1: Ten Probability Points for Demands

i	α(i)	z(i)	y(i)	d(i)
1	.05	–1.645	–1.131	0.322
2	.15	–1.036	–0.549	0.578
3	.25	–0.674	–0.202	0.816
4	.35	–0.385	0.074	1.077
5	.45	–0.125	0.322	1.380
6	.55	0.125	0.562	1.754
7	.65	0.385	0.810	2.248
8	.75	0.674	1.087	2.965

9	.85	1.036	1.433	4.192
10	.95	1.645	2.015	7.504

In a similar way, the ten IOQ points are obtained. Since the lead time is L = 2 months, the mean and standard deviation of the lead time demands are obtained as $\mu_{dL} = 4.92$ and $\sigma_{dL} = 4.25$. The counterpart normal distributed statistics become $\mu_y = 1.314$ and $\sigma_y = 0.747$. Now following the same steps described above, the list below is generated.

Table 10.2: Ten Probability Points for Lead Time Demands

i	α(i)	z(i)	y(i)	dL(i) = q(i)
1	.05	-1.645	0.084	1.088
2	.15	-1.036	0.539	1.715
3	.25	-0.674	0.810	2.247
4	.35	-0.385	1.026	2.790
5	.45	-0.125	1.220	3.387
6	.55	0.125	1.407	4.084
7	.65	0.385	1.601	4.958
8	.75	0.674	1.817	6.155
9	.85	1.036	2.088	8.068
10	.95	1.645	2.542	12.714

For simplicity in Table 10.3, the ten demand points and ten quantity points are listed in closest integers. So the integer demand points (d) are: 0, 1, 1, 1, 1, 2, 2, 3, 4, 8. The ten quantity points (q) become: 1, 2, 2, 3, 3, 4, 5, 6, 8, 13. Subsequently, in the computations, the fractional values are used.

The computations continue to find the optimal quantity to buy (IOQ). The parameters used in the example are: gw = 0.2, sr = 0.5, h = 0.24, Co = 24 and mu = 1.25. Further recall L = 2 months and c = \$1356. So, when q = 1.088 and d = 0.322, for example, the annual costs become the following: K(order) = 112.6, K(hold) = 138.0, K(goodwill) = 0.0 and K(scrap) = 0.0 and thereby K(q, d) = 250.6 (see Table 10.3 below).

The ten (average monthly) demand points (d) are listed in the left column (in integers), and the ten candidate initial buy quantities (q) are given in the first row (in integers). Recall, d and q are both shaped like a lognormal distribution. For brevity, the table lists only the integer portion of d and q; but in the computation of the cost model, the corresponding fractional values are used throughout. The body of the table gives the values of K(q, d) = annual cost when the initial buy quantity is q and the average monthly demand is d. The bottom row gives the values of K(q), the expected annual cost when the initial order quantity is q. Note, the minimum of K(q) is 1311 and this occurs when q = 4. Thereby, IOQ = 4.

Table 10.3: K(q, d) and K(q) for L = 2

d/q	1	2	2	3	3	4	5	6	8	13
0	251	285	339	420	537	866	1743	2943	4862	9524
1	352	341	365	403	461	551	695	950	2291	6953
1	576	396	409	433	470	529	625	798	1174	4541
1	812	600	459	474	500	541	610	736	1012	2066
1	1078	863	687	523	541	571	622	716	924	1730
2	1398	1182	1003	825	635	615	652	723	881	1500
2	1810	1593	1412	1232	1037	815	702	753	871	1342
3	2393	2176	1994	1811	1613	1386	1108	814	898	1242
4	3368	3151	2967	2783	2582	2350	2064	1680	1086	1209
8	5916	5698	5515	5329	5125	4889	4595	4198	3574	2112
K(q)	1795	1628	1515	1423	1350	1311	1342	1431	1757	3222

Note: L = 2

All Time Requirements

In the assembly of a finished good item, many parts and components are needed in the process. Each part has a supplier that replenishes the plant as needed. As time passes, the collection of parts in the assembly is ever changing due to engineering and model changes. The parts are also needed in the service parts distribution center, DC, to satisfy the demands for maintenance and repair of the finished good item. This is where the parts are stocked to fill dealer demands. Eventually, a part is dropped in assembly and thereby no longer needed in the plant; but the demands for the part continue as a service part and so the supplier continues to replenish the DC as needed. But as time passes, and the service demand falls, the supplier may request one last replenish buy from the distribution center. At this time, the DC management is obliged to determine the quantity to stock and this quantity is called the all time requirement, ATR.

When a request for an ATR occurs on a part, a first step is to generate the forecast over the future time horizon. The time horizon is in conformance with the service obligation on the part. This is the number of future years the service parts management is obliged to cover the part.

Consider a finished good item that is produced and sold to customers. The finished good is composed of many parts and components that make-up its bill-of-material. But because of various models, options and engineering changes, not all finished good units have the same set of parts and components. Of particular interest is to determine how to estimate the life cycle curve for an individual part and the associated all-time-requirements (ATR).

Background

In searching the literature, little has been written on estimating the population size on a finished good item and a need for such an estimate. A review on the closest references is summarized here: In his book, Brown [1959] has a section entitled "All-time supplies" and describes the following: "There is a typical pattern to the life cycle of demand for a spare part, used to repair some piece of equipment such as an automobile, an appliance, or a construction machine. When the new model of the equipment is first built, there is a gradual rise in demand for parts. Some of the rise is caused by the larger population of equipment needing the part; some by the increasing probability that the part will have to be replaced. The renewal equation can be used to estimate the distribution of the quantities required in this phase of the life cycle. Ultimately, the average rate of usage per unit of equipment in the population will reach a steady state, when the effects of the different ages of the population disappear." In a [1980] book, I have stated the following in a section called "All-time requirements": "Typically, when a new item is introduced into the inventory, the demand gradually rises from time period to time period until it reaches an equilibrium level. Eventually, the need for the item drops and the demand steadily dwindles to zero. The latter event occurs because the item has been replaced or is no longer in style. For a service part, the parent machine(s) may be out of production, and the need for the part drops as the population of the machine becomes less and less."

Time Horizon

The time horizon is represented by an index t and ranges from t = 1 to T. t = 1 represents the first year the part is included on the bill-of-materials of the finished good; and $t = t_o$ represents the last year (since introduction) the part is included on the bill-of-material. T identifies the current year of the part since introduction. To illustrate, suppose the time horizon is 20 years, and a part is introduced on the bill-of-material in the year 2000 and dropped in 2003. For this part, t = 1 (represents 2000), $t_o = 4$ (2003) and T = 9 (2008) identifies the current year.

Probability Distribution on Active Life

Consider the life cycle of an individual unit (of a finished good). The life of the unit begins after it is produced in the plant and enters the population of active units. The life of the unit ends when it is scrapped or junked.

The probability model follows the life of an individual unit (of a finished good item) for the years after it is produced and sold to a customer. The model assumes no units are scrapped for the years just immediately after the active life begins. Thereafter, a steady annual scrap rate takes place from year to year. In essence, the annual scrap rate is assumed as zero (or near zero) for the immediate years just after the unit begins its active life. The number of scrap-free years is denoted as j_o. After j_o, the finish goods unit has a probability of being scrapped at a probability of r per year. That is, for each year beyond j_o, the probability is r that the unit will be scrapped in the year. In the same manner, the probability is (1 – r) that the unit will not be scrapped in the year.

The probability is stated in the following way: Let j designate the year the unit is scrapped where j begins as j = 1, the year the unit starts its active life. So the probability of j becomes:

$$p(j) = \begin{cases} 0 & j = 1 \text{ to } j_o \\ r(1-r)^{(j-jo-1)} & j = j_o \end{cases}.$$

In essence, j is a discrete index with $j \geq 1$ and where j_o acts as a location parameter. The probability distribution is the same as a *geometric distribution* for the years $j > j_o$.

The probability the unit is scrapped in year j or sooner is the following:

$$F(j) = \Sigma_{i=1,\, j}\, p(i)$$

This is the probability the unit is scrapped in year j or sooner.

The complementary probability H(j) is obtained from H(j) = 1 − F(j). This gives the probability the unit survives beyond year j.

Life Cycle

Let x(t) represent a generic shape of the life cycle for a part with parameters (t_o, r, j_o) known. For t = 1 to t_o,

$$x(t) = H(1) + \ldots + H(t)$$

and for the years $t > t_o$,

$$x(t) = H(t - t_o + 1) + \ldots + H(t)$$

Life Cycle Fit

Suppose the part of interest has been in use for T years and the history demands for the past few years, d(t) ($t = t_1$ to T) are known and $t_1 \geq 1$. The sums Σd(t) and Σx(t) for ($t = t_1$ to T) are computed to yield the ratio

$$a = \Sigma d(t) / \Sigma x(t)$$

This ratio is used to give a life cycle fit for the part for all the years of interest, history plus future. The fit of demands per year becomes $d(t) = a \times x(t)$ for t = T + 1, T + 2, ...

Computing the All-Time-Requirements (ATR)

The all-time-requirement (ATR) for the part becomes

$$ATR = \Sigma_{t>T} d(t)$$

Example: Assume a part where r = 0.20 (annual scrap rate), j_o = 2 (scrap free years), t_o = 3 (part production years) and T = 9 (years since introduce part). The table below lists the probabilities p(j), F(j) and H(j) for the years j = 1 to 20. For simplicity, the table entries are rounded to two decimal places.

Table 10.4: Worksheet for Life Cycle Curve

j	p(j)	F(j)	H(j)
1	0.00	0.00	1.00
2	0.00	0.00	1.00
3	0.20	0.20	0.80
4	0.16	0.36	0.64
5	0.13	0.49	0.51
6	0.10	0.59	0.41
7	0.08	0.67	0.33
8	0.07	0.74	0.26
9	0.05	0.79	0.21
10	0.04	0.83	0.17
11	0.03	0.87	0.13
12	0.03	0.89	0.11
13	0.02	0.91	0.09
14	0.02	0.93	0.07
15	0.01	0.95	0.05
16	0.01	0.96	0.04
17	0.01	0.96	0.04
18	0.01	0.97	0.03
19	0.01	0.98	0.02
20	0.00	0.99	0.02

The generic life cycle curve, x(t), for the part is listed in the table below. They are obtained by x(1) = H(1), x(2) = H(1) + H(2), x(3) = H(1) + H(2) + H(3), x(4) = H(2) + H(3) + H(4), x(5) = H(3) + H(4) + H(5), and so forth.

Note the current year is T = 9 and the demand history on the part is known for the three years, t = 7, 8, 9. In the example, the demands are d(7) = 100, d(8) = 70 and d(9) = 60. The table notation for the years are the following: p = part in production years, d = part demand history years, and f = part demand forecast years. The sum of the three year demands are 230 and the corresponding three years of the life cycle fit rounds to 3.05. So the ratio of demands over life cycle is a = 230/3.05 = 75.45. This yields the forecast for the part for the years t = 10 and beyond from the relation d(t) = 75.45x(t) for t = 10 to 20. Because of rounding, the numbers listed on the table are not always exact.

The ATR for the part is the sum of the forecasts for the planning horizon over future years. In the example, if the planning horizon are the years from t = 10 to 20, then the all-time-requirement is approximately ATR = 221.

Table 10.5: Worksheet for ATR Forecast

t		x(t)	d(t)
1	p	1.00	
2	p	2.00	
3	p	2.80	
4		2.44	
5		1.95	
6		1.56	
7	d	1.25	100
8	d	1.00	70
9	d	0.80	60
10	f	0.64	48.26
11	f	0.51	38.61
12	f	0.41	30.89
13	f	0.33	24.71
14	f	0.26	19.77
15	f	0.21	15.81

16	f	0.17	12.65
17	f	0.13	10.12
18	f	0.11	8.10
19	f	0.09	6.48
20	f	0.07	5.18

Summary

When a part is new and is to be stocked in the inventory system, the buy quantity is called the initial order quantity. This happens for service parts and concerns the new (never been used before) parts that are installed on the finished good units in assembly. These are the parts that are new due to engineering changes or are installed on new models. On the other hand, the last buy for a part is called the all time requirements. This happens when the supplier will no longer replenish the part, and where the stocking location is obliged to continue stocking the part and thereby is forced to call for a final buy.

References

Brown, R.G., *Statistical Forecasting and Inventory Control*, McGraw Hill, New York, 1959.

Fortuin, L., "Initial Supply and Re-order Level of New Service Parts", *European Journal of Operations Research*, 15(3), March 1984.

Lentz, G.J. and N.T. Thomopoulos, *Expert System for Service Parts Initial Order Quantities*, Decision Sciences Institute Proceedings, 1996.

Thomopoulos, N.T., *Applied Forecasting Methods*, Prentice Hall, 1980.

——, "Optimal Order Point for Dated Items", *Strategic Inventory Management and Planning*, 1990, Hittchock Publishing Co., Carol Stream, Il.

——, "The Population Shape and Size for Finished Good Items", *Emerging Issues in Business and Technology*, Western Illinois University, 1999.

——, "The Initial Buy Quantity", *The International Journal of Operations and Quantitative Management*, March 2009.

Thomopoulos, N.T. and A.V. Johnson, *Tables and Characteristics of the Standardized Lognormal Distributions*, Decision Sciences Proceedings, November 2004.

11

Late Delivery and Lost Sales

In this chapter, the reader will learn the relation between the lead time and the service level, and how a late delivery of stock from the supplier is harmful and could cause a decrease in the service level by way of an out-of-stock condition. The chapter shows how to measure the service level when the lead time is longer than planned, and also how extra stock, here called safety time stock, can be used to offset this loss in the service level. The chapter further describes how the service level is related to backorders and lost sales. In the analysis, the demands on a part are partitioned as follows: filled demand, backorder demand, lost sales demand, unfilled demand, and effective demand. The service level and the effective service level are also described.

Introduction

Two sensitivity relations concerning the service level on a part are described in this chapter. The first pertains to the relation between the service level and late delivery of stock. When the replenish stock does not arrive on-time, the service level decreases. The second relation pertains to the service level and lost sales. When stock is not available to fill a customer demand, a backorder or lost sales occurs.

In a typical inventory holding location along the supply chain, safety stock is needed to yield a desired service level of the type (demand filled/total demand). To determine the safety stock, the computations are based on a planned lead time provided by the supplier. In reality, however, the actual lead time may vary from the planned lead time and often is longer. This chapter explores how the actual service level may fall when the lead time varies in this way; and shows how to determine the safety time stock needed to offset the longer than planned lead time.

When a customer demand is not filled because stock is not available, the unfilled demand becomes a backorder or lost sales. Lost sales demand is often not known or measured by the stocking facility. The chapter shows how to estimate and control the lost sales demand; and also how to compute a related measure, here called the effective service level.

Late Delivery

Consider a stocking facility where customer orders arrive and require immediate fill. The flow of these orders is unknown in advance, and their uncertainty is measured by the standard deviation of the forecast errors, denoted as σ. The management generally sets a desired service level, and seeks to have the proper amount of stock to achieve this desired level. This requires finding the minimum amount of safety stock to offset the forecast error that is associated with the planned supplier lead time duration. A difficulty occurs when the actual delivery time is longer than the planned lead time, and thereby causes the service level to suffer. This section shows how to measure the service level when late deliveries of this type occurs; and further shows how an extra layer of stock (safety time stock) can be provided to offset the lead time uncertainty.

Safety Stock for a Desired Service Level

Recall (from Chapter 4) how the safety stock is obtained to yield the service level desired by the management. The data used in the computations is listed below:

SL = desired service level

F = average monthly forecast

L = lead time to procure the part from the supplier

Q = size of the order quantity

σ = standard deviation of the one-month ahead forecast error

The lead time forecast is measured by $F_L = L \times F$, and the corresponding lead time standard deviation is $\sigma_L = \sqrt{L}\sigma$. The partial expectation is computed from $E(k) = (1 - SL)Q/\sigma_L$, and E(k) yields the safety factor k by way of a table look up as described in Chapter 4. Finally, the safety stock becomes $SS = k\sigma_L$.

Going further, the above measures are used to find the order point and order level. The order point is obtained from $OP = F_L + SS$, and the order level by $OL = OP + Q$. A buy is called when the on-hand plus on-order (OH + OO), inventory is at OP or lower, and thereby the buy quantity, q, becomes: $q = OL - (OH + OO)$. Note, $q \geq Q$.

For convenience in the following analysis, the order size and forecast error are converted into units of the average monthly forecast as shown below:

M = Q/F = months-in-buy

cov = σ/F = coefficient of variation

This way, the data is independent from the forecast size and is defined in relative terms. The data to determine the safety stock is now reduced to the following:

SL = desired service level

L = lead time in months

M = order size in months supply

cov = coefficient of variation

The procedure to find the safety stock in months supply is as follows:

First, the partial expectation becomes $E(k) = (1 - SL) M/(\sqrt{L}\ \text{cov})$. Second, a table look up yields the safety factor k. So now, thirdly, the safety stock (in months supply) is computed by: $(k\sqrt{L}\ \text{cov})$. Note, in months supply, the lead time forecast is L, and the order point is $OP = L + k\sqrt{L}\ \text{cov}$.

Service Level when Late Delivery

Suppose a situation with desired service level SL, and where the safety stock, lead time forecast, and the order point from the planned lead time L are computed as shown above. But now assume the actual (delivery) lead time is w instead of L. The following shows how to find the actual service level. Note, with w, the delivery time forecast becomes $F_w = w \times F$, and the corresponding standard deviation is $\sigma_w = \sqrt{w}\sigma$. So, the associated safety factor is measured from $k = (OP - F_w)/\sigma_w$. Using k, in a table look up, the corresponding partial expectation E(k) is found. Thereby, the conditional service level becomes: $SL|w = 1 - E(k)\sigma_w/Q$.

Half-Normal Distribution

Recall the standard normal distribution where the variable z is N(0, 1) with $\mu_z = 0$ and $\sigma_z = 1$. Thomopoulos [1980] explores the left-truncated normal where the only values of z that occur are those when $z \geq k$. The variable $t = (z - k)$ is used and $t \geq 0$. In the special situation when $k = 0$, the left-truncated normal distribution becomes the half-normal distribution. When $k = 0$, the above reference shows the expected value of t is $E(t) = 0.7979$, and the associated standard deviation is $\sigma(t) = 0.6078$. Thereby, for the half-normal, $E(t) \sim 0.8\sigma_z$, and $\sigma_z = 1.25E(t)$. Figure 11.1 depicts the half-normal distribution.

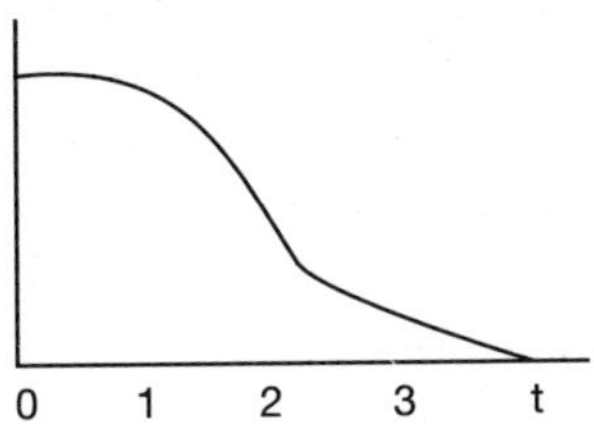

Figure 11.1: The Half-Normal Distribution

Delivery Time Distribution

In the analysis to follow, the delivery time (denoted as w) is assumed as a mixed discrete and continuous variable where $P(w = L) = Po$, $P(w > L) = (1 - Po)$, and $w \geq L$. The distribution of the variable w is shaped like the right-hand side of the normal distribution. For convenience, w is listed in monthly units, and a related (conditional) measure is ML = expected months late given the delivery is late.

The values of w begin at the mode L and seldom fall beyond (L + 3 × 1.25ML). The distribution of w is listed below and is depicted in Figure 11.2.

$$f(w) = Po \quad \text{at } w = L$$
$$\text{Half-normal} \quad \text{at } w > L$$

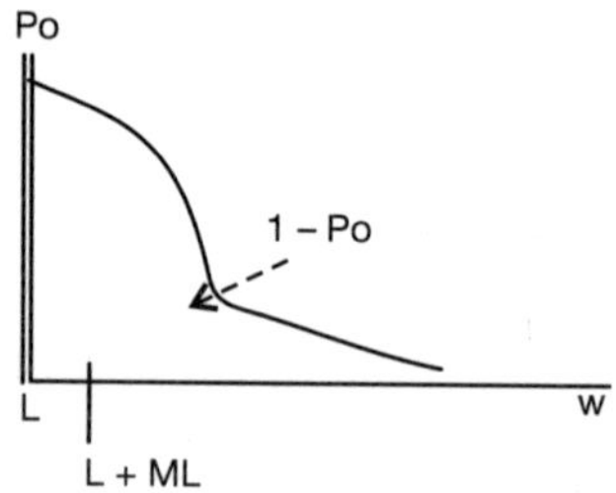

Figure 11.2: The Lead Time Distribution

Lead Time Sensitivity on the Service Level

To illustrate how the lead time affects the service level, consider the following scenario when the planned lead time is L = 3.00 months, but the actual delivery times can vary from 3.00 to 3.75 months. Thereby, the late time ranges from 0.00 to 0.75 months. The computations to follow assume the average monthly forecast is F = 100, and the associated standard deviation is σ = 30, hence, cov = 0.30. Further, assume the order quantity is Q = 100, whereby M = 1.00. Using the method described above to find SL|w, the table below lists the conditional service levels for selected values of w.

w	3.00	3.15	3.30	3.45	3.60	3.75
late	0.00	0.15	0.30	0.45	0.60	0.75
SL|w	0.950	0.915	0.861	0.792	0.709	0.640

Note how the achieved service level dramatically drops as the delivery time increases above the planned lead time L. For example, when the delivery time is 3.30, the service level becomes 0.861.

Safety Time and Safety Time Stock

Safety time (ST) is used as a parameter that allows the inventory management to hold added stock to offset the increase in delivery time. When the safety time is one or less (months), the safety time stock (STS) for month t is computed by $STS_t = ST \times F_{t+1}$ where F_{t+1} is the forecast for month (t + 1), and so forth. The total safety stock for a part in month t becomes $TSS_t = SS + STS_t$. In the examples, the forecasts are assumed horizontal ($F = F_t$) and so STS = ST × F is used throughout all months. In this way, the order point becomes: $OP = TSS + F_L$.

Recall when w = L, $F_w = L \times F$ and $\sigma_w = \sqrt{L}\sigma$. Further, when the delivery-time is w = L + ML, $F_w = w \times F$, and $\sigma_w = \sqrt{w}\sigma$. In either case, the safety factor becomes $k = (OP - F_w)/\sigma_w$ and the corresponding partial expectation, E(k) is found by a table look up. With E(k), the service level is now measured by $SL|(w) = 1 - E(k)\sigma_w/Q$.

In the computations below, the safety time parameter in use is ST = k(1.25ML) where k is the safety factor related to E(k). So, for a particular combination of Po and ST, an estimate of the service level is obtained as follows:

$$SL(Po, ST) = SL|(w = L)Po + SL|(w = L + ML)(1 - Po)$$

The six scenarios listed below are used to measure the sensitivity of the service level with the supplier lateness and the safety time.

Scenarios	SL	cov	M	L	ML
1	.90	0.3	0.25	0.25	0.10
2	.90	0.5	0.50	0.50	0.20
3	.95	0.3	1.00	1.00	0.40
4	.95	0.5	1.00	3.00	0.50
5	.97	0.3	1.00	1.00	0.40
6	.97	0.5	1.00	3.00	0.50

For brevity, only the detail results for scenario 3 is listed in Table 11.1. The rows pertain to the portion of deliveries not late,

Po (0.0 to 1.0), and the columns identify the safety time parameter, ST = k × 1.25ML (0.0 to 2.0). The cells in the body give the service level achieved with each combination of Po and ST. The right-hand column lists the safety factor, k′, that yields the minimum safety time needed to bring the achieved service level, SL(Po, ST), up to the desired service level, (SL). For example, when ML = 0.40 and Po = 0.4, k′ = 0.78 is the minimum safety factor needed to bring the achieved service level up to the desired service level of 0.95.

Table 11.1: Scenario 3

Po/k	0.0	0.5	1.0	1.5	2.0	k′
0.0	0.723	0.874	0.957	0.990	0.998	0.96
0.1	0.746	0.886	0.961	0.991	0.998	0.93
0.2	0.769	0.897	0.965	0.992	0.999	0.89
0.3	0.791	0.909	0.970	0.993	0.999	0.84
0.4	0.814	0.920	0.974	0.994	0.999	0.78
0.5	0.837	0.932	0.978	0.995	0.999	0.70
0.6	0.859	0.944	0.982	0.996	0.999	0.58
0.7	0.882	0.955	0.986	0.997	0.999	0.46
0.8	0.905	0.967	0.990	0.998	1.000	0.37
0.9	0.927	0.978	0.995	0.999	1.000	0.22
1.0	0.950	0.990	0.999	1.000	1.000	0.00

Note: SL(Po, ST) when SL = .95, cov = 0.30
M = 1.00, L = 1.00, ML = 0.40, ST = k(1.25ML)

Table 11.2 summarizes the minimum safety factors obtained from the right-hand columns of scenarios 1 to 6. Recall these factors give the minimum safety time needed to bring the achieved service level up to the desired service level. In general, the safety factors needed for each Po are relatively consistent. The right-hand column gives the minimum safety factor needed for each Po.

Table 11.2: Minimum Safety Factors (k′) from Scenarios 1 to 6

Po	1	2	3	4	5	6	(average k′)
0.00	1.09	1.17	0.96	0.99	0.98	1.01	1.03
0.10	1.01	1.08	0.93	0.94	0.95	0.96	.98
0.20	0.94	0.98	0.89	0.89	0.92	0.91	.92
0.30	0.86	0.90	0.84	0.82	0.88	0.85	.84
0.40	0.78	0.81	0.78	0.74	0.83	0.77	.78
0.50	0.67	0.70	0.70	0.64	0.76	0.68	.69
0.60	0.54	0.57	0.58	0.53	0.66	0.57	.57
0.70	0.43	0.44	0.46	0.43	0.51	0.45	.45
0.80	0.31	0.32	0.37	0.32	0.41	0.35	.33
0.90	0.17	0.18	0.22	0.18	0.26	0.20	.20
1.00	0.00	0.00	0.00	0.00	0.00	0.00	.00

The entries in the right-hand column of Table 11.2, average k′, are used to generate a quadratic fit via regression methods. The equation that results is listed below.

$$k = 1.022 - 0.360Po - 0.642Po^2$$

The above regression equation can now be applied to the parts in the inventory by the following six steps:

1. For each vendor that supplies parts to the inventory, measure Po and ML from the past deliveries.
2. Use Po and the above quadratic equation to find the (minimum) safety factor, k, for the vendor.
3. Use ML and k to determine the safety time, ST, for the vendor.
4. For each part of the vendor, apply the safety time, ST, with the forecasts to yield the safety time stock, STS.
5. For each part, apply the regular safety stock, SS, with the safety time stock, STS, to get the total safety stock, TSS = SS + STS.
6. The order point for the part becomes $OP = F_L + TSS$.

Example 11.1. Suppose a vendor with Po = 0.50 and ML = 0.40 months. Using the equation to get k for Po = 0.50, yields k = 0.6815, and the corresponding safety time for the vendor becomes ST = k × 1.25ML = 0.341 months. Now assume a part of the vendor has F = 100, σ = 30, Q = 100, L = 3.00 months, and SL = 0.95. Applying the methods of Chapter 4, the safety stock becomes 48, and the lead time forecast is 300 pieces. Further, the safety time stock is STS = ST × F = 34.1. So now, the order point for the part becomes OP = 300 + 48 + 34 = 382. Finally, the order level is OL = 382 + 100 = 482.

Lost Sales

Most companies are unaware of the amount of lost sales that they incur, and have no way to measure this important demand. This section formulates a lost sales demand model, and shows how to measure this demand, and also how to set limits to control lost sale demands.

One of the key measures that management uses to gauge their inventory performance is by way of the service level. A common way to measure the service level (sl) is the ratio of (demand filled) over the (recorded demand). This measure is also referred to as the percent fill. Generally a service level of .95 or higher is sought by the management. The reported measure of service level is often computed over all or a portion of the parts in the inventory, and for a particular time period as one week, one month or one year.

A fault in the above service level measure is that sometimes all of the demands on the items are not known or are recorded. This happens when a customer has need for an item and the item is not available in stock, and the sale is lost. Here the demand is not satisfied and this unfilled demand becomes either a backorder or a lost sale. It is called a backorder when the customer will wait for the stock to be replenished, whereby the demand is subsequently filled. It is a lost sale when the customer does not wait for the stock to be replenished and drops the demand. In this latter case, the demand is mostly not recorded.

Demand Model

Consider the demands associated with a stocking facility that are tallied over a fixed period of time (here called a review time), and over a group of items. Often the demands known are only those that are recorded as sales. In this model, the demands are classified in more detail, using categories as: filled demands, unfilled demands, backorder demands, lost sales demands, and effective demands. This demand model identifies the category of demands, shows how they are related, and also how they can be measured. The model also describes the service level (demand filled over total demand) and how it is related to the various demand categories.

Some stocking facilities measure and know exactly what their service level is over all the items, and over various review times. Other facilities do not measure or know this measure. In the typical industrial system, the planned service level is set as a parameter and the safety stock needed is determined and applied accordingly.

Below is a review on the various category of demands, the service level and also on the percent of unfilled demands that become backorders.

Demand Categories. The recorded demand (dr) is the aggregate of customer demands that is ultimately filled by a stocking facility over a period of time (year, month) and for a category of items (parts, products). The quantity could be stated in units of pieces, dollars or lines. The filled demand is from the customer orders that are received and are filled immediately (df). The customer orders that are not filled immediately—are placed on backorder—and are filled ultimately (dbo) are here called backorder demands. Note another category of demand is when the customer orders are not filled immediately and the customers cancel the order. This latter demand is here called the lost sales demand (dls). In this model, the total demand recorded is derived from dr = (df + dbo) and does not include the lost sales demand. In most situations, the lost sales demands (dls) are not recorded or known. All the demands noted here are measured in the same units (pieces, dollars or lines).

Service Level. The service level (sl) is a measure of the portion of the demands that are immediately filled from the stock available. This measure is an aggregate over all the items in the category and over the time period under review. This is denoted as sl and computed by the ratio of: sl = (df/dr). Notice the lost sales demand is not included here since this demand is really not known. In essence, dr is not the total demand, it is only the demand that is known and for convenience, it is here called the total demand recorded. In the event the lost sales demand (dls) was known, the real total demand would also be known. This total demand is denoted here as the total effective demand (de). This would be de = (df + dbo + dls). The service level associated with the effective demand is called the effective service level and is computed by sle = (df/de).

Backorder Portion of Unfilled Demands. This backorder portion is really not known by the management and is like a probability with a value falling between zero and one. Although the exact value of this factor is not known, most managements can provide reasonably close estimates. When a customer order comes in and the stock is not available to fill the order, the customer order is unfilled demand (du) and the customer order becomes either a backorder or a lost sales. So, pbo is the portion of the unfilled demand that becomes a backorder. This is pbo = (dbo/du). The portion of the unfilled demand that becomes a lost sale thereby is derived from pls = (dls/du). Note where pbo + pls = 1.

So using only the data typically known for a stocking facility (dr, sl, pbo), the other measures described above can be determined. This is in the following way:

df = sl × dr = demand filled (immediately)

pls = 1 – pbo = portion of unfilled demand that becomes a lost sale

dbo = dr – df = backorder demand

dls = dbo × (pls/pbo) = lost sales demand

du = dbo + dls = unfilled demand

de = df + du = effective (total) demand

sle = df/de = effective service level

Example 11.2. Consider a location where the annual sales is worth \$1,000,000 and the service level is measured as 0.90. Further, assume the management estimates that 50% of unfilled demands are lost and 50% go on backorder and are ultimately filled. With this notation, we have:

dr = 1,000,000 = demand recorded

sl = 0.90 = service level

pbo = 0.50 = portion of unfilled demand that becomes a backorder

Now using the relations given above, the following measures are computed:

df = sl × dr = 900,000 = demand filled immediately

pls = 1 – pbo = 0.50 = portion of unfilled demand that becomes a lost sale

dbo = dr – df = 100,000 = backorder demand

dls = dbo × (pls/pbo) = 100,000 = lost sales demand

du = dbo + dls = 200,000 = unfilled demand

de = df + du = 1,100,000 = effective total demand

sle = df/de = 0.818 = effective service level

Hence, when the service level is set to sl = 0.90, the annual lost sales is worth \$100,000 and the effective service level is 0.818.

Lost Sales Model

Using the structure from the model presented above, it is possible for the management to specify a limit on the lost sales demand (dls), and then find the service level (sl) that is needed to accomplish this goal.

In reviewing the above demand model, the data that remains constant regardless of the setting of the service level (sl) are the effective demand (de) and the portion of backorders (pbo) from unfilled demand. First note the effective demand is de = (df + du), and although df and du will change with sl, the sum (de) remains the same. Hence, de is a constant. Further, the portion of backorders and the portion of lost sales from unfilled demands (pbo, pls) are not related to the service level. So now (de, pbo, pls) are constants and are included as data available to carry on the lost sales model. A list of the known data is below:

dls = (specified) lost sales demand

de = effective demand

pbo = portion of backorders from unfilled demands

pls = portion of lost sales from unfilled demands

Continuing with the model, the following relations lead to finding the service level (sl) needed to achieve the goal specified on lost sales demand (dls).

dbo = dls × pbo/pls = backorder demand

du = dbo + dls = unfilled demand

df = de – du = filled demand

sle = df/de = effective service level

dr = df + dbo = recorded demand

sl = df/dr = service level

Example 11.3. Continuing with the earlier example, de = 1,100,000, pbo = 0.50, and pls = 0.50 are known. Suppose management also sets an upper limit on lost sales demand to dls = 40,000 (from 100,000). So now the computations to find the service level (sl) needed to accomplish are as follows:

dbo = dls × pbo/pls = 40,000 = backorder demand

du = dbo + dls = 80,000 = unfilled demand

df = de – du = 1,020,000 = filled demand

sle = df/de = 0.927 = effective service level

dr = df + dbo = 1,060,000 = recorded demand

sl = df/dr = 0.962 = service level

The results show when the limit on lost sales demand is set to dls = 40,000, the service level needed to achieve this goal becomes sl = 0.962. Further, the effective service level is sle = 0.927.

Estimating Potential Sales

Table 11.3 lists the potential sales relative to measures of the service level and lost sales. In this context, potential sales are the percent of the effective (total) demand that becomes filled demands. The sales are the same as the recorded demands (dr) since they are the customer orders that are filled either immediately or later as backorders. The service level (sl) and the lost sales portion of unfilled demands (pls) have been defined earlier. The table serves as a guide on how to estimate the relation between sales and the service level. Although not listed in the table, when pls = 0.00, the table entries would be 100.0.

Note, for example, when sl = .80 and pls = .5, then dr = 83.3 percent. This means that 83.3 percent of the real total demands are achieved (as recorded demands) without lost sales; or 16.7 percent of the demands are lost.

For comparison sake, the above example continues with three associated scenarios shown below:

A dealer with pls = .5 and sl = 0.80 yields dr = 83.3 percent.

Scenario 1: When pls = .5 and sl = .90, then dr = 90.9 percent; and this is a (90.9 – 83.3)/83.3 = 9.1% increase in sales.

Scenario 2: When pls = .5 and sl = .95, then dr = 95.2 percent; and this is a (95.2 – 83.3)/83.3 = 14.3% increase in sales.

Scenario 3: When pls = .5 and sl = .975, then dr = 97.6 percent; and this is a (97.6 – 83.3)/83.3 = 17.2% increase in sales.

Example 11.4. Suppose a dealer with $10,000,000 annual sales, pls = .5 and sl = .80.

When pls = .5 and sl = .90, then a 9.1% increase in sales yields annual sales of $10,910,000.

Scenario 1: When pls = .5 and sl = .95, then a 14.3% increase in sales yields annual sales of $11,430,000.

Scenario 2: When pls = .5 and sl = .975, then a 17.2% increase in sales yields annual sales of $11,720,000.

The results show how to estimate the potential sales from measures of the service level and the lost sales portion of unfilled demands. In the example, the annual sales increase 17.2% when the service level increases from 0.80 to 0.975.

Table 11.3: Percent of Demand (de) that Becomes Sales (dr) as Related to Service Level (SL) and Lost Sales Portion (pls) of Unfilled Demands

SL pls	0.1	0.2	0.3	0.4	0.5	0.6	0.7	0.8	0.9
.975	99.7	99.4	98.9	98.4	97.6	96.4	94.5	90.9	81.6
.950	99.4	98.8	97.9	96.8	95.2	93.0	89.6	83.3	69.0
.925	99.2	98.2	96.9	95.2	93.0	89.9	85.1	76.9	59.7
.900	98.9	97.6	95.9	93.8	90.9	87.0	81.1	71.4	52.6
.875	98.6	97.0	94.9	92.3	88.9	84.2	77.4	66.7	47.1
.850	98.4	96.4	94.0	90.9	87.0	81.6	74.1	62.5	42.6
.825	98.1	95.8	93.0	89.6	85.1	79.2	71.0	58.8	38.8
.800	97.8	95.2	92.1	88.2	83.3	76.9	68.2	55.6	35.7
.775	97.6	94.7	91.2	87.0	81.6	74.8	65.6	52.6	33.1
.750	97.3	94.1	90.3	85.7	80.0	72.7	63.2	50.0	30.8
.725	97.0	93.6	89.5	84.5	78.4	70.8	60.9	47.6	28.8
.700	96.8	93.0	88.6	83.3	76.9	69.0	58.8	45.5	27.0

Summary

When the supplier is late in the delivery of replenish stock to a stocking facility, the service level for the stocking facility suffers. This chapter shows how to measure the late delivery by supplier; and how to set safety time stock to overcome the fault in on-time-delivery. The chapter also describes how to measure lost sales in a stocking facility and how to reduce the lost sales over a set of parts in a stocking facility.

References

Baker, K.R. and J.W.M. Bertrand, "A Comparison of Due-Date Selection Rules", *AIIE Transactions*, Vol. 13, 1981, pp. 123-32.

Chen, Zhi-long and Nicholas G. Hall, "Supply Chain Scheduling: Conflict and Cooperation in Assembly Systems", *Operations Research*, Vol. 55, No. 6, Nov.-Dec. 2007, pp. 1072-89.

Downs, B.R. Meters and S. Semple, "Managing Inventory with Multiple Products, Lags in Delivery, Resource Constraints and Lost Sales", *Management Science*, Bo. 47, No. 3, 2001, pp. 464-79.

Janaskiraman, G. and R. Roundy, "Lost Sales Problems with Stochastic Lead Times", *Operations Research*, Vol. 52, 2004, pp. 795-805.

Nahmias, S. "Simple Approximations for a Variety of Dynamic Lead Time Lost Sales Inventory Models", *Operations Research*, Vol. 27, No. 5, 1979, pp. 904-24.

Thomopoulos, Nick T., "Supplier Lateness, Safety Time and Service Level", *Journal of Research in Engineering and Technology*, Vol. 3, No. 4, 2006.

——, *Applied Forecasting Methods*, Prentice Hall, Inc., 1980.

——, "Demands, Backorders, Service Level, Lost Sales and Effective Service Level", *Journal of Business and Economics Research*, Vol. 2, No. 11, November 2004.

12

Reusable Inventory

In this chapter the reader will learn some of the terminology and methods of queuing theory and how they are associated with reusable inventory in the plants, offices, stocking and retail locations. These are systems with one or more service facilities where customers arrive to the system in random time intervals and desire to use one of the service facilities. The efficiency of the system is measured by the service level. Two scenarios are described, one when backorders occur and another when lost sales. When backorders, the service level measures the probability a new arrival will not need to wait in the queue before being serviced. When lost sales, the service level measures the probability the system is not full and the unit can immediately enter the system, and therefore is not a lost customer. Another measure, the utilization ratio, evaluates how busy the system is based on the average time between the arrivals and the average time of service. The chapter shows where the number of service facilities and the utilization ratio, in combination, affect the level of service for the system.

Introduction

This chapter concerns another form of inventory that is present in most firms, but does not leave the firm's possession once a demand is fulfilled. The demands on this type of inventory are mainly time related. When a demand occurs, the customer uses an item (resource or service facility) to fulfill a task of some sort, and when finished, the item is released and remains to meet the next customer demand. For purposes here, these items are labeled as reusable inventory items. If all of the reusable inventory items are occupied when a demand arrives, and if the customer demand will wait its turn in a queue, in essence the demand is in a backorder state. Examples of reusable items with backorders are tools (in a shop), lift trucks, pallets, molds, binding machines, order picking personnel, fixtures, so forth. In the event, the demand will not wait, the customer demand becomes a lost sale. Could be tables in a restaurant, pumps at a gas station, or items at a rental agency. Queuing theory is the tool used to develop the solutions presented in this chapter.

Reusable Inventory When Backorders

In queuing theory, the inventory items are called service facilities, (sometimes channels), and these facilities provide some type of service to each arrival unit. In this backorder section, when a unit arrives for service and finds all the service facilities busy, the unit will wait in a queue in a backorder state until one of the service facilities becomes available.

For notation sake, suppose a service system with N service facilities are available to the customers, where n (n = 0, 1, 2, ...) designates the number of (customer) units in the system at any moment of time. Of the n units, some are being serviced, and others are waiting in the queue. When n is less or equal to N, no units are in the backorder state. When n is larger than N, (n – N) units are in the queue waiting to be serviced in a backorder state.

The model in this chapter, assumes the arrivals to the system have inter-arrival times that follow an exponential density with an average time of $\tau_a = 1/\lambda$. The service time also follows an exponential density with an average service time of $\tau_s = 1/\mu$. The utilization ratio for the system is denoted by $\rho = \tau_s/\tau_a = \lambda/\mu$.

The probability of n units in the system is referred to as P(n) and is computed as follows:

$$P(n) = \begin{cases} P(0)\,\rho^n/n! & n = 0 \text{ to } N-1 \\ P(0)\,\rho^n/(N!\,N^{n-N}) & n \geq N \end{cases}$$

where

$$P(0) = 1/(\Sigma_{(n<N)}\, \rho^n/n! + \rho^N/[(N-1)!(N-\rho)])$$

The probability that a new arrival will not have to wait in a backorder state prior to service is called the service level, and is signified as SL. The service level is computed from the probability of n less than N whereby, $SL = P(n < N)$. Note, when $n < N$, a new arrival will not need to wait; but when $n = N$, new arrivals will need to wait, and thereby the above definition of SL is used.

Table 12.1 pertains to a backorder system and contains a list of utilization ratios ρ, and shows the minimum number of service facilities, N, needed to yield the desired service level for SL = .85, .90, .95 and .99. The utilization ratios range from $\rho = 0.1$ to 700. Some examples on how the table results can be used in industry are provided below.

Example 12.1. When a car windshield is broken, a firm in Minnesota is a major supplier to replace the windshield. A significant portion of the inventory in this firm concerns the many windshield molds. A unique mold is needed for each model and year of the car. With the vast models and years of the past, this inventory is indeed expensive.

Suppose, the facility is open eight hours a day, and a mold for a particular windshield is used in the manufacturing process. Assume a windshield where the average demand is 8 per day and the average processing time per windshield is 4 hours. The management wants to know how many molds should be in stock to yield a 90 percent service level. To seek out the answer with the data provided, the arrival and service times must be measured with the same time units. In this example, the unit of time is set to hours, and thereby $\tau_a = 1$ hour and $\tau_s = 4$ hours. Therefore, the utilization ratio is $\rho = \tau_s/\tau_a = 4/1 = 4.00$. So now, Table 12.1 is searched, and shows when $\rho = 4$ and $SL = 0.90$, $N = 8$. Hence, eight molds are needed to yield a 90 percent service level for the windshield.

Example 12.2. Consider a distribution center with a large number of parts, and a pool of order pickers, that receive on average 10,000 lines a day. A customer order lists the parts and quantity needed for each. The individual part on the order is called a line. The order picker locates the bin (of the part), collects the pieces and puts them on a cart. Suppose further, the industrial engineer at the center estimates the average time to locate and pick a line is 2 minutes. The orders steadily arrive to the center and the management desires a service level of SL = 0.85. This way, the lines are filled fairly quickly and do not cause an unduly delay in delivery to the customers. The management wants to know how many order pickers are needed to yield the desired service level. To accomplish, note the average time between the arrival of a line in a 480 minute day is $\tau_a = 480/10{,}000 = 0.048$ minutes. Also, note the average service time (to process a line) is $\tau_s = 2$ minutes, and so, the utilization ratio becomes $\rho = 2.000/0.048 = 41.67$. With this information, Table 12.1 is searched and shows N = 50 order pickers are needed.

Example 12.3. Consider a warehouse receiving department where trucks arrive with goods for unloading at a rate of 3 per hour. Suppose also, the average time required to unload a truck is 16 minutes. The management wants to know how many loading crews are needed to attain a service level of SL = 0.85. In this situation, the service level is the portion of new arrival trucks that do not have to wait in a queue to begin unloading. Note, the time between arrival of trucks is $\tau_a = 20$ minutes, and the average time to unload a truck is $\tau_s = 16$ minutes. Thereby, the utilization ratio becomes $\rho = 0.80$. So, Table 12.1 is searched with $\rho = 0.80$ and SL = 0.85 to find N = 3 loading crews are needed.

Reusable Inventory When Lost Sales

Queuing theory is also used to find reusable inventory solutions when lost sales are encountered. This type of situation occurs when a new arrival to a system, will not wait, should it find all the service facilities busy. The arrival does not wait for service and therefore leaves the system forever as a lost sale. To formulate the system, consider a service system with N service facilities. As before, n designates the number of units in the system where n = 0, 1, 2, ..., N. Here, n is always less or equal to N because no unit will enter the system when all the service facilities are busy. All arriving units that try to enter the system when the system is full become lost sales.

As before, the arrivals to the system have inter-arrival times that follow an exponential density with an average time of $\tau_a = 1/\lambda$. The service times also follow an exponential density with an average service time of $\tau_s = 1/\mu$. The utilization ratio for the system is denoted by $\rho = \tau_s/\tau_a = \lambda/\mu$.

In this situation, the probability of n units in the system is represented by P(n) where

$$P(n) = P(0)\,\rho^n/n! \qquad n = 0 \text{ to } N$$

and

$$P(0) = 1/(\Sigma_{(n \le N)}\,\rho^n/n!)$$

The probability that a new arrival will find an open service facility to use, is the probability that n is less than N, and in the lost sales scenario, this probability is the service level of the system. Hence, in the lost sales case, SL = P(n < N), and represents the probability a new arrival to the system will enter the system. If a new arrival unit finds the system full, the unit cannot enter the system and is lost forever. Table 12.2 gives the minimum value of N needed to yield the desired service level of SL = .85, .90, .95 and .99 when the utilization ratios range from $\rho = 0.1$ to 700. Some examples on how the table results can be used in industry are provided below.

Table 12.1: Minimum Number of Service Facilities to Achieve the Service Level (SL) with the Utilization Ratio (ρ) for the Backorder Queuing System

	SL			
ρ	.85	.90	.95	.99
0.1	1	1	2	2
0.2	2	2	2	3
0.3	2	2	2	3
0.4	2	2	3	3
0.5	2	2	3	4
0.6	2	3	3	4
0.7	3	3	3	4
0.8	3	3	4	4

0.9	3	3	4	5
1.0	3	3	4	5
1.2	3	4	4	5
1.4	4	4	5	6
1.6	4	4	5	6
1.8	4	5	5	7
2.0	5	5	6	7
2.5	5	6	6	8
3.0	6	6	7	9
3.5	7	7	8	10
4.0	7	8	9	10
4.5	8	9	9	11
5	9	9	10	12
10	15	16	17	19
15	21	22	23	26
20	26	27	29	32
25	32	33	35	39
30	38	39	41	45
35	43	44	47	51
40	49	50	52	57
45	54	56	58	63
50	60	61	64	66
55	65	67	69	74
60	70	72	75	80
65	76	78	80	86
70	81	83	86	92
75	86	88	91	97
80	92	94	97	103
85	97	99	102	109
90	102	105	108	114
95	108	110	113	120

100	113	115	119	125
150	166	168	173	181
200	218	221	226	235
250	270	274	279	289
300	322	326	331	343
350	374	378	384	396
400	425	429	436	449
450	477	481	488	502
500	528	533	540	555
550	579	584	592	607
600	631	636	644	660
650	682	687	696	712
700	733	739	747	765

Example 12.4. Suppose a rental agency is open seven days a week and includes a number of small cargo trailers for rent. Assume the average number of requests is 10 per week and the average rental time is 2 days. Customers who request a trailer when all are out will not wait and will go elsewhere. The store owner wants to know how many trailers to have in stock to provide a service level of 95 percent (SL = 0.95). In this situation, $\tau_a = 7/10 = 0.70$ days and $\tau_s = 2$ days. Therefore $\rho = 2.00/0.70 = 2.86$. A search in Table 12.2 shows that SL = 0.95 and $\rho = 2.5$ gives N = 6. When SL = 0.95 and $\rho = 3.0$, N = 7. Thus, the number of trailers needed to give a 95 percent service level is about seven.

Example 12.5. A bicycle dealer wishes to maintain a system of continuous availability for each model bike where, as soon as a bike is sold, another is ordered from the supplier. If the bike is not in stock when a customer demand arrives, the sale is lost. For a particular model, suppose the average demand is 2 per week and the average procurement lead time is 2 weeks. The store owner wants to know how large should the order point and order level be set for the bike model to attain a 99 percent service level? Note, the average time between customer demands is

τ_a = 1/2 = 0.5 weeks and average time to receive a new bike is τ_s = 2.0 weeks; so the utilization ratio is ρ = 4.0. A search in Table 12.2 with ρ = 4.0 and SL = 0.99, shows N = 10 bikes are needed in stock (on-hand plus on-order) at any one time. Thereby, the order level is 10 and the order point is 9.

Table 12.2: Minimum Number of Service Facilities to Achieve the Service Level (SL) with the Utilization Ratio (ρ) for the Lost Sales Queuing System

	SL			
ρ	.85	.90	.95	.99
0.1	1	1	2	2
0.2	2	2	2	3
0.3	2	2	2	3
0.4	2	2	3	3
0.5	2	2	3	4
0.6	2	3	3	4
0.7	3	3	3	4
0.8	3	3	3	4
0.9	3	3	4	5
1.0	3	3	4	5
1.2	3	3	4	5
1.4	3	4	4	6
1.6	3	4	5	6
1.8	4	4	5	6
2.0	4	4	5	7
2.5	4	5	6	7
3.0	5	6	7	8
3.5	6	6	7	9
4.0	6	7	8	10
4.5	7	7	8	11
5	7	8	9	11
10	12	13	15	18

15	16	18	20	24
20	21	23	26	30
25	25	28	31	36
30	30	32	36	42
35	34	37	41	47
40	38	42	46	53
45	43	46	51	58
50	47	51	56	64
55	51	56	61	69
60	56	60	66	75
65	60	65	71	80
70	64	69	76	85
75	69	74	81	91
80	73	78	86	96
85	77	83	90	101
90	81	88	95	107
95	86	92	100	112
100	90	97	105	117
150	133	142	154	170
200	175	188	202	221
250	218	233	250	273
300	261	278	298	324
350	303	323	346	375
400	346	368	394	426
450	388	413	442	476
500	431	458	489	527
550	473	503	437	577
600	516	549	585	628
650	558	594	632	678
700	601	639	680	728

Summary

Inventory that does not leave the firm's possession once a demand is fulfilled is here called reusable inventory. This type of inventory takes place (for items) when a demand (to temporarily use the item) occurs and upon completion, the item remains in the facility to meet the next demand. This chapter describes the methods to determine how much of this type of reusable inventory to have available for two separate situations: when backorders occur, and also when lost sales occur.

Reference

Thomopoulos, Nick T., *Strategic Inventory Management and Planning*, Hitchcock Publishing Co., Carol Stream, Il, 1990.

13

Statistical Process Control

Statistical process control was pioneered by Walter Shewhart in the 1920s. Using carefully designed experiments, Shewhart created control charts and the concept of statistical control. This chapter describes how to monitor and control a process to meet specification standards that management designates. The reader will learn about processes where the output products are of the attribute type and of the variable type. Four tests are described for the attribute type process and four for the variable type process. At the outset of each test, a pre-study is performed to measure the average and variability of the process. This is done by taking samples at regular time intervals called subgroups. An initial goal measures the process in statistical stability, and then computes control limits. The control limits are used to monitor the process ensuring the system is producing units that conform with the desired specifications. The reader will also learn about center lines, and how to measure the capability of the process.

Introduction

A process is any system that produces an output of a given product or service. Statistical process control (SPC) is the function that analyzes the outputs of such a process to take appropriate action to achieve and maintain a state of statistical control, and to improve the process capability. Process capability is a measure of the proportion of the output that will be within the product specification tolerances.

Two important measures of a process are the quality of the units, and the quantity of units produced. The key philosophy of

SPC is that the quality has the highest importance, even at the risk of slowing down the quantity.

The data are of two types: attribute and variable. The attribute type is when an item is identified as either defective or non-defective, conforming or non-conforming, good or bad. The variable type is when a measure is taken, like strength of a cord, the weight of a can, so forth.

The basic tool of SPC is depicted by way of control charts as in Figure 13.1. The charts give a graphic representation of the characteristics of a process in a time line manner showing plotted values of a characteristic, a center line and two control limits. The center line is the average, and the limits are upper and lower control limits. When a measure falls outside of one of the control limits (UCL, LCL), the system is deemed as out of statistical control. Note, if the lower control limit (LCL) is below zero in the computations, the limit is reset to zero, i.e., LCL = max(LCL, 0).

There are several types of control charts that are in use for various process situations. In this chapter, eight charts are described, four for attribute type data and four for variable type data. The charts for attribute type data are called: p charts, np charts, c charts and u charts; and the charts for variable type data are called: x-Bar and R charts, x-Bar and s charts, median charts and individual charts.

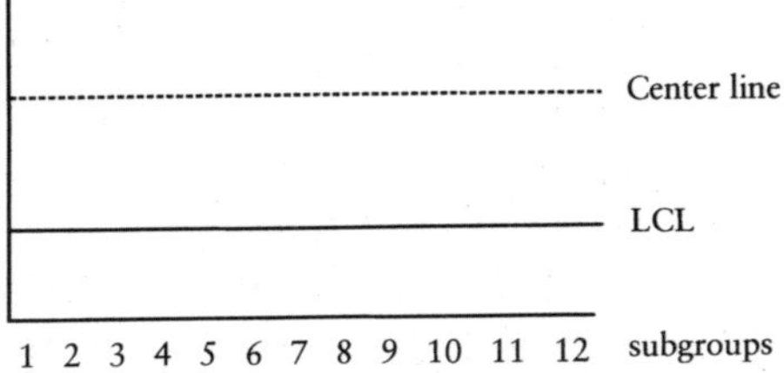

Figure 13.1: Control Chart

The five basic steps in carrying out the SPC for a process are the following: gather data, calculate control limits, analyze for process control, interpret the process capability and monitor the process. More detail is given below. Steps 1 to 4 below are pre-study steps.

1. **Gather data:** Choose the size (number units in a sample), frequency (timing between taking a sample), and number in a subgroup (number of samples). For example, 6 units are tested each hour for 36 hours.
2. **Calculate control limits:** Use the data from above to measure the average and the control limits.
3. **Analyze for process control:** From the data in Step 1, if any sample has a measure out of control, find the cause in the process and fix accordingly. Eliminate the samples that are out of control and recalculate the average and control limits.
4. **Interpret for process capability:** Now that the process is in statistical control, measure if the process is performing in accordance with the specification tolerances.
5. **Monitor the process:** After the pre-study, use the same sample size and frequency to monitor the process in an ongoing manner.

Attribute Type Data

Attribute type charts apply when a unit inspected is identified as either conforming or nonconforming. The four common charts for attribute type data are the following: p chart, np chart, c chart and u chart. The p and np charts are used when each individual unit inspected in a subgroup is either conforming or non-conforming. Further, the np chart applies when, the number of units inspected is the same for each subgroup; and the p chart is used when the number of inspected units may vary from one subgroup to another. The c and u charts are used when an individual item inspected can have more than one defect. The c chart is used when one item is inspected in a subgroup, whereas the u chart applies when one or more items are inspected in each subgroup.

For attribute type data, the capability is a measure on the percent of units in a process that are conforming. The goal is to achieve a 100% capability measure for each process.

p Chart

The p chart is used when the units of the process have attribute type data, and during the monitoring stage, the number of units in each subgroup may vary.

Pre-Study

Consider the example below with pre-study results from N = 8 subgroups. The subgroup samples are taken each hour for eight hours. The subgroups are denoted by i, the number units per subgroup is n, and the number defected in a subgroup is x. The portion defective per subgroup is p = x/n. The sums over all subgroups are also listed.

i	1	2	3	4	5	6	7	8	sum
n	25	25	20	25	25	30	25	25	200
x	0	1	0	6	1	0	0	1	9
p	0	.04	0	.24	.04	0	0	.04	.045

The pre-study averages are now computed as below. The average percent of defective units is $\overline{p}$, and the average number of units sampled in a subgroup is $\overline{n}$. In the example,

$$\overline{p} = \Sigma x/\Sigma n = 9/200 = .045 \text{ (center line)}$$

$$\overline{n} = \Sigma n/N = 200/8 = 25$$

The standard deviation on the percent defective is measured by:

$$\sigma = \sqrt{\overline{p}(1-\overline{p})/\overline{n}} = .041$$

So now, the lower and upper control limits on the percent defective units are computed as below. The lower limit should be zero or larger.

$$LCL = \overline{p} - 3\sigma = -.078 \text{ (LCL = 0)}$$

$$UCL = \overline{p} + 3\sigma = .168$$

Process control. The pre-study data shows one subgroup (i = 4) is out of statistical control since the percent defected (0.24) is larger than the upper control limit of UCL = 0.168. The cause for the subgroup is sought and corrective action is taken, accordingly. The subgroup is eliminated from the study and the averages are recalculated, with results as below:

Σn = 175

Σx = 3

$\bar{p}$ = $\Sigma x / \Sigma n$ = 3/175 = .017 (center line)

σ = .026

LCL = 0

UCL = .095

Process capability. The capability is a measure on the percent of units that are conforming (non-defective). In the example, the process capability is computed as

Process capability = $(1 - \bar{p}) = (1 - .017) = .983 = 98.3\%$.

Monitoring. Having completed the pre-study, the process is now monitored with a steady frequency of subgroups, and the same sample size as in the pre-study. See the example below. As long as the percent defective in the subgroups are within the lower and upper control limits, the process is in statistical control.

i	1	2	3	...
n	25	20	25	
x	0	0	1	
$\bar{p}$	0	0	.04	

np Chart

The np chart is used when the units in the process have attribute type data, and during the monitoring stage, the number of units inspected are the same.

Example 13.1. Suppose a pre-study with N = 30 subgroups as below. Consider the notation and hourly data as listed:

i = subgroup

n = 20 = sample size per subgroup

np = number non-conforming units in subgroup i hour

i	1	2	3	...	30	sum
np	0	1	0		0	10

$\overline{np} = \Sigma(np)/N = 10/30 = 0.33$ = average non-conforming units per subgroup = (center line)

The percent of units that are non-conforming and the associated standard deviation are computed below:

$$\bar{p} = \overline{np}/n = 0.33/20 = .0165$$

$$\sigma_{np} = \sqrt{\overline{np}(1-\bar{p})} = 0.57$$

The lower and upper control limits of np are obtained as follows.

$$LCL_{np} = \overline{np} - 3\sigma_{np} < 0,$$

and thereby, LCL_{np} is reset to zero.

$$UCL_{np} = \overline{np} + 3\sigma_{np} = 2.04$$

In the monitoring stage, if three or more non-conforming units are found in a subgroup, the process is deemed out of control. This is because $UCL_{np} = 2.04$ and $3 > UCL_{np}$.

The process capability is $(1 - \bar{p}) = .9835 = 98.35\%$.

c Chart

The c chart is used for a process, when the units have attribute type data, and more than one defective can be found on each unit inspected, e.g. bubbles on a plate of glass, c = number of non-conformities per subgroup. The number of units inspected per subgroup is one.

Example 13.2. Consider the pre-study example where N = 40 subgroups, c = number non-conformities in subgroup i and with one sample per subgroup.

hour

i	1	2	3	...	40	sum
c	2	1	0	...	0	64

The average c, and the associated standard deviation are obtained by the following:

$\bar{c} = \Sigma c/N = 64/40 = 1.6 = \text{(center line)}$

Using the Poisson distribution,

$$\sigma_c = \sqrt{1.6} = 1.26$$

So now, the control limits of c are computed as below:

$LCLc = \bar{c} - 3\sigma_c < 0$, and reset to zero

$UCLc = \bar{c} + 3\sigma_c = 5.38$

In the monitoring stage, if any subgroup has c > 5.38 (six or more non-conformities), the process is deemed out of control.

u Chart

The u chart is used for a process, when the units of the process have attribute type data, and more than one defective can be found on each unit inspected, and where one or more units can be inspected in a subgroup.

Example 13.3. Consider a pre-study example with N = 50 subgroups, and with n = sample size in subgroup i, c = number non-conforming units in subgroup i, and u = average non-conformities per item.

i	1	2	3	...	50	sum
n	2	4	3	...	2	150
c	0	1	0	...	0	30

The averages of u and n are found as below:

$\bar{u} = \Sigma c/\Sigma n = 30/150 = 0.20 = \text{(center line)}$

$\bar{n} = \Sigma n/N = 150/50 = 3 = \text{average sample size}$

The standard deviation of u becomes,

$$\sigma_u = \sqrt{\bar{u}/\bar{n}} = 0.258$$

Finally, the control limits on u become:

$LCL_u = \bar{u} - 3\sigma_u < 0$, and reset to zero

$UCL_u = \bar{u} + 3\sigma_u = 0.97$

In the monitoring stage, if the average number of non-conformities in a subgroup is more than $UCL_u = 0.97$, the process is deemed out of control.

Variable Type Data

Variable type charts apply when a measure (of some type) is taken to determine whether the unit is conforming with the specifications of the unit. The four basic charts for variable type data are the following: x-Bar and R chart, x-Bar and s chart, median chart, and individual chart. The first three charts are used when more than one unit is inspected in each subgroup; the individual chart is used when only one unit is inspected in a subgroup.

For variable type data, the capability of a process is measured by how many standard deviations separate the center line from the closest specification limit. The measure is commonly denoted at cpk and the larger cpk, the better. When cpk is close to 3 or above, the capability is assumed as excellent, indicating, the probability of a unit exceeding the specification limits is very small.

Six-Sigma Limits

Six-sigma limits occur when the cpk reaches six or higher and thereby the probability of producing a non-conforming unit is almost impossible. The goal in many manufacturing facilities is to achieve this six-sigma-limit for all processes, whether attribute or variable type data.

Below is a table of coefficients that are used with variable type data.

Table 13.1: Statistical Coefficients for Variable Type Data

n	A_2	A_3	B_3	B_4	c_4	d_2	D_3	D_4
2	1.88	2.66	–	3.267	0.7979	1.128	–	3.27
3	1.02	1.95	–	2.568	0.8862	1.693	–	2.57
4	0.73	1.63	–	2.666	0.9213	2.059	–	2.28
5	0.58	1.43	–	2.089	0.9400	2.326	–	2.11
6	0.48	1.29	0.300	1.970	0.9515	2.534	–	2.00
7	0.42	1.18	0.118	1.882	0.9594	2.704	0.08	1.92
8	0.37	1.10	0.185	1.815	0.9650	2.847	0.14	1.86
9	0.42	1.03	0.239	1.761	0.9693	2.970	0.18	1.82
10	0.31	0.93	0.284	1.716	0.9727	3.078	0.22	1.78

x-Bar and R Chart

The x-Bar and R chart is used in a process, when the units of the process have variable type data, and during the monitoring stage, the same number of units are inspected in each subgroup. The average (x-Bar), and range (R) are measured for each subgroup.

To apply this method, the following five steps are carried out. An example with N = 20 subgroups are used in this context.

1. Gather data in a pre-study where i = subgroup, n = sample size, x = measure, $\bar{x}$ = average and R = range. Note, there are n = 4 measures of x within each subgroup.

i	1	2	3	...	20	sum
n	4	4	4		4	
x	3,1,5,4	6,2,1,1	2,3,2,2		3,5,2,2	
$\bar{x}$	3.25	2.50	2.25		3.00	52.48
R	4	5	1		3	64.24

2. Compute the control limits as follows:

$$\bar{\bar{x}} = \Sigma\bar{x}/N = 52.48/20 = 2.624 \text{ (center line)}$$

$$\bar{R} = \Sigma R/N = 64.24/20 = 3.212 \text{ (center line)}$$

In the equations below, use the coefficients given earlier with n = 4.

$$UCL\bar{x} = \bar{\bar{x}} + A_2\bar{R} = 4.97$$

$$LCL\bar{x} = \bar{\bar{x}} - A_2\bar{R} = 0.28$$

$$UCLR = D_4\bar{R} = 7.32$$

$$LCLR = D_3\bar{R} = 0.$$

3. Analyze for statistical control. Check each subgroup for outliers, and also look for any trend or cyclical pattern from subgroup to subgroup. If any fault, find the cause and correct. Eliminate any subgroup data that is out of control and re-compute the control limits.

4. Now interpret for process capability in the following way:

First, note when n = 4 in Table 13.1, $d_2 = 2.059$, and thereby the standard deviation of x-Bar is obtained by the relation below:

$$\sigma = \bar{R}/d_2 = 3.212/2.059 = 1.56$$

Second, gather the process specification limits and denote USL = upper specification limit, and LSL = lower specification limit. In the example, assume (LSL, USL) = (0, 9).

Third, measure the number of standard deviations separating the average (x-Bar) and the specification limits.

$$kU = (USL - \bar{\bar{x}})/\sigma = 4.087$$

$$kL = (\bar{\bar{x}} - LSL)/\sigma = 1.682$$

Fourth, the process capability is the minimum k and is denoted as cpk (this is the number of standard deviations separating the center line with the closest specification limit). In the example,

$$cpk = \min(kU, kL) = 1.682$$

The higher cpk, the better and when cpk > 3, the process capability is excellent. In the example, with cpk = 1.682, the process is likely to produce units outside of the specification limits. This is not an acceptable situation.

Upon completing the pre-study, and eliminating any out-of-control subgroup, the process is now ready for regular monitoring as described below.

5. Monitor the process and use the same sample size and frequency as in the pre-study. Check each subgroup to see if any x-Bar or R falls outside of the control limits. If any, the process is deemed out of control and the process should be halted and corrected.

Future subgroups

i	1	2	3	...
n	4	4	4	
x	2,1,1,2	3,4,2,5		

$\bar{x}$	1.5	3.5
R	1.0	3.0

x-Bar and s Chart

The x-Bar and s chart is used in a process, when the units of the process have variable type data, and the same number of units (n) are inspected in each subgroup. The mean (x-Bar) and standard deviation (s) are measured for each subgroup.

Consider the example below with pre-study data of N subgroups, and n = 4 samples per subgroup.

i	1	2	...	N	sum
x	2,3,1,5				
$\bar{x}$	2.75	X_2		X_N	$\Sigma\bar{x}$
s	1.71	S_2		S_N	Σs

The standard deviation(s) for each subgroup is computed as below: For subgroup 1,

$$s^2 = (\Sigma x^2 - n\bar{x}^2)/(n - 1) = (39 - 4(2.75)^2)/3 = 2.92$$

$$s = 1.71$$

The control limits and associated standard deviation are computed by the following relations:

$$\bar{\bar{x}} = \Sigma\bar{x}/N \text{ (center line)}$$

$$s = \Sigma s/N$$

$$UCL\bar{x} = \bar{\bar{x}} + A_3 s$$

$$LCL\bar{x} = \bar{\bar{x}} - A_3 s$$

$$UCL_s = B_4 s$$

$$LCL_s = B_3 s$$

From Table 13.1 with n, get the corresponding coefficient c_4 and then,

$$\sigma = s/c_4$$

As before, the number of standard deviations separating the average (center line) and the specification limits are computed,

$$kU = (USL - \bar{\bar{x}})/\sigma$$

$$kL = (\bar{\bar{x}} - LSL)/\sigma$$

Thereby, the process capability is determined as below:

$$cpk = \min (kU, kL)$$

Median Chart

The median chart is used for a process, when the units have variable type data, and during the monitoring stage, the same number of units (n) are inspected in each subgroup. The median and range R are measured for each subgroup.

Consider the pre-study example below with N subgroups, n = 4, x = n measures per subgroup, $\tilde{x}$ = median, and R = range for each subgroup.

i	1	2	...	N	sum
x	8,7,2,3				
$\tilde{x}$	5				$\Sigma \tilde{x}$
R	6				ΣR

Suppose, the pre-study results yield the averages and control limits listed below.

$$\bar{\tilde{x}} = \Sigma \tilde{x}/N \quad \text{(center line)}$$

$$\bar{R} = \Sigma R/N \quad \text{(center line)}$$

$$UCL\tilde{x} = \bar{\tilde{x}} + A_2\bar{R}$$

$$LCL\tilde{x} = \bar{\tilde{x}} - A_2\bar{R}$$

$$UCL_R = D_4\bar{R}$$

$$LCL_R = D_3\bar{R}$$

From Table 13.1, use n to get the corresponding d_2. Note, at n = 4, d_2 = 2.059. The standard deviation of the median is computed by the relation below:

$$\sigma = \bar{R}/d_2$$

As in the prior systems, the number of standard deviations (kU, kL) separating the average (center line) and the specification limits are computed, and the process capability becomes cpk = min(kU, kL).

Individual Chart

The individual chart is used in a process, where the units of the process have variable type data, and only one unit is inspected in each subgroup.

This chart is commonly used for homogeneous data, such as paint, milk or beer. The size of each subgroup is one. x is the measure taken on the unit in the subgroup.

Consider the pre-study example data with N subgroups.

i	1	2	...	N	sum
x	30	24		x_N	Σx
R	–	6		R_N	ΣR

For subgroup 2, the range is $R_2 = |x_1 - x_2| = |30 - 24| = 6$; for subgroup 3, it is $R_3 = |x_2 - x_3|$, and so forth.

Below are the averages for the median and range over the total pre-study.

$$\bar{x} = \Sigma x/N \qquad \text{(center line)}$$

$$\bar{R} = \Sigma R/(N-1) \qquad \text{(center line)}$$

Note, from Table 13.1, when n = 2, d2 = 1.128. The control limits are computed as follows:

$$\text{UCL } \bar{x} = \bar{x} + (3/d_2)\bar{R} = \bar{x} + (3/1.128)\bar{R}$$

$$\text{LCL } \bar{x} = \bar{x} - (3/d_2)\bar{R} = \bar{x} - (3/1.128)\bar{R}$$

$$UCL_R = D_4\bar{R}$$

$$LCL_R = D_3\bar{R}$$

Finally, the standard deviation for the median is computed as below:

$$\sigma = \bar{R}/d_2$$

As in the prior methods, the number of standard deviations (kU, kL) separating the average (x-bar) and the specification limits are computed, and the process capability becomes cpk = min (kU, kL).

Summary

This chapter describes the methods to control the quality of the manufactured items. These methods are commonly used at the parts and component suppliers and also at the plants. The goal is to produce items with zero defects. Two types of control measures are considered and labeled as: variable and attribute. Four control charts are described for data of the attribute type, and four for data of the variable type.

References

Amsden, Robert T., Howard E. Butler and Davida M. Amsden, *SPC Simplified, Practical Steps to Quality*, 1997.

Doty, Leonard, *Statistical Process Control*, Industrial Press, Inc., 1996.

Oakland, John S., *Statistical Process Control*, Butterworth-Heinemann, 1996.

Stapenhurst, Tim, *Mastering Statistical Process Control: A Handbook for Performance Improvement Using Cases*, Elsevier, 2005.

14

Supply Chain Management

This chapter describes some of the key goals that confront a supply chain management team in a company. Examples are presented on how the parts flow from one location to another until they reach the customer. The chapter shows some essential data needed to coordinate the overall flow of inventory. The concepts of vendor-managed-inventory, continuous-replenishment, pallet-size, truck-load delivery, master-production-scheduling, level-load production are important to generate an efficient system in all locations across the supply chain. The ultimate is to meet the customer needs with the least inventory cost, and with a high service level throughout. The chapter also shows, in a statistical way, how the demands flow across the supply chain from the customers to the supplier.

Introduction

A typical role of the supply chain management (SCM) team in a company is to study the needs of their customer base, and determine the associated flow of inventory from origin to customer. The goal is to provide a high level of service to the customers, while minimizing the time and cost of all activities involved in their products. The activities pertain to the procurement, transportation, storage and production of any related raw materials, work-in-process and finish goods, and often takes place within the company (in-house) and across (outside) companies, both upstream and downstream. To achieve, cooperation, control and planning is needed between the in-house facilities, suppliers, third party service providers and retail outlets.

The in-house activities are in continual review to determine if they can be outsourced with efficiency and with reduced cost. When feasible, without disturbing the flow of inventory and the customer service, third party entities are used in place of the in-house counterparts. Consistent measures of all activities are maintained to ensure the system flow is in control as planned.

Trust and collaboration is needed between all the extended partners of the supply chain (SC)—in-house, suppliers, third party providers, retail outlets—so that information can be shared to provide efficiency for all. Common systems are encouraged so that information can flow as needed from one entity to another.

With international competition gaining throughout industry, the customers are ever more demanding products with low cost and high quality. This pressures the companies to use offshore suppliers and manufactures to attain lower costs throughout. At the same time, quality control of the parts and products; and the associated storage and transportation become more complicated and vital than ever.

Three supply chain management examples are described below. In all of these, the main goal is to pass the inventory from one entity to another in a way where the inventory needs are fulfilled and the costs are minimized in all locations. Data sharing is needed from one location to another in both the upstream and downstream locations.

Plant to Warehouse to DC to Stores and to Customers

Consider an original equipment manufacturer (OEM) with K products that are produced in the plant with an adjoining warehouse. The plants schedule product runs based on the warehouse forecasts and inventory status. This is by a master production scheduling (MPS) system that generates schedules over the planning horizon yielding a level load for each day, i.e. the schedule satisfies all the warehouse orders while balancing the plant work load each day. The plant produces each product in pallet sizes and stocks in the warehouse in pallet sizes. The warehouse gets its orders from a distribution center (DC) of a large retailer that operates many stores throughout the DC region. The distribution center buys the products from the OEM in pallet sizes. The DC has a vendor managed inventory (VMI) arrangement with every store, whereby it has access to the demands, on-hand and on-order for each product at each store (i.e., each sku). Software at the DC generates the forecast by sku and determines which products need replenishment by day and how much. The replenishments are shipped in pallet sizes and the goal is to send one truckload (say, 20 pallets) to every store each day in a continuous replenishment manner. So the software determines which products to send for the day. The store receives the stock and sells to the customers in a one-unit-at-a-time manner.

The diagram below describes seven stages that depict the flow from plant to customers.

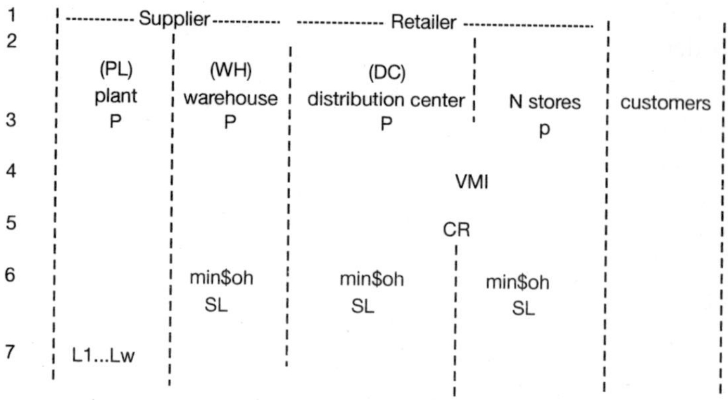

1. The supplier facilities are the plant (PL) and warehouse (WH). The supplier produces K parts in the plant on a make-to-stock basis, and stocks in the warehouse. The warehouse is the source to the distribution center, and the DC is the source to the retail stores.

2. The retailer has the DC and N stores, and each store stocks the parts for sale to its customers.

3. Each part is produced, handled and stored in full pallet size (P) from the plant to the stores. At the plant, each part is produced in pallet size and wrapped accordingly. The pallets are sent to the warehouse in pallet sizes and stored waiting the replenish needs from the distribution center. The DC orders in pallet sizes and when they need stock, the warehouse delivers to the DC in pallet sizes. The DC stocks the parts in pallet sizes and when a store is in need of a replenish order, the DC ships a full pallet of the part to the store. The store then sells the part to the customers in unit sizes of one piece or more as needed.

4. The DC and the retailer have a VMI arrangement in replenishing the store inventory. This way, for the supplier parts, the DC has access to each store's current inventory status [on-hand (oh) and on-order (oo)], and their demands. The DC maintains a database on the part demand history and current inventory. With this data, the DC generates the forecast and computes the order point op and order level ol on each part at every store. When (oh + oo) ≤ op, a quantity of size q = ol – (oh + oo) is needed. Because deliveries are only in pallet sizes, the order quantity is adjusted to meet the pallet size for the part.

5. The replenishments from the DC to the stores are planned with continuous replenishments (CR) arrangement and truckload (TL) deliveries. The DC plans to ship a truckload of stock to each store every day. The trucks have a capacity on M pallets and thereby M parts (one part per pallet) are scheduled for delivery to each store each day. A routine determines which parts to deliver each day to a store, and when demands are low and the truck is not filled, no delivery is scheduled for the day.

6. A replenish software system, located at the supplier and at the DC controls the replenishments at each of the main stocking locations (WH, DC, stores). Separate database tables are maintained for each location and the software determines when a replenish quantity is needed at a location and the size. The goal is to maintain the minimum investment in inventory by part and location to yield the desired service level.

7. The plant production is determined from the build schedule on each part by week over the planning time horizon. This schedule requires software that generates a master production schedule (mps) in a way that meets the replenish needs of the warehouse, and also yields a level load for each of the planning future weeks. A level load is achieved when the aggregate load from the mps is compliant with the resource needs in the plant. The plant load for the next w weeks is denoted as L1, ..., Lw.

Parts DC and Direct Ship Suppliers to Retailer Master Location to Branch Locations and to Customers

An offshore dealer has K stores where one is a master location (ML) and the others are branch locations (BL). The master location has a software system with access to all the demands and inventory at all locations. On a daily basis, the software determines which skus by BL need replenishment and how much. The ML is the only location to receive replenishments from the suppliers. The main supplier is an OEM DC that stocks all the parts. The lead time is one month and the shipment comes by boat in container sizes. Another source of stock is a direct-ship supplier(s) that offers bulk discounts to the dealer if the order for the day reaches a target level. To take advantage of the discount, the dealer must order more than the normal quantity of stock from the collection of the supplier's parts. The ML software determines when and how much to order from the DC and from the direct-ship supplier(s). Since the ML is the source for each BL, the ML orders sufficient stock to satisfy the orders from each BL and also the demands from its own customers. The software system at the ML determines how much to order for the ML to satisfy all of these needs. The software at the ML also runs a transfer routine each week to determine if any location is short of stock, and seeks if another location has excess stock. When a pair is found, a transfer order is generated. A series of trucks start at the ML each day and stop at each BL to deliver any replenish stock from the ML. It also picks up and delivers any transfer stock from one location to another.

The seven stages below describe this system.

1. The dealer has K locations, one master location (ML) and K-1 branch locations (BL). Each location holds inventory for the needs of its customers. The ML is the only location that buys and receives replenish stock for the dealer. The ML then serves as the source for all the BLs. This is called 2-level-service (2LS), since the BLs get their inventory from the ML, who receive their inventory from a supplier. Note, the two replenish levels needed for the BL to receive its stock.

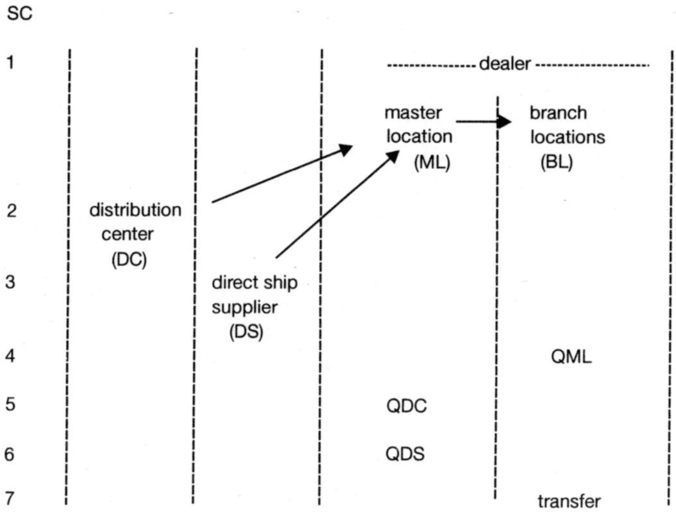

2. The distribution center (DC) is the main source for the dealer. It holds all the parts that are needed at the dealer. The dealer can order one part at a time as needed. The lead time from the DC is denoted here as LDC.

3. A direct ship supplier (DS) produces N parts and these parts are available to the dealer from both the DC and the DS. The supplier entices the dealer to buy more from him by offering discount terms for group buys over the N parts. To gain the discount, the dealer must buy, at each order, from the collection of N parts, an aggregate quantity that meets a target level set by the DS.

4. A replenish software system is run at the ML and keeps the status of the demands and inventory status, on-hand (oh) and on-order (oo), at each BL. On a once a month basis, this system determines the order point (op) and order level (ol) for each part. When the (oh + oo) $\leq$ op, a replenish order is generated as QML = ol – (oh + oo). The quantity is placed on a truck at the ML for the next day delivery to the BL.

5. The ML buys stock for all the locations in the dealership. For this purpose, the software replenish system uses the aggregate data from all locations. The dealer demand history is D(i, t) =

Σd(i, j, t) where i = part, j = location and t = month. The corresponding inventory for part i is OH = Σoh(i, j) and the on-order is OO = oo(ML). The demands are used to generate the forecast for the part over the total dealership. The lead time and cost per unit from the DC are now applied to generate the order point (OP) and order level (OL) for each part. If OH + OO ≤ OP, a replenish order for the DC is needed as QDC = OL – (OH + OO).

6. On a periodic basis, the dealer considers a buy to a DS supplier. The N parts from the DS are noted and any buy quantities on these parts to the DC are halted. The aggregate of the buy quantities (Q1, ..., QN) are compared to the target quantity specified by the DS to gain the discounts offered. Should the current aggregate buy be near of above the target quantity, then a buy to the DS is called. When the total buy is sufficiently close to the target, the part buy quantities are nudged up, by a software routine, to just satisfy the target quantity. Then, the (group) buy order is placed with the DS supplier.

7. On a once a week basis, a transfer routine is run at the ML to determine if any BL inventory on a part is dangerously low, and further, if another location has adequate stock to cover this low stock. If a pair is identified, a transfer order is created, and the next day, a delivery truck picks up the stock from the sender location and delivers to the receiver location.

Parts DC to Parts Supplier to Packager with a Link to Component Supplier and to Parts DC

The service parts distribution center (SPDC) from an OEM orders replenish stock from a Parts-and-Components supplier (PCS). The order comes with a due quantity and date. Upon completion at the PCS, the stock is sent in bulk and in raw form to a packager (PKG) that places the pieces in containers with labels that are specified by the OEM. When the packager receives the stock, they must act quickly to meet the OEM due date and to complete the packaging process. A packaging bill-of-material for each part is needed that calls for all the items required in packaging. The packager is obliged to carry sufficient stock on all package components that are used for this purpose. The package components are not always unique to one part and may be shared on a number of parts. The packager software system must monitor the package component's inventory and project the needs of each from all the parts that require the component. The software determines when new stock is needed and how much. The order quantities (QCS) from the packager to a component supplier are placed in a timely way to allow replenishments to arrive as needed. In this situation, it is essential that the SPDC notifies the PCS and the packager for each replenish order (quantity due and due date) so the packager can plan appropriately to have the component stock available.

The eight stages shown in the diagram below describe the flow of the system.

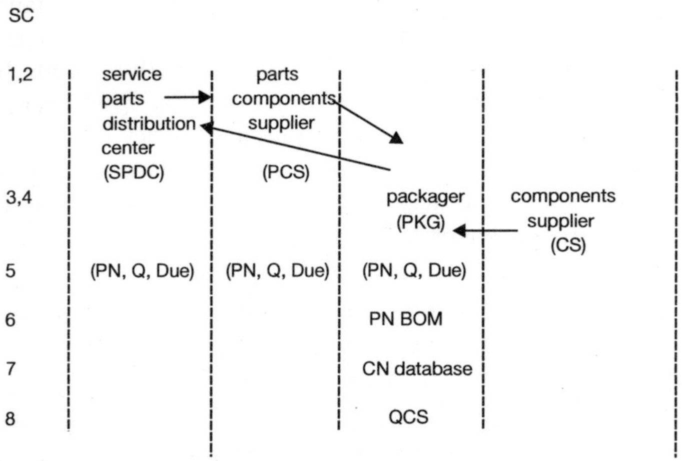

1. The service parts distribution center (SPDC) holds stock to meet its customer demands. When it needs replenish stock, it sends a purchase order to a parts and components supplier (PCS) giving the part number and quantity needed.

2. When the part and component supplier receives the purchase order, it begins the process to fabricate the part in the quantity ordered. Upon completion, some parts are shipped directly to the SPDC. Others need packaging and these are shipped to a packager for further processing.

3. The packager's (PKG) role is to place the units in containers with labels and in a way that prevents damage and are amenable to stocking and storage. The packager needs a supply of components to carry out the process. The source of these components is here called the component supplier. Typically the packager has to coordinate its work load and maintain the component inventory so that it can quickly process the parts and ship to the SPDC. The packager's on-time-deliver (OTD) is measured from the time it takes to carry out the process. This time begins when the parts come to the packager receiving dock and ends when the packager sends the completed stock to the SPDC. The OTD measure is based on how often this time meets the desired process time.

4. The component supplier (CS) is the source of the component parts that are needed by the packager.

5. The purchase order (PO) that begins this flow is generated at the SPDC and contains the information (PN, Q, Due) = (part number, quantity, due date). The purchase order is sent to the part supplier to start the process. For the parts that require packaging, it is good practice to also send the PO to the packager. This way, the packager has advance notice on when and how much is coming and can prepare accordingly.

6. The packager requires a packaging bill-of-material (BOM) for each part. This BOM contains the part and a list of the components needed to package the units of the part.

7. The components used to package are here called component numbers (CN). The packager must maintain an inventory on these and calls for replenish orders from the component supplier when new stock is needed. To do this, the future requirements on each CN are placed on file. This data comes from combining the POs for the future months with the part BOM. All of the future requirements on a CN are combined by due date and this yields a list of the requirements by CN for each of the weeks in the planning horizon.

8. The component part database holds each of the CN's used by the packager and the future requirements over the planning weeks in the near future. It also lists the lead time from the component supplier, the cost per unit and the multiples to buy. The CN table should also hold the on-hand plus on-order inventory (oh + oo) for each CN. With this data, the order point and order level are computed. For each CN, the oh + oo is compared to the order point and order level to determine when to replenish and how much.

Demands along the Supply Chain

Consider a dealer that carries inventory on parts to meet the oncoming customer demands. Assume the monthly demands from the customers are horizontal (no trend or seasonal pattern); and also, the monthly demands at a dealer are low volume and thereby are distributed like a Poisson probability distribution. The dealer receives replenish stock on the part from a distribution center (DC) and the DC is replenished from a supplier. The replenish quantities Q at a location depends mostly on the forecast of demands and the cost per unit. For simplicity, the replenish order quantity can be stated in month-in-buy (mib) terms where $Q = mib \times \mu$ and μ is the forecast of the average monthly demands at the location. When mib is 1.0, Q is one month supply; when mib = 2.0, Q is two months supply, and so forth. The aggregate flow of replenishments from all the dealers are the demands at the DCs; and the flow of demands from all the DCs are the demands at the supplier. It has been shown below how the demands along the supply chain—from customers to dealers, DCs and supplier—are related.

All Customer Monthly Demands

Assume an item where μ_0 represents the aggregate average monthly demand from customers on a part (or product). In the examples shown later in the chapter, $\mu_0 = 10$, 100 and 1000.

Average Dealer Monthly Demands

The monthly demand for an average dealer is denoted as d_1, and when N_1 is the number of dealers, the mean monthly demand for an average dealer is $\mu_1 = \mu_0/N_1$.

Recall the monthly demand to an average dealer from its customers is assumed Poisson distributed with an average of μ_1. Thereby, since Poisson, the associated standard deviation is

$\sigma_1 = \sqrt{\mu_1}$. Further, the coefficient of variation (cov) of a random variable is defined as the ratio of the standard deviation over the average. So in this situation, the coefficient of variation becomes $cov_1 = \sigma_1/\mu_1$.

Table 14.1 lists values μ_1, σ_1 and cov_1 as the average monthly demands range from 1 to 1000. Note how cov_1 is largest (1.00) when $\mu_1 = 1$, and becomes increasingly smaller as μ_1 rises. Further, when the demands are all positive and normally distributed, the cov attains a value is 0.33 or less. This is because the mean is at least three standard deviations larger than zero. On the other extreme, when the cov is as large as one, the monthly demands are distributed as an exponential distribution, since for the exponential, the standard deviation is the same as the mean. So in essence, as the average monthly demands (from customer's) increase, the monthly demand tends like a *normal* distribution; and as the average monthly demands go down, the monthly demands are of the lumpy type, and are shaped more like an *exponential* distribution.

Table 14.1: Monthly Demand Statistics for an Average Dealer

μ_1	σ_1	cov_1
1	1.00	1.00
5	2.24	0.45
10	3.16	0.32
50	7.07	0.14
100	10.00	0.10
500	22.36	0.04
1000	31.62	0.03

Average DC Monthly Demands

The monthly demand for an average distribution center (DC) is here denoted as d_2. The associated mean monthly demand is μ_2, and corresponding standard deviation is σ_2. Also, the coefficient of variation becomes $cov_2 = \sigma_2/\mu_2$. To compute the measures (μ_2, σ_2, cov_2) for an average DC, the analysis below is presented.

Analysis

When a dealer needs replenish stock, he buys from its assigned distribution center (DC). Each buy quantity is in a lot size that is economical for the location. Suppose the lot size is denoted as q and this quantity is sufficient for the forecast of demands over the next mib months. In this analysis, mib = months-in-buy and represents the buy amount of replenish stock in monthly requirements. Of interest here is to measure the mean and variance for the average monthly replenish quantities from the dealer to the DC. For notation, E(q) = expected replenish quantity per month and V(q) is the associated variance of q.

Consider the general situation when the months-in-buy, mib, is an integer of size m = 1, 2, 3, ... Suppose the dealer demands for the most recent m months are: d(1), ..., d(m). Also, assume the stock at the dealer is sufficient for the first month (m–1) months, and the dealer needs replenish stock at month t = m, for a quantity size that covers the next m month requirements. So the replenish quantity from the dealer to the DC will be q(t) = 0 for months t = 1 to m–1, and will be approximately q(m) = (d(1) + ... + d(m)) at the end of month m. Since mib = m, this pattern will repeat as the subsequent months move along. Of interest now is to determine the expected value and variance of the monthly replenish quantities, q(t). Note (m–1) of the quantities are zero, and one quantity is an m-month supply. The expected value of q is:

$$\begin{aligned} E(q) &= ((m-1)/m) \times 0 + 1/m \times E(d(1) + \dots + d(m)) \\ &= 1/m \times m\,E(d) \\ &= E(d) \end{aligned}$$

In a similar way, the expected value of q^2 becomes

$$\begin{aligned} E(q^2) &= 1/m\, E[(d(1) + \dots + d(m))^2] \\ &= 1/m(mE(d^2) + m(m-1)E(d)^2) \\ &= E(d^2) + (m-1)E(d)^2 \\ &= V(d) + E(d)^2 + (m-1)E(d)^2 \\ &= V(d) + mE(d)^2 \end{aligned}$$

Finally, the variance of q becomes

$$V(q) = E(q^2) - E(q)^2$$
$$= V(d) + (m-1)\,E(d)^2$$

Returning to the notation for the average DC, the following substitutions are made: $\mu_2 = E(q)$, $\sigma_2^2 = V(q)$, $\mu_1 = E(d)$ and $\sigma_1^2 = V(d)$. Also, the month-in-buy from the dealer to the DC is denoted as M_1. Further, N_2 = the number of dealers and N_3 is the number of DCs. The statistics for the mean monthly demands, d_2, at an average DC are as below:

$$\mu_2 = (N_2/N_3)\mu_1$$
$$\sigma_2^2 = (N_2/N_3)\,(\sigma_1^2 + (M_1 - 1)\mu_1^2)$$
$$cov_2 = c_2 = \sigma_2/\mu_2$$

Table 14.2 shows how cov_1 and $M_1 \doteq$ mib are related to cov_2 as cov_1 ranges from (0.1 to 1.0) and M_1 from (1 to 6) and when $N_2 = N_3 = 1$. Recall, cov_1 is a measure of the variation in demands from the customers to an average dealer, and cov_2 is the counterpart measure of the variation in demands from the dealer to an average DC. Note how cov_2 increases significantly as M_1 increases beyond one month. Also, when M_1 is two or larger, cov_2 increases gradually as cov_1 goes from 0.1 to 1.0.

Table 14.2: Values of cov_2 as Related to cov_1 and M_1 at $N_2 = N_3 = 1$

				cov_1						
M_1	.1	.2	.3	.4	.5	.6	.7	.8	.9	1.0
1	0.10	0.20	0.30	0.40	0.50	0.60	0.70	0.80	0.90	1.00
2	1.00	1.02	1.04	1.08	1.12	1.17	1.22	1.28	1.35	1.41
3	1.42	1.43	1.45	1.47	1.50	1.54	1.58	1.62	1.68	1.73
4	1.73	1.74	1.76	1.78	1.80	1.83	1.87	1.91	1.95	2.00
5	2.00	2.01	2.02	2.04	2.06	2.09	2.12	2.15	2.19	2.24
6	2.24	2.24	2.26	2.27	2.29	2.32	2.34	2.37	2.41	2.45

Average Monthly Demands for all DCs

In this section, assume N_3 is the number of DCs and d_3 is the aggregate monthly demand for all DCs. Further μ_3 is the average monthly demand, σ_3 is the standard deviation, and c_3 is the coefficient of variation of d_3. So now, $\mu_3 = N_3 \times \mu_2$, $\sigma_3^2 = N_3 \times \sigma_2^2$, and $cov_3 = c_3 = \sigma_3/\mu_3$.

Average Monthly Demands for Supplier

The monthly demand for the supplier is denoted as d_4. In the same way, μ_4 is the associated average monthly demand, σ_4 the standard deviation, and c_4 is the coefficient of variation of d_4. In the calculations, M_3 is the month-in-buy from the DC to the supplier.

So now,

$$\begin{aligned} \mu_4 &= \mu_3 \\ \sigma_4^2 &= \sigma_3^2 + (M_3 - 1)\mu_3^2 \\ c_4 &= \sigma_4/\mu_4 \end{aligned}$$

Summary Statistics across the Supply Chain

In summary, the demand statistics across the supply chain are listed in Tables 14.3 and 14.4. The tables show how the demand flows from the customers to the dealers, onto the DCs and to the supplier. The measures are the average monthly demand, the standard deviation, and the coefficient of variation. The monthly demands at an average dealer are assumed as Poisson. The tables show how the shape of the monthly demands can range from normal to exponential and beyond. Recall, when cov ≤ 0.33, the monthly demands could be shaped like a normal distribution, and when cov ≥ 1.00, the monthly demands are the lumpy type.

A summary of the notation used is listed below:

N_2 = number of dealers
N_3 = number of DCs
M_1 = dealer month-in-buy (to DC)
M_3 = DC month-in-buy (to supplier)
d_0 = monthly demands all customers
d_1 = monthly customer demands per dealer
μ_1, σ_1 = the mean and standard deviation of d_1
c_1 = cov of d_1
d_2 = monthly demands for an average DC

μ_2, σ_2 = the mean and standard deviation of d_2
c_2 = cov of d_2
d_3 = monthly demands all DCs
μ_3, σ_3 = the mean and standard deviation of d_3
c_3 = cov of d_3
d_4 = monthly demands to supplier
μ_4, σ_4 = the mean and standard deviation of d_4
c_4 = cov of d_4

Table 14.3: Average Monthly Demands (μ) and cov (c) for all Customers, per Dealer, per DC, all DC's and Supplier When Number of Dealers is $N_2 = 100$ and number of DC's is $N_3 = 1$

		All	per dealer		per DC		all DC's		supplier	
M_1	M_3	μ_0	μ_1	c_1	μ_2	c_2	μ_3	c_3	μ_4	c_4
1	1	10	0.1	3.16	10.0	0.32	10.0	0.32	10.0	0.32
1	1	100	1.0	1.00	100.0	0.10	100.0	0.10	100.0	0.10
1	1	1000	10.0	0.32	1000.0	0.03	1000.0	0.03	1000.0	0.03
1	2	10	0.1	3.16	10.0	0.32	10.0	0.32	10.0	1.05
1	2	100	1.0	1.00	100.0	0.10	100.0	0.10	100.0	1.00
1	2	1000	10.0	0.32	1000.0	0.03	1000.0	0.03	1000.0	1.00
2	1	10	0.1	3.16	10.0	0.33	10.0	0.33	10.0	0.33
2	1	100	1.0	1.00	100.0	0.14	100.0	0.14	100.0	0.14
2	1	1000	10.0	0.32	1000.0	0.10	1000.0	0.10	1000.0	0.10
2	2	10	0.1	3.16	10.0	0.33	10.0	0.33	10.0	1.05
2	2	100	1.0	1.00	100.0	0.14	100.0	0.14	100.0	1.01
2	2	1000	10.0	0.32	1000.0	0.10	1000.0	0.10	1000.0	1.01

Table 14.4: Average Monthly Demands (μ) and cov (c) for all Customers, per Dealer, per DC, all DC's and Supplier When Number of Dealers is $N_2 = 1000$ and number of DC's is $N_3 = 5$

		All	per dealer		per DC		all DC's		supplier	
M_1	M_3	μ_0	μ_1	c_1	μ_2	c_2	μ_3	c_3	μ_4	c_4
1	1	10	0.0	10.00	2.0	0.71	10.0	0.32	10.0	0.32
1	1	100	0.1	3.16	20.0	0.22	100.0	0.10	100.0	0.10
1	1	1000	1.0	1.00	200.0	0.07	1000.0	0.03	1000.0	0.03
1	2	10	0.0	10.00	2.0	0.71	10.0	0.32	10.0	1.05
1	2	100	0.1	3.16	20.0	0.22	100.0	0.10	100.0	1.00
1	2	1000	1.0	1.00	200.0	0.07	1000.0	0.03	1000.0	1.00
2	1	10	0.0	10.00	2.0	0.71	10.0	0.32	10.0	0.32

2	1	100	0.1	3.16	20.0	0.23	100.0	0.10	100.0	0.10
2	1	1000	1.0	1.00	200.0	0.10	1000.0	0.04	1000.0	0.04
2	2	10	0.0	10.00	2.0	0.71	10.0	0.32	10.0	1.05
2	2	100	0.1	3.16	20.0	0.23	100.0	0.10	100.0	1.01
2	2	1000	1.0	1.00	200.0	0.10	1000.0	0.04	1000.0	1.00

Summary

This chapter describes three supply chain management applications where inventory is passed along the chain from one entity to another. The examples consider plants, plant warehouse, distribution centers, retailers, packagers, component suppliers, service parts suppliers, service parts distribution centers, direct ship suppliers, master stock location, branch locations and customers. Methods to control the inventory flow in each location and between the locations are shown. The chapter also measures how the demand flows from the customers to the dealers to the DCs and to the supplier. The demand measures are the average monthly demand, the standard deviation and the coefficient of variation.

References

Bolstorff, Peter, *Supply Chain Excellence*, AMACOM Publishing, 2003.

Cohen, Shoshanah and Joseph Roussel, *Strategic Supply Chain Management*, McGraw Hill, 2005.

Hugos, Michael, *Essentials of Supply Chain Management*, John Wiley & Sons, 2002.

15

Software and the Supply Chain

This chapter shows how software is used along the locations (links) of the supply chain to gain efficiency in cost, timing, and the flow of inventory. The reader will become aware of the variety of routines available, how they are related, and where the output from one routine sometimes serves as the input to another. The concepts of location cluster and supplier cluster are introduced so that a collection of parts (supplier cluster), and/or a set of locations (location cluster) can be processed together as a group to achieve a common gain for the cluster. The chapter describes the various links in the supply chain and shows how the inventory flows from one link to another.

Introduction

FIC Inc. is a typical software company that specializes in building supply chain routines that concern forecasting and inventory. The name of the software is called FIRM (Forecasting for Inventory Replenishment Management). There are twelve routines under the FIRM system. Below is a short description on the FIRM routines. Forecast-Replenish is the vital routine because the output results from the routine is used in all of the other routines. The source of this chapter comes from the website: www.ficfirm.com.

Supplier Cluster and Location Cluster

In the discussion below, FIRM uses the concept of 'supplier cluster' and 'location cluster'. A supplier cluster is a collection of parts from a particular supplier. A location cluster is a collection of locations that are managed together. For example, when one store operates independently, the location cluster has only one location. But when the customer market is large and consists of N distribution centers, the location cluster has N locations. When decisions are needed on a group of parts, usually from one supplier, the supplier cluster contains all the parts in the group.

Forecast and Replenish

Forecast and Replenish (FR) is the main program, typically run monthly, generates the forecasts, order quantity, safety stock and related replenish measures (order point, order level) on each part and location. It identifies the parts that need immediate attention, those with low (on-hand plus on-order) inventory; as well as those parts with high on-order inventory; and those with surplus inventory. A summary report on all the parts, and various detail reports on individual parts are printed allowing management to monitor the inventory in total and on single parts. A report on lost sales is also provided. The key results are stored in the database by part and location and are available for use in the other routines.

Compare

Compare (CO) could be run throughout the month to determine if any forecast on a part and location is out-of-line with the demands. This routine monitors (month-to-date demands) with (current month forecasts) and identifies the parts where the forecasts are not consistent with demands. The parts that are out-of-line are placed on a table and are candidates for rerun in FR.

Buy

Buy (BUY) is run daily during the month, comparing the on-hand plus on-order inventory with the order-point and order-level for each part and location. This routine determines if a replenishment quantity is needed now and, if so, the quantity to buy. When full bin and/or job quantity constraints are noted, the buy quantities are adjusted to be compliant with the constraints. Full bin constraints give the max number of units allowed in a bin, and job quantity gives the number of units needed for a typical customer line order, like four tires on a car.

Returns

Return (RT) identifies any part by location with excess stock and lists the amount in excess for possible return to the supplier. This routine is typically run once a month.

Allocate

Allocate (AL) is needed when the location cluster has two or more locations. This routine is run for those parts where a replenish quantity is received from the supplier and the quantity is to be shared by the locations in the cluster. The current inventory is compared with the safety stock, the forecasts and other requirements by location to determine the fairest way to allot the new stock to the locations. This process is important to avoid mal-distribution of stock in the cluster.

Transfer

Transfer (TR) applies for location clusters that have two or more locations. This routine is run about once a week and processes each part searching for a mal-distribution situation among the locations. The system seeks if any location(s) is short in stock, and, if so, searches if any location(s) has excess stock to send. Should a match be found, the part, receive location, send location and the transfer quantity are placed on a table of parts that call for transfer. The routine is designed to minimize the number of lines of transfer to a receiver, and when possible, the senders are selected from a sequenced list of preferred send locations to each receive location. This way, the travel distance of the transfers is in control.

Share

Share (SH) applies for location clusters with two or more locations. This routine is run, as needed, for a particular location cluster and supplier cluster, and a specific location named as the share location. The routine scans each part in the supplier cluster to determine if any excess stock is in the share location—and if excess stock is found—the routine determines how to spread this stock to the other locations in a fair share manner. The results are placed on tables that name the part, the send and receive locations, and the send quantity.

Multi Part Buy

Multi Part Buy (MPB) pertains to the collection of parts in a supplier cluster when the supplier of the parts offers a discount on the total buy. The routine determines buy quantities for each part in the supplier cluster. The supplier has a pool of parts and offers discounts so that the customer buys enough stock on the parts to meet various total target quantities. The target quantities could be in pieces, dollars or weight. As the target quantities are met, the prizes are free freight and price discounts. The customer could be one location, or a group of locations in a location cluster. Sometimes two or more location clusters join together to accomplish the buy and gain the discount benefits. Often the target quantities are consistent with supplier full truckload quantities.

Limit Buy

Limit Buy (LB) is associated with a collection of parts grouped into a supplier cluster. A limit is placed on the total buy—covering all parts—and the best combination of part buy quantities is generated to conform with the limit constraint. The limit could be in pieces, dollars or weight.

OPOL

OpOl (OPOL) is developed for applications—where a second tier of skus are called—and control of this level of sku inventory is needed. Here the items stocked are variations of a basic product (e.g., size, color, model, accessory) and these are the skus of concern. The skus could be the sizes of a style shoe, the color of a sweater, the model of a hearing aid, or the accessories of a bicycle. The forecast is developed for each product in FR and the order point, order level and replenish quantity are determined for every sku that corresponds with the product in OPOL.

Firm Weekly

Firm Weekly (FW) takes the 12 monthly forecasts from FR and converts them to 52 weekly forecasts. The method applies for calendar months and for fiscal (4:4:5) months. The weekly forecasts can recognize shifts in demands for weekly cycles in a month, holiday demand build-up, shutdowns and even leap year. This routine is popular in plants when the (MPS and MRP) scheduling takes place over the future horizon in weeks.

Master Production Scheduler

Master Production Scheduler (MPS) is a level loading tool for the plants. This routine is typically run each week (in the plant) to determine the production schedule for every end-item produced in the plant. The system schedules the end-item parts for manufacture by quantity and time periods in a way where the assignments yield an aggregate load (over all parts) that is compatible with the desired loads for each future time period. This way, the aggregate work load by week across all part numbers in the plant is consistent with the plant desired load capability. The latter is here called the target load. MPS takes on these more difficult tasks and leads the way on production scheduling in a cost efficient manner.

Note that the computations in the routines: FR, Buy, Compare and Returns are performed for each part and location independent of concerns for the other parts and locations. The routines: Transfer, Share and Allocate are for businesses with multi-storage sites that do not make independent replenishment decisions. The computations in the routines: Multi-Part Buy and Limit Buy are used in either single location or multi-location configurations where buy quantities are based on an analysis of the requirement for a group of parts.

Two related utility routines, Updateohoo (update on hand and on order) and Updated 25 (d25 = the month-to-date demand) are used regularly to refresh the part-location data of on-hand, on-order and month-to-date demand. Another routine (Plot) is called to plot the monthly demand history and forecasts for any part and location combination.

OPOL is used in situations where the units are stocked in stores or distribution centers in various skus. Examples are, a style shoe with various sizes, sweaters with different colors and sizes, various models and brands of a products (catsup, toothpaste, TV's), accessory items on bicycles, and so forth.

Firm Weekly (FW) applies in production and retail situations in industry. Some examples are below:

Firm Weekly in Production

FW pertains especially for plants that schedule their production on a weekly basis and use production planning tools like the master production scheduler (MPS). The history demands of the part are gathered in monthly buckets and these are the input to FR where 12 monthly forecasts are generated. The monthly forecasts are converted to 52 weekly forecasts in the routine Firm Weekly. Finally the weekly forecasts are applied in subsequent production planning routines.

Firm Weekly in Retail

FW also pertains to retail situations that reorder stock each week. Again, the history on each part is housed in monthly (calendar or fiscal) buckets. This monthly history is input to FR where the monthly forecasts are generated from one of the forecast models: (horizontal, trend, seasonal or promotion). The monthly forecasts are then processed through the Firm Weekly routine to generate the forecasts for the 52 future weeks as needed. For the parts with strong holiday ties (e.g., Christmas, Easter), the routine allows the forecasts to ramp up to the week of the holiday. For parts with weekly demand cycles inside each month, the routine allots the forecasts to react accordingly within a month.

To run any of the routines above, a run command is activated and the command identifies the location or location cluster(s) to run and the supplier cluster(s) to process.

The Supply Chain

Below is a depiction of a typical supply chain. The chain begins with the raw good supplier (rgs) and ends with the customer (cu). In between are the basic good supplier (bgs), component part supplier (cps), plant (pl), service part distribution center (spdc), finish good distribution center (fgdc) and dealer (dlr).

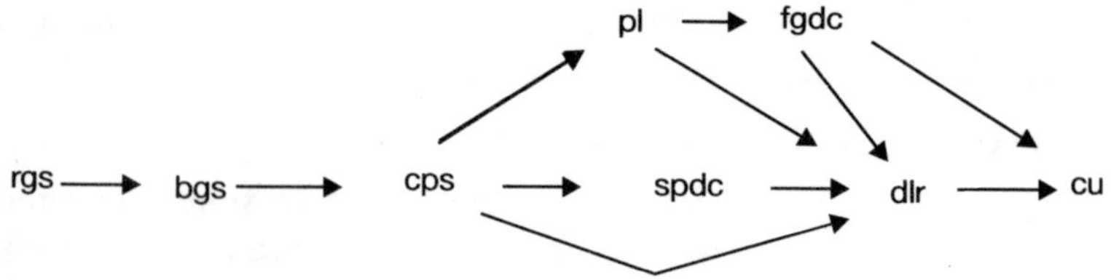

Figure 15.1: A Typical Supply Chain

Note:

rgs = raw goods supplier

bgs = basic goods supplier

cps = component part supplier (often includes: plant & distribution center)

pl = plant

spdc = service part distribution center

fgdc = finish good distribution center

dlr = dealer (store, branch, retailer)

cu = customer

A description on the links from the above supply chain is provided below.

Raw Goods Suppliers (rgs). The suppliers of the raw goods are farms, ranches, mines, the land and oceans. The mines are the suppliers that take from the ground the key raw goods such as coal, ores and salt. Other raw goods are items like: cotton, lumber, cattle, fish, oil and marble.

Basic Goods Suppliers (bgs). These are the firms that take the raw good and process them to a higher level of product—generally in a standard form of size, weight and/or grade. They are sold to producers at the next level of production. Lumber becomes cut wood (e.g., 2 × 4) of various standard lengths, parts of the cattle become food and leather and cotton become yarn and cloth, and so forth. The ores from the mines are processed to obtain iron and steel and all other metals.

Component Part Suppliers (cps). These are the producers of stand-alone parts and of components that are made up from a bill-of-material of parts. They buy the basic goods and produce the parts and component parts for sale to the next higher level of manufacture.

Plants (pl). The plants are the producers of the finished goods. They buy the components and parts, and produce the final product by processing, assembly or manufacture.

Service Parts Distribution Centers (spdc). The original equipment manufacturer (OEM) that sells the finished goods to customers are obliged to carry stock on parts and components for service parts needs. In this way, the OEM maintains a service part distribution center to hold the parts and components inventory for this purpose. Their customers are primarily the dealers that have direct contact with the customer.

Finished Goods Distribution Centers (fgdc). Some distribution centers serve as the source for the finish goods to dealers and customers. These are the locations that receive the finish goods from the plants and ship to the dealers and customers as the demands arrive. For example, they hold stock on TV's, computers, carpets, food products and so forth.

Dealers, Stores and Branches (dlr). The dealers carry stock of the finish good for sale to the customer. Some carry a supply of parts and components for use in the maintenance and repair of their customer's finish goods.

Customers (cu). This is the final link in the supply chain. The customers are the buyers of the finish good items. They typically buy from the dealer. When they need repair or maintenance on the finish good, they go to the dealer for service.

Special for Dealers and the MPB Routine

Sometimes the dealer has a choice of two suppliers on the same part: the service part distribution center, and the component part suppliers. Further discussion is below.

Buying from Component Part Suppliers

The component part supplier ships directly to the dealer and specifies contract terms of the following type. In order for the dealer buys a total quantity Q (target quantity) from the N parts of the supplier, the component part supplier will give the dealer a discount on the total buy. Often the contract terms have two or more target quantities. The first target often spells the minimum total quantity to buy; the second target is free freight, and the target quantities beyond are discount rates—the more you buy the better the discounts.

Buying from the Distribution Centers

The dealer can also buy each individual part from the distribution center. Typically, the lead time from the distribution center is 1-3 days and from the component part supplier, it is 1-6 weeks. The cost from the distribution center could be 120% to 200% over the cost from the component part supplier. It is an advantage to buy from the component part supplier for the sake of price, but a disadvantage with respect to high inventory on-hand. The routine, MPB, determines whether to buy from the distribution center or from the component part supplier. When the buy is from the component part supplier, MPB finds the best buy for each part such as the total buy—over all parts—meets the target constraints.

Special for Distribution Centers and Dealers

This application is used in various situations. When a distribution center or a store carries the finished good in various sizes, colors, and models (called skus), decisions are needed on when, and how much to buy for each sku. FR generates the forecast for the basic product, and the OPOL routine determines the forecasts, order-point, order-level, and buy quantity for each sku.

Accessories

Another situation is when a distribution center holds stock for finish goods and also for the associated accessories to the finish goods. OPOL is used to forecast and replenish for the finish goods, and for each of the accessories. The distribution center stocks the finished goods, and the FR routine generates the forecast and replenish needs for each finished goods. The OPOL routine determines the order point and order level for every accessory that is associated with the finished good. Since the accessory can be used on more than one finished goods, OPOL recognizes and determines the order point and order level for each accessory over all of the finish goods. This way, the on-hand and on-order on each accessory is compared to the order-point and order-level to determine when and how much to buy for each accessory.

Firm and the Supply Chain

Below is a table of the FIRM routines, and lists how they typically apply to the entities (links) along the supply chain. Note some routines apply when an entity has one or more locations and, some routines apply only when there are two or more locations. Some of the routines are optional and not always needed.

The Supply Chain

FIRM routines	dlr	spdc	fgdc	pl	cps	bgs
FR	x	x	x	x	x	x
compare	x	x	x	x	x	x
buy	x	x	x	x	x	x
mpb	x					
transfer	2	2	2			
allocate		2				
share	2					
limit buy	o	o	o			
return	o	o	o			
OPOL	o					
firm weekly	o			o	o	o
mps				x		

x = routine applies

2 = routine applies when entity has 2 or more locations

o = routine is optional

cu = customer

dlr = dealer

dc = distribution center

spdc = service part distribution center

fgdc = finish goods distribution center

pl = plant

cps = component part supplier

bgs = basic goods supplier

rgs = raw goods supplier

Summary

This chapter describes some typical computer software routines that are used to control the inventory at the links along the supply chain. The links are the dealers, service parts distribution center, finished goods distribution center, plants, component and parts suppliers, and basic goods suppliers.

16

Transportation and Logistics

Introduction

Transportation and logistics are two topics that are closely related since they both pertain to the movement of products from a source to a destination. Transportation concerns the movement of goods from one location (plant, factory, shop) to another (warehouse, store, customer); whereas logistics is the management of the flow of goods, information and other resources between the point of origin, and the point of consumption in order to meet the requirements of consumers. The transport may take place via air, water, rail, road, pipeline, or cable routes, using planes, boats, trains, trucks, and telecommunications equipment as the means of transportation. The goal for any business owner is to minimize transportation and storage costs while also meeting all demands for the products. These are important issues to transportation and to logistics and thereby this chapter describes the topics together.

Transportation

Transportation is the movement of goods from one location to another by the various transport modes, such as: air, rail, road, water and pipeline. An accompanying infrastructure includes facilities like roads, railways, airways, waterways, canals, pipelines, terminals (airport, truck, railway, bus, seaports), warehouses, and a range of refueling stations. Various networks are established that connect the facilities and allow the transport system to flow efficiently as the needs evolve. The units (vehicles) that travel along the networks include: trucks, buses, trains, barges, ships and aircraft. Regulations are established for the vehicles that deal with the various operation procedures of financing, legalities and policies. In the transport industry, the operation and ownership of the infrastructure facilities are either public or private, depending on the country and mode.

Freight transport, is the catalyst in achieving the value chain in manufacturing. The value chain refers to the progression of manufacturing activities where a product passes from one stage to another and gains value with each stage. With globalization on the rise, various stages of production are located further away from consumption, increasing the demand for transport services worldwide.

Passenger and freight transport needs continue to grow in both the domestic and global spheres. Passenger transport is shared between public and private ownership and provide a schedule of services to satisfy the public needs. In freight transport, the majority of goods are shipped by containers; and when large volumes of durable goods are shipped, bulk transport is used. Because transportation is an essential service and is a main catalyst to economic growth and globalization, it is often subsidized by domestic governments. The goal of transport planning is to yield a smooth and efficient flow of traffic in a manner with minimal urban congestion and pollution, and where all the transport needs are fulfilled.

Modes of Transport

The mode of transport is a general term used to identify the different types of facilities that are used to transport people or cargo. The most typical modes of transport are air, road, rail, water and pipeline. A description of each is below:

Air. Aircraft takes on many forms from large commercial jets to single engine planes to helicopters. To function, they require a network of airports with facilities for maintenance, restocking, refueling and for the loading and unloading of crew, cargo and passengers. Almost all aircraft land and take off on land; some, however, have the ability to ascend and descend from ice, snow and still water. The use of aircraft to transport goods continues to grow. Commercial jets can reach over 500 miles per hour, while single-engine aircraft attain over 100 miles per hour. Aviation is the favored way to transport people over long distances, and is used in a limiting way for cargo. A drawback for cargo is the high costs and energy use. Helicopters are sometimes used when short distances with difficult places to land.

Road. A road is a marked corridor that allows vehicles to travel from one location to another. In the majority of situations, the roads are smoothly paved and allow easy travel. The most common vehicle for transporting goods is the truck. Sometimes goods are transported by bus and automobiles. Automobiles are high flexibility but are limited in capacity. Buses are cost efficient and can be used when small goods are shipped, but have limited storage space and flexibility in scheduling and destinations.

Rail. Transport by rail is where a train travels along a two parallel steel rails known as a railway or railroad. A train consists of one or more connected vehicles that run on the rails. The driving force is provided by a locomotive that is connected to a series of unpowered cars, that carry passengers or freight. Some individual units have their own motors to provide power. The train moves with much less friction than rubber tires on paved roads, and thereby are more energy efficient than automobiles, buses and trucks.

Intercity trains are a common way to transport passengers and goods over long distances between cities. Regional and commuter trains are used daily to transport people between a city and its surrounding suburbs. Freight trains use a combination of boxcars, container and dedicated cars. The boxcars require manual loading and unloading of the cargo. The container car is much easier to load and unload cargo and has become the dominant method for general freight. Large quantities of bulk are transported by dedicated trains (like cattle and refrigerated cars).

Water. Watercraft are vehicles that transport goods by water, such as a barge, boat or ship. These vehicles are transported over a body of water, such as: sea, ocean, lake, canal or river. This mode of transport is slow, but is an effective way to transport large quantities of non-perishable goods. Water transport is far more economical than air transport for trans-continental shipping.

Pipeline. Liquid and gases are commonly transported through tubular means from their source to their destinations. These include chemically stable substances such as sewage, slurry and water. By far, however, the most common transported goods are oil and natural gas.

Vehicles of Transport. Vehicles traveling on these networks include conveyances of various types such as automobiles, buses, trains, trucks, helicopters and aircraft. A description on each is given below.

Trucks. A truck is a motor vehicle mainly used for carrying goods and materials. Light trucks are not much bigger than a passenger automobile. Commercial trucks are often large and are capable of transporting many forms of cargo and specialized equipment. The larger trucks are built to tow one or more trailers or semi-trailers. Trucks could be very elaborate and complex vehicles depending on the need.

The majority of small trucks (SUV's, pickups, light medium-duty) have gasoline engines; others have diesel engines. The heavier trucks mainly use diesel engines. Small trucks use the same type of (automatic or manual) transmissions with synchronizers as cars. Bigger trucks mainly use manual transmissions with and without synchronizers. Automatic and semi-automatic transmissions for heavy trucks are becoming more and more common, due to advances both in transmission and engine power. Automatic transmissions give a driver more time to concentrate on the road and traffic conditions than manual transmissions.

Trains. A train is a connected series of rail vehicles that move along the track. The thrust for the train is provided by a separate locomotive, or from individual motors in self-propelled multiple units. Most trains carry a revenue (pay) load. The railroad engineer (engine driver) controls the locomotive and any other power cars.

A freight train hauls cargo using freight cars specialized for the type of goods. These are highly economic, with economy of scale and top energy efficiency. The main difficulty is the loss of flexibility due to the lack of tracks at the pick-up and delivery points of the trip. A public advantage for the use of cargo rail transport is its environmental friendly profile.

Container trains are now the dominant type in the U.S. for non-bulk haulage. Containers transship easily to other modes, such as ships and trucks, using cranes. Containers have replaced the boxcar, where the cargo must be loaded and unloaded into the train manually. Other types of cars include refrigerator cars, stock cars for livestock and auto-racks for road vehicles. When rail is combined with road transport, a semi-trailer can be driven onto the train giving easy transshipment between road and rail.

Bulk cargo is mostly by rail transport, since rail has low transshipment costs, is energy efficient and allow trains to handle bulk in a cost effective way. Bulk cargo includes coal, ore, grains and liquids. Bulk is transported in open-topped cars and tank cars.

Barge. A barge is a flat-bottomed boat, built mainly for river and canal transport of heavy goods. Most barges are not self-propelled and need to be towed by tugboats or pushed by towboats. Self-propelled barges operate successfully in still water when traveling downstream or upstream. Sometimes they need assistance from a tugboat, when traveling upstream in faster waters. In some situations, the barges are made for the particular canal in which they will operate.

Barges are used for low-value bulk items and for very heavy or bulky items. The cost of hauling goods by barge is very low. The typical barge measures 195 feet by 35 feet, and can carry up to 1,500 tons of cargo. Large items can either be shipped in sections and assembled onsite, or shipped in assembled form to avoid construction labor at the delivery.

Cargo Aircraft. A cargo aircraft plane (freight aircraft or freighters) is a fixed wing aircraft designed or converted for the carriage of goods. They do not have passenger amenities, and generally have one or more large doors for the loading and unloading of cargo. Freighters are operated by civil passenger, cargo airlines, private individuals, or by the armed forces of individual countries. Air-freight can also be carried in a special ULD (Unit-Load-Device) container in the cargo hold of a passenger aircraft.

Aircraft designed for cargo flight have features different from passenger aircraft. They have a "fat" looking fuselage, a high-wing to allow the cargo area to sit near the ground and a large number of wheels to allow it to land at non-standard airport locations. Plane conversions are often carried out on older aircraft that are no longer suitable for passenger use. These planes are converted from aircraft that no longer meet the passenger safety or noise requirements, or have become uncompetitive in the passenger airline service. There is also a market for new-build freighter designs. Freighter aircraft are designed with strong cabin floors, a broad top-hinged door on the port fuselage and no cabin windows for passengers.

Cargo Handling. Various facilities and equipment are used in cargo transport and handling. These are needed for the tasks of loading, unloading, transferring and stocking the cargo. Below is a description on the following: ports, forklift trucks, cranes, pallets, containers and dunnage.

Ports. A port is a facility that receives ships and has facilities to load and unload the cargo. They are located where the land and water meet on an ocean, sea, river or lake and where the water is deep enough to receive the ships. Ports require cargo-handling equipment likes cranes and forklifts for use in loading and unloading of ships. These facilities are managed by private or public enterprises. They employ longshoremen to carry out the labor needs. Various types of processing facilities (like canneries) are strategically located nearby. The larger ships may need to be guided in and out of the tight port facility with the help of a harbor pilot or tugboat. A customs office is available should the port handle cargo from international ships.

Forklift Trucks. A forklift is a powered industrial truck used to lift and transport materials. These vehicles are necessary to carry-out the operations in facilities like ports, manufacturing, distribution centers and warehouses. They are designed for efficiency and safety in the movement of material. The forklift must be able to retrieve or place a pallet from low to high locations in a rack of a narrow aisle and also maneuver turns of 90 degrees. Well trained forklift drivers are essential to maneuver the material in and out of the often tight storage facilities and to do this without damage to the material or the facility.

Cranes. A crane is a lifting machine, generally equipped with wire ropes or chains or sheaves that are used both to lift and lower materials and also to move them horizontally. It uses simple machines to create mechanical advantage allowing the movement of heavy loads. Cranes have a multiple of uses; in the transport industry they load and unload freight. There are many types of cranes. Deck cranes are located on ships and boats and are used for cargo operations or boat unloading and retrieval where no shore unloading facilities are available. Gantry cranes are located on the port and are designed for loading and unloading containers from the ships.

Pallets. This is a flat structure that supports goods that are being lifted by a forklift, or other device; and may also serve as the base in the racks where the goods are stored. The pallet is designed to hold all sort of goods, and when necessary, they can be secured with straps or stretch-wrapped plastic film. Most pallets are wooden, while others are made of plastic, metal and paper.

Containerization for transport has increase the use of pallets because the shipping containers have clean and level surfaces that allow for easy pallet handling. Most pallets can carry a load of 2,000 pounds. Pallets make it easy to move heavy stacks by forklift trucks and by various hand-pumped or hand-drawn pallet jacks.

The International Organization for Standardization (ISO) sanctions six pallet dimensions. The flat pallets for intercontinental materials handling are the following (by width, length, inches): 48.00 × 40.00, 39.37 × 47.24, 44.88 × 44.88, 42.00 × 42.00, 43.00 × 43.00 and 31.50 × 47.24. Freight handling expenses for international trade incur increase costs when multiple pallet sizes are in use.

Containers. Containerization is a system of intermodal freight transport using standard intermodal containers that are standardized by the International Organization for Standardization (ISO). These can be loaded and sealed intact onto container ships, railroad cars, planes and trucks. Container usage have greatly improved port handling efficiency, and have lowered costs and freight charges and, thereby, have increased the flow of trade. Most manufactured products are shipped in containers.

There are five common standard lengths: 20, 40, 45, 48 and 53 foot containers. U.S. domestic standard containers are generally 48 and 53 foot (rail and truck). Container capacity is often expressed in twenty-foot equivalent units (TEU). An equivalent unit is a measure of containerized cargo capacity equal to one standard 20 foot (length) × 8 foot (width) container. The height of the box is not considered. For example, a 20 foot container with a 9 foot 6 inch height and with a 4 foot by 3 inch height are also called one TEU.

The maximum gross mass for a 20 foot dry cargo container is 67,000 pounds, and for a 40 ft (9 ft 6 in) high cube container, it is 75,000 pounds. Allowing for the tare mass of the container, the net maximum payload mass is therefore reduced to approximately 62,000 pounds for 20 foot, and 66,000 pounds for 40 foot containers.

Since the 1950s, the use of ISO standardized containers on all vehicles and all ports has been progressing. This achievement has streamlined international and domestic trade, gaining large reductions in transport costs. The need to manually load and unload material in a vehicle's storage space is gone. With standard containers, the handling and transfer between modes tremendously reduces all the labor and handling times.

Dunnage. In transporting cargo, dunnage is the packing of material (wood, inflatable bags) between items to avoid damage to the vehicle and the cargo. In trucks, rubber bags were originally used to brace pallets, but more recently, paper bags with a plastic bag interior are favored. Metal strapping of the cargo is now less popular, giving way to the less expensive.

Transport Security

The Transportation Security Administration (TSA) is a U.S. Government law enforcement agency that is responsible for security in all modes of transportation (highways, railroads, buses, mass transit systems, pipelines, ports and airports). Most of TSA's efforts are in aviation security; they employ Transportation Security Officers (TSOs), Federal Air Marshals (FAMs), Transportation Security Inspectors (TSIs) and oversees the training and testing of explosives detection canine team polythylene or vinyl based bags. Dunnage includes inflatable air bags, plastic films, jute coverings, tarpaulins, wood, rice matting, nonwovens, liner bags and so forth. Dunnage is used on all sides of the cargo: on the floor, on top, in-between in layers and on the side.

In rail transport, more-and-more railroad freight carriers are equipping their boxcars with load-securing devices to avoid shifting of the pallets during transit. These cars are labeled as damage free and negate the need of customer-supplied dunnage.

In shipping, because of the frequent ship motion, securing the cargo is essential, and a variety of dunnage is used from wooden boards to modern mechanical spring loaded post-and-socket systems. The role of the dunnage is to separate the cargo in the hold to prevent any shifting of the material. A Transportation Security Officer performs security screening of persons and property and controls entry and exit points within an airport. A Federal Air Marshal, blends in with passengers, and is assigned to detect, deter, and defeat terrorist or other criminal hostile acts within the US's general transportation systems. Transportation Security Inspectors perform thorough inspections, assessments and investigations of passenger and cargo transportation systems to determine their security fitness. TSA employs aviation inspectors, cargo inspectors and surface inspectors. TSA's National Explosives Detection Canine Team Program trains dogs and handlers to act as teams that are mobile and can rapidly detect and identify dangerous materials to transportation systems.

Operations

The transport operations pertain to the legalities, strategies and tools on how the material is moved from one location to another. These concern the following: dispatchers, bill-of-lading, tariffs, truckload, container load, break bulk and air freight. A description on each is provided below.

Dispatchers. There are many types of dispatchers and their role varies by industry. In general, dispatchers take immediate action on emergency and service calls, synchronize transportation schedules, and coordinate the delivery of materials. Truck dispatchers are vital to trucking companies in the pickup and delivery of freight. They schedule and monitor the movement on the non-local deliveries and manage the pickup and drop-off progress on the local deliveries. Bus and train dispatchers observe the progress in the daily operations of their vehicles and attend to any problems that arise, seeking high compliance with the posted schedules. A flight dispatcher is responsible in planning and monitoring the progress of every aircraft flight in its territory. He and the command pilot of the aircraft are legally accountable for the safety of the flight. The flight is released for take off only when the dispatcher and pilot give authority. The dispatcher can delay, divert or cancel a flight at any time.

Bill of Lading. This is a document issued by the carrier to a shipper that specifies the goods that are on-board as cargo for transport to a destination location to a specific consignee. When two or more modes of transport (road, rail, air, sea) are involved, it is called a through bill of lading. The bill of lading is named since it also identifies the transport cost of service (bill) and the load of cargo (lade).

For example, suppose that a logistics company will transport cargo from a plant in Illinois to a location in Ohio via a truck. After the cargo is loaded onto the truck, a plant person from Illinois and the driver will sign the bill of lading. Upon delivery of the cargo to the specified location, the truck driver requires a representative at the Ohio location also to sign the document.

Tariff. A tariff is a duty imposed on foreign goods. The tariff acts as an economic policy to limit trade between nations. This is a political act that is imposed on certain imported goods, and sometimes on exported goods. The purpose is to protect a country's major industries from foreign competition, to avoid the loss of jobs and tax revenue that can hurt the country's economy and cause poverty.

A nation with high industrial regulations will find it is impossible for the domestic industries to compete with the trade from inferior nations that have low regulations and costs unless duties are imposed on the imported goods. Protective tariffs of this type are used for this purpose. The protective tariff can also cause harm to the home market, since it does not allow the populace to benefit with the lower prices in purchasing imported goods like food and clothing and thereby may add to their poverty. Because of the tariff, the domestic manufacturers pay a higher price on imported components they require to make their finished goods and thus cause their goods to be more costly and less competitive. A domestic country that imposes a tariff on a foreign country's goods, may find the foreign country reciprocates by imposing other tariffs back onto the goods of the domestic country, causing a trade war with a disadvantage to both countries.

Truckload. Truckload shipping is the transport of homogeneous cargo that fills an entire semi-trailer or intermodal container. A truckload carrier is a trucking company that mainly serves customers with large quantities that require shipment of an entire trailer-load to a single customer. A less-than truckload (LTL) carrier may mix the freight from several customers in each trailer. The freight from a full truckload carrier is never handled *en route*; while the freight from the LTL carrier is often transferred onto different trailers on the way to the final destination.

Full Container Load. A full container load (FCL) in shipping is when the transport goods fill a standard container (20 or 40 feet). This is called a stuffed (load) with one shipper and where the entire container is intended for one consignee. FCL container shipment yields lower freight rates than an equivalent weight of cargo in bulk. FCL means the loading reaches its allowable maximum weight or full measurement—some exceptions are allowed in ocean freight transactions.

The process of loading and unloading freight that fulfills the FCL limit requires special care to avoid cargo and container damage. The container should be inspected inside and outside, before loading. The container must be loaded to the required weight, and at the same time, the cargo should be packed properly with special dunnage for sea and air shipment to avoid damage. The proper equipment should be used to load and unload the cargo in the container; not heavy forklifts since they risk damage to the container floor.

Break Bulk Cargo. In shipping, break bulk cargo (general cargo) is a term that covers a wide variety of goods that must be loaded individually, and not in intermodal containers or in bulk as with oil or grain. Ships that carry this sort of cargo are often called general cargo ships. The term comes from the phrase breaking bulk, meaning the unloading a portion of the cargo from a ships hold. The goods may be in bags, cases, crates, drums, barrels, or they are held together by baling or loaded onto pallets.

A break-in-bulk point is a place where goods are transferred from one mode of transport to another, for example the docks where goods transfer from ship to truck. Compared to containerization, break bulk cargo handling is more expensive and has more theft and damage. Before the 1960s, break bulk was the most common form of worldwide cargo shipping. Containers are now favored over bulk since they are much more efficient in moving the cargo on and off ships, and thereby require (the ships) less time in port.

Bulk transport is the common way to ship cargo that is not sensitive to careful handling and spoilage; like coal, ore, grains and petroleum. Because of the homogeneity of the product, mechanical devices can process very large quantities in a quick and efficient manner. When the volume of quantity to ship is very large and the unit value is low, bulk transport by large ships or whole trains are desired. Liquid products with large volume can be transported by pipeline.

Air Freight. For high value items (electronics, fashion clothing), air freight is the common mode of transport. In manufacturing, to achieve the benefits from applying the strategies of postponement and just-in-time, the speed of air delivery is sometimes essential, particularly for components of the finished product that have high value and low weight. The very small percent of the air transport volume represents a much higher percent of the total transport value.

Logistics

Logistics refers to the way personnel acquire, transport and store supplies and equipment along the supply chain. With an efficient supply chain and proper logistical procedures, a company can cut costs and increase efficiency. Logistics is the management of transferring products between the point of origin and the point of consumption in order to meet the requirements of consumers and satisfy all legal requirements. It pertains to the coordination from producer to consumer, including the storage, transport, transshipment, warehousing, material-handling, packaging, and the associated exchange of information. Logistics is a business concept that became apparent to industry sometime after World War II, as complexity grew with the domestic and global flow of parts and components coming-in and finished goods going-out. This slogan (and goal) of logistics is as follows: having the right item in the right quantity at the right time at the right place for the right price in the right condition to the right customer. In this respect, the logistics management goal is to create a system that implements and controls, in a most efficient way, the forward and backward flow and storage of goods, services and associated information between the point of origin and the point of consumption.

Cross-Docking

This is a logistics practice where goods are unloaded from incoming vehicles (trucks, semi-trailers, rail cars) and loaded onto (trucks, semi-trailer, rail cars) with little to no storage in-between. In the LTL trucking industry, cross-docking is done by moving cargo from one transport vehicle directly onto another, with minimal or no warehousing. In retail practice, cross-docking operations may utilize staging areas where inbound materials are sorted, consolidated, and stored until the outbound shipment is complete and ready to ship.

Cross-dock operations have been in practice in the U.S. trucking industry since the 1930s for goods that are transported in LTL. The logistics branch of the U.S. military have successfully used this method since the 1950s. Beginning in the 1980s, Wal-Mart has become a heavy user of cross-docking in the supply operations of its retail stores.

Postponement

Postponement (delayed differentiation) is a business strategy that pertains to products that are offered with a variety of options. In the inventory operation of these products, the units are produced and stocked in a stripped-down form (generic model) that only includes the standard components. As each customer order is received with the exact specifications known, a generic unit (in stock) is then customized by including the components as called. This strategy delays adding value to the product until the last possible moment, and as such, reduces inventory cost and risk and increases profit. Postponement also allows companies to respond quickly to market opportunities and offer greater customization options.

The strategy requires a high degree of cooperation and data transfer across the supply chain. Many manufacturers and retailers are now using postponement to hold inventory in a less finished state in the product assembly until actual customer demand is known. The inventory in the warehouses, in stripped-down form, requires light assembly and packaging before the order is filled. This policy has been implemented successfully in the consumer electronic industry by leaders such as Dell and Hewlett-Packard. For those products that are adaptable, this supply chain strategy reduces inventory and improves customer service.

Third Party Logistics (3PL)

Third party logistics is when an external organization is contracted to perform (outsource) a logistics function that is normally performed in-house. An example is when a company, with a trucking fleet, hires an outside trucking company to deliver some of its products.

Outsourcing

Outsourcing occurs when a company contracts another company to provide services that are otherwise performed by employees in-house. These jobs are assigned to separate companies that specialize in each service, and often are located overseas. With the services taken care of by outside experts, outsourcing allows companies to concentrate more on their main business issues. The specialized outsource provider company often is equipped with the most current technologies which often are expensive and time consuming for the company to provide on its own. However, it is important to ensure that the outside company builds all of the parts and components to the company specifications and to the government standards. This assurance becomes more difficult when the outsource company is foreign. Outsourcing can lead to a loss of jobs in some countries as the work is often given to underdeveloped or slower developing countries, that utilize a much cheaper labor force. Outsourcing is also used in contract packaging where other companies are hired to package the products.

Warehouse Management Systems (WMS)

This is a system that plans the inventory activities for all the parts in a warehouse or distribution center. It may generate the forecasts, safety stock, order point and order level for all the parts, and compares these measures to the current on-hand and on-order inventory levels, then determine which parts need a replenishment now and how much.

Production Logistics

This term is used for describing logistic processes within an industry. The purpose is to ensure that each machine and workstation is being fed with the right product in the right quantity and quality at the right point in time. The issue is not the transportation itself, but to streamline and control the flow through the value adding processes and eliminate non-value adding ones. Machines are exchanged and new ones added, which give the opportunity to improve the production logistics system accordingly. Production logistics is getting more and more important with decreasing batch sizes. In many industries batch size one is the short term aim.

Tracking and Tracing

Tracking and tracing, is the part of production logistics that provides a way to determine the current and past locations and other status of property in transit. This concept requires a way to recognize and report the position of the vehicles that are transporting containers with the property of concern in real-time. Another approach is to report the arrival or departure events of the object by location, time and status. The integrity of this data is based on the consistency and completeness of the reports as they come in on a real time basis. An example of this method is the package tracking procedure that is used by specialized shippers (UPS, FedEx).

Barcode

A barcode (bar code) is an optical machine-readable representation of data. Since the beginning, bar codes represent data in the arrangement of widths (lines) and spacing of parallel lines in a one-dimensional format. Some barcodes are now represented in a variety of patterns (squares, dots, hexagons) and within 2-dimensional codes or symbols. Barcodes are read by scanners called barcode readers and they may be scanned from an image by way of special software. Some smart phones now have the ability to scan and read the barcodes.

Prior to 1970, barcodes were mainly used to identify railroad cars. Starting in the 1970s, barcodes gained widespread popularity when they were used to automate supermarket checkout systems. They are now used in a wide variety of ways with tasks referred as Auto ID Data Capture (AIDC). Other systems, like RFID, are attempting to make inroads in the AIDC market, but the simplicity, universality and low cost of barcodes have limited the role of these other systems. The costs to implement a barcode compared to a passive RFID system is far less expensive.

Radio Frequency Identification

Radio-frequency identification (RFID) is the use of an object (RFID tag) integrated into a product, animal, or person for the purpose of identification and tracking using radio waves. Some tags can be read from several meters away and beyond the sight of the reader. The RFID tags have two main parts: the integrated circuit that stores and processes information and the antenna that receives and transmits a signal. There are two type of RFID tags: active RFID tags, have a battery and can transmit signals independently; passive RFID tags, have no battery and require an external source to cause the signal transmission. RFID is a principle tool used in enterprise supply chain management to improve the efficiency of inventory tracking and management.

Incoterms

Incoterms (international commercial terms) are a series of international sales terms, published by International Chamber of Commerce (ICC) and widely used in international commercial transactions. They are used to divide transaction costs and responsibilities between buyer and seller and reflect state-of-the-art transportation practices. They closely correspond to the U.N. Convention on Contracts for the International Sale of Goods. The first version was introduced in 1936 and the date of the present version is 2010. The list of terms is partitioned into four groups: (E—departure, F—main carriage unpaid, C—main carriage paid, D—arrival). The terms are listed below:

E—Departure

EXW Ex Works (named place)

The seller makes the goods available at his premises. The buyer is responsible for all charges.

F—Main Carriage Unpaid

FCA Free Carrier (named place)

The seller hands over the goods, cleared for export, into the custody of the first carrier (named by the buyer) at the named place. This term is suitable for all modes of transport, including carriage by air, rail, road, and containerized/multi-modal transport.

FAS Free Alongside Ship (named loading port)

The seller must place the goods alongside the ship at the named port. The seller must clear the goods for export; this changed into the 2000 version of the Incoterms. Suitable for maritime transport only.

FOB Free on Board (named loading port)

The classic maritime trade term. The seller must load the goods on board the ship nominated by the buyer, cost and risk being divided at ship's rail. The seller must clear the goods for export. Maritime transport only.

FOT Free on Truck

FOR Free on Rail

C—Main Carriage Paid

CFR Cost and Freight (named destination port)

Seller must pay the costs and freight to bring the goods to the port of destination. However, risk is transferred to the buyer once the goods have crossed the ship's rail. Maritime transport only.

CIF Cost, Insurance and Freight (named destination port)

Exactly the same as CFR except that the seller must in addition procure and pay for insurance for the buyer. Maritime transport only.

CPT Carriage Paid To (named place of destination)

The general/containerized/multimodal equivalent of CFR. The seller pays for carriage to the named point of destination, but risk passes when the goods are handed over to the first carrier.

CIP Carriage and Insurance Paid (To) (named place of destination)

The containerized transport/multimodal equivalent of CIF. Seller pays for carriage and insurance to the named destination point, but risk passes when the goods are handed over to the first carrier.

D—Arrival

DAF Delivered At Frontier (named place)

This term can be used when the goods are transported by rail and road. The seller pays for transportation to the named place of delivery at the frontier. The buyer arranges for customs clearance and pays for transportation from the frontier to his factory. The passing of risk occurs at the frontier.

DES Delivered Ex Ship (named port)

Where goods are delivered ex ship, the passing of risk does not occur until the ship has arrived at the named port of destination and the goods made available for unloading to the buyer. The seller pays the same freight and insurance costs as he would under a CIF arrangement. Unlike CFR and CIF terms, the seller has agreed to bear not just cost, but also Risk and Title up to the arrival of the vessel at the named port. Costs for unloading the goods and any duties, taxes, etc…are for the Buyer. A commonly used term in shipping bulk commodities, such as coal, grain, dry chemicals...and where the seller either owns or has chartered, their own vessel.

DEQ Delivered Ex Quay (named port)

This is similar to DES, but the passing of risk does not occur until the goods have been unloaded at the port of destination.

DDU Delivered Duty Unpaid (named destination place)

This term means that the seller delivers the goods to the buyer to the named place of destination in the contract of sale. The goods are not cleared for import or unloaded from any form of transport at the place of destination. The buyer is responsible for the costs and risks for the unloading, duty and any subsequent delivery beyond the place of destination. However, if the buyer wishes the seller to bear cost and risks associated with the import clearance, duty, unloading and subsequent delivery beyond the place of destination, then this all needs to be explicitly agreed upon in the contract of sale.

DAP Delivered At Place (named destination place)

This term means that the seller delivers when the goods are placed at the disposal of the buyer on the arriving means of transport ready for unloading at the named place of destination. This is exactly what the old Incoterm DDU stipulated.

DDP Delivered Duty Paid (named destination place)

This term means that the seller pays for all transportation costs and bears all risk until the goods have been delivered and pays the duty. Also used interchangeably with the term 'Free Domicile'. The most comprehensive term for the buyer.

Summary

This chapter is a review on the basic fundamentals on transportation and logistics as they are used in business. Transportation concerns the movement of materials from a source to a destination along the supply chain. Logistics pertains to the acquisition, transport and storage of the material along the supply chain. The transportation manager and the logistics manager have overlapping goals, where they both seek the optimal movement of material from one location to another in a way that satisfies all the customer demands.

References

Cooper, Andre R., "Cooper's Comprehensive Environmental Desk Reference." *International Thomson Publishing*, Inc. 1996.

Ewing, Reid. "Measuring Transportation Performance." *Transportation Quarterly*. Winter 1995.

Gordon, Cameron. "Putting Transportation Investments in Context." *Transportation Quarterly*. Summer 1997.

Hoch, L. Clinton. "Find the Best Ways to Your Markets." *Transportation and Distribution*. March 1998.

Weiss, Howard J. and Mark E. Gershon. *Production and Operations Management*. Allyn and Bacon, 1989.

Problems

Chapter 2

1. Part A has a forecast of 100 and a standard deviation of 20. Part B has a forecast of 50 and a standard deviation of 20. Compute the coefficient of variation for parts A and B.
2. A part has five history demands: 3, 2, 5, 4, 6 where 3 is the oldest and 6 is the most recent. If the horizontal model is to apply with a discount parameter of 0.90, find the forecast for each of the five future months. Show the integer forecasts for the first five future months.
3. Find the cumulative two and a half month forecast for the part is problem 2.
4. Assume the same data as in problem 2, but now the trend forecast is to be generated with a discount parameter of 0.90. Find the forecast coefficients for the level and slope. What are the forecast for future months 1 and 2?
5. Suppose the horizontal forecast model is in use and the smoothing parameter is 0.10. Consider a part with a one period ahead forecast of 10 and the actual demand is 12. Find the revised forecast for the future month one. Find the integer forecasts for each of the next 6 months.
6. Suppose the trend forecast model with smoothing is in place at time t = 8 with the coefficients for the level and slope as 10 and 1, respectively. Also, the smoothing parameters are 0.10 for the level and 0.20 for the slope.

If the demand at t = 9 is nine pieces, find the forecast for each of the next two months.

7. Consider the example trend seasonal model of this chapter and suppose the demand for month t = 25 is 28 pieces. Find the revised coefficients for the level, trend and seasonal ratios. Also find the forecast for months t = 26, 27 and 28.
8. Assume a part is stocked in five locations (1, 2, 3, 4, 5) with portion of demands as follows: (10, 15, 20, 25, 30) percent. The lead time is 1.5 months and the aggregate forecast is 200 pieces for future month 1 and 220 for month 2. Find the lead time forecast for each location.

Chapter 3

1. Suppose a part with annual demand of 600 pieces, cost per unit of $20, cost per order $25, and annual holding rate of 0.15. Find the economic order quantity, and the associated annual order plus holding cost. Also find the associated stocking rate and the effective cost per unit. If the order quantity is 50 pieces, find the associated annual cost of hold plus order.
2. Suppose the annual demand for an item is 1200 pieces and the associated eoq is 200 pieces. If the annual demand drops to 600 pieces, what is the associated eoq? If the annual demand increases to 1800 pieces, what is the associated eoq?
3. A product has an eoq of 200 pieces and the cost per order is $40. If the cost per order drops to $20, find the associated eoq.
4. A part has an eoq of 100 pieces and the cost per unit is $100. If the cost per unit increases to $150, what is the revised eoq?
5. A part has an eoq of 100 pieces and the annual holding rate is 0.10. If the holding rate is increased to 0.15, what is the revised eoq?
6. Suppose the economic order size is 10 pieces and the annual cost of hold plus order is $200. If the order size

changes to 15 pieces, what is the associated annual hold plus order cost? If the order size drops to 5 pieces, what is the corresponding annual hold plus order cost?

7. Suppose a part with annual demand of 60 pieces and the cost per order is $10. Also assume the annual holding rate is 0.24. Suppose also, the supplier contract has four price tiers as follows:

Quantity	cost per unit
1-10	$100
11-20	95
21-30	90
31-	85

Find the economic order quantity.

8. Consider a part where the cost per unit is $10, the annual holding rate is 0.25 and the cost per order is $20. Also, the current on-hand plus on-order is 6 pieces and the safety stock is 10 pieces. The future 12 monthly forecasts are the following: 20, 30, 20, 10, 0, 0, 20, 30, 30, 10, 0, 40. Find the quantity that yields the least unit cost.
9. A firm seeking the spirit of Just-in-Time wants to lower the order sizes on all its parts in half. How can it achieve this by way of adjusting the cost per order?
10. A firm wants to reduce the inventory on all items by 20 percent. How can it achieve this by adjusting the annual holding rate?
11. What happens to the order size when a supplier increases the cost per unit by 5 percent?
12. Suppose the forecast for an item will increase by 15 percent for a set of parts. What effect will this have on the order sizes and the inventory?

Chapter 4

1. Suppose a part where the trend forecast model is f(t) = 20 + 2t (t = 1, 2, ...) and the months supply method is used with parameter set at 1.4 months. Find the safety stock needed.

2. Consider a part where the forecast is 10 per month, the lead time is 2 months, the one month standard deviation is 5 pieces and the order quantity is 15 pieces. The availability method is used to find the safety stock. If the availability parameter is set to 0.93, find the safety stock needed. What is the order point and order level for the part?
3. Consider the part in Problem 2, but suppose the safety stock is 2 pieces.
   (a) Find the months supply for this part.
   (b) Find the availability for this part.
   (c) Find the service level for this part.
4. Assume the same part in Problem 2 above, but now the service level method is used to find the safety stock and the service level parameter is set to 0.93. Find the safety stock needed and the order point and order level.
5. Consider a product with an annual forecast of 240 pieces, the one month standard deviation is 10 pieces, the lead time is 2 months, the order size is 15 pieces, and the cost per unit is $10. Further, the Lagrange method is used to find the safety stock and the Lagrange parameter is 0.04. How much safety stock is needed? What is the corresponding service level for this part?
6. A part has a lead time on 2 weeks (0.50 months), and the months-in-buy is 1.0 month, the coefficient of variation is 0.70 and the service level is 0.95.
   (a) Find the months of safety stock needed.
   (b) If the lead time is reduced to one week (0.25 months), how much safety stock (in months) is needed?
   (c) If the coefficient-of-variation improves to 0.50, how much safety stock (in months) is needed?
   (d) If the months-in-buy changes to one week, how much safety stock (in months) is needed?

Chapter 5

1. Consider a part where the forecast is F = 20 pieces per month, the safety stock is SS = 10 pieces, the lead time is L = 1 month and the months-in-buy is M = 1 month. Also the opening on-hand and on-order quantities are OH = 45 and OO = 0, respectively. Project the replenish quantities for the future six months.
2. Suppose a part where the forecast is 10 per month, the safety stock is 8 pieces, the lead time is L = 2 months, the months-in-buy is M = 2 months and the opening on-hand plus on-order is 12 pieces. Project the replenish schedule for this part for the future six month time horizon.
3. Assume a part is stocked in three locations (1, 2, 3) and has the following data per location: the prior 12 month demand per location are: 50, 150 and 300 for locations 1, 2 and 3, respectively. The total forecast over all locations is 40 per month and the corresponding one month standard deviation is S = 20 pieces. Further, the lead time is L = 2 months, the months-in-buy is M = 1 and the desired service level is SL = 0.95. Find the order point and order level for each location.
4. A style sweater has three sizes, S, M, L. The aggregate forecast for the sweater is 20 pieces per month, and the corresponding standard error is 6.0. The portion of demands by size are estimated as: 20, 50, 30 percent, respectively. The lead time is 0.75 months, the order size is always one-month buy quantities, and the desired service level is SL = 0.90. What are the safety stock, order point and order level for each size?

Chapter 6

1. Suppose a store stocks an item with a lead time of one week and the demand is estimated as one piece per month. The store manager would like the service level to be 0.95. Find the order point and order level needed for the item.

2. Consider a stocked item in a store where the lead time is three weeks and the demand is four units per month. If the desired service level is 0.90, find the order point and order level for the item.
3. Using the Poisson probability tables, verify the results found in Problem 2.
4. Consider a store that stocks a style shoe that come in 10 sizes. Assume the average demand for the style shoe is 20 units per month and the lead time is 4 weeks. Suppose further that size 10 receives 20 percent of the demand for this style shoe. What setting of the order point and order level are needed to maintain a service level of 90 percent for the size 10 shoe?
5. Suppose a dealer holds stock for a service part with a forecast of 0.4 units per month. The replenish lead time is two weeks and the desired service level is 0.95. Find the order point and order level for this part.
6. Consider a sweater that comes in three sizes (S, M, L) and the aggregate forecast is 10 pieces per month. The lead time is one-half month (0.50) and the portion of demands per size are estimated as: 20, 50, 30, percent, respectively. The desired service level is 0.95. Find the order point and order level for each size.

Chapter 7

1. **Location Assignment.** Suppose a network of five locations (1, 2, 3, 4, 5) with location 1 as the master location. The 12 month forecast is 120 pieces and the average pieces per order is ppo = 2.40. The estimates on the portion of demand by location are: 0.20, 0.25, 0.35, 0.05 and 0.15, for locations 1 to 5, respectively. Which locations should stock the part if the policy on minimum lines per year is set to 4 pieces?
2. **Allocate.** Assume a part with five stocking locations (1, 2, 3, 4, 5) and associated data as listed below. Suppose the supplier ships a replenish quantity of Q = 55 pieces and the supplier's multiple quantity is 5 pieces. Find how to allocate the replenish quantity to the locations.

Locations	OH	IT	SS	F(1)	F(2)	F(3)	F(4)
1	10	0	6	12	12	12	12
2	5	0	3	6	6	6	6
3	25	0	4	8	8	8	8
4	20	0	8	16	16	16	16
5	0	0	2	4	4	4	4

3. **Transfer.** Suppose a part is stocked in five locations (1, 2, 3, 4, 5) with data as listed below. Also the transfer multiple quantity is 4 pieces. Determine if a transfer is needed in the network, and if so, find the locations and the quantity to transfer.

Locations	OH	IT	SS	F1	F2	F3	F4
1	34	0	4	8	8	9	9
2	25	0	6	12	12	12	13
3	9	0	5	10	10	10	11
4	30	0	7	14	14	15	15
5	20	0	4	8	8	8	9

Chapter 8

1. Find the make-to-stock production plan for the following situation.

Months (t)	0	1	2	3
forecast of sales (F)	–	200	240	180
desired ending inventory (I)	300	310	320	300
production plan (P)				

2. Find the make-to-order production plan using the data shown.

Months (t)	0	1	2	3
forecast of sales (F)	–	500	530	512
desired ending backlog (B)	270	310	270	320
production plan (P)				

3. Find the mixed make-to-stock and make-to-order production plan.

Months (t)	0	1	2	3	4
forecast of sales (F)	–	360	340	380	420
desired ending backlog (B)	80	80	120	120	110
desired ending inventory (I)	370	400	420	440	480
production plan (P)					

4. With the data provided, find the requirements (R), projected balance (PB), available to promise (AP), and the master production schedule (MPS) for the time horizon t = 1 to 7.

Q = 100 order size OH = 80 on-hand L = 0 lead time

t	0	1	2	3	4	5	6	7
F		10	0	0	10	0	0	10
PF		8	17	25	30	30	30	30
AD		22	13	5	0	0	0	0
R								
PB								
AP								
MPS								

5. With the data provided below, complete the rough cut capacity plan.

End item	Resource per unit		Months 1	2	3
A	1.2	planned order release	200	190	300
		resource usage			
B	0.8	planned order release	250	300	300
		resource usage			
		Load total cumulative			
		Capacity total cumulative	500	500	500
		Variance total cumulative			

Chapter 9

1. Suppose a single model assembly with $\Sigma t_i = 100$ minutes, and $T = 440$ minutes. List a table that shows the measures: (n', n, c', $\bar{c}$, d) for N = 50 to 55.
2. Consider an assembly of a single model line where the total unit time is $\Sigma t_i = 100$ minutes, the number of operators is n = 10 and the assigned operation times for the ten operator are as follows: (10.0, 9.6, 10.2, 9.9, 9.7, 10.3, 10.0, 9.6, 10.3, 10.4). Find the cycle time and the effective balance delay for the line.
3. Consider the precedence diagram of Figure 9.2 and the corresponding element times listed below for elements 1 to 17. Balance the line as best as you can for two stations. Measure the balance delay.
4. In problem 3, balance the line as best as you can for four stations. Measure the balance delay.
5. Consider the 17 element example in the chapter and the associated element times. Assume two stations and two models (A, B), are assigned to the line with the shift production schedule of 10 units for model A and 20 units for model B. The total time for a shift is 440 minutes. Elements 1, 4, 7, and 15 are only used on A, elements 2, 3, 6, 12 and 16 are only used on B. All other elements are used on A and B. Balance the line as best as you can for the shift.

Chapter 10

1. Consider the IOQ example of the chapter. Find the annual costs for order, hold, goodwill and excess when q = 1.715 and d = 2.248.
2. Use the same data from the ATR example in the chapter, but now suppose the annual scrap rate is r = 0.30. The other data are the following: $j_o = 5$ (scrap free years), $t_o = 2$ (part production years) and T = 9 (years since introduce part). Develop the table that lists the probabilities p(j), F(j) and H(j) for the years j = 1 to 15.

3. Using the results from problem 2, list the generic life cycle curve, x(t), for the part. Note the current year is T = 9 and suppose the demand history of the part is (200, 140, 100) for the three years: t = 7, 8, 9, respectively. Find the forecast for each year of t = 10 to 15. What is the ATR?

Chapter 12

1. A shoe manufacturing facility is open 8 hours a day and a mold, called a 'last', for a particular style shoe and size is used in the manufacturing process. Suppose the style and size has an average demand of 6 per day and the average processing time is 4 hours. The management wants to know how many lasts (for the style and size) should be held in their stock to yield a 90 percent service level.
2. A distribution center is open 8 hours a day and receives 1000 customer orders a day for processing. The average processing time is 10 minutes per order. How many order pickers are needed to yield a service level of 85 percent?
3. Trucks arrive to a warehouse receiving department at a rate of 5 per hour and the average unloading time per crew is 30 minutes. How many crews are needed to attain a service level of SL = 0.85?
4. Suppose a truck rental agency is open seven days a week and the average number of requests is 5 per week for a small size truck. The average rental time is 1.5 days. Customers who request a truck when all are out will not wait and will go elsewhere. The agency wants to provide a service level of 95 percent. How many small size trucks should they have available?
5. A motorcycle dealer wishes to maintain a system of continuous availability for each model bike where, as soon as a bike is sold, another is ordered from the supplier. If the bike is not in stock when a customer demand arrives, the sale is lost. For a particular model,

suppose, the average demand is 2 per month and the average procurement lead time is 6 weeks (1.5 months). The store owner wants to know how to set the order point and order level for the bike model to attain a 99 percent service level?

Chapter 13

1. Consider the p-chart with the pre-study results listed below from N = 8 subgroups.

i	1	2	3	4	5	6	7	8
n	30	25	28	22	34	30	30	30
x	1	1	2	6	1	0	0	1

   For the measure of p, find the average, standard deviation and the upper and lower control limits. What is the process capability (pc) for this item?

2. Consider the np-chart where the pre-study of 30 subgroups yields results as below with the sample size per group of 10. The sum of defects over the 30 subgroups is 20.

   For the measure np, find the average, standard deviation and the upper and lower control limits. What is the process capability (pc) for this item?

3. Consider the c-chart where a pre-study has 50 subgroups and the sum of non-conformities is 84. For the measure of c, find the average, standard deviation and the upper and lower control limits.

4. Consider the u-chart where a pre-study example has 40 subgroups, the sum of the samples is 120 and the number of non-conforming units is 25. For the measure of u, find the average, standard deviation and the upper and lower control limits.

5. Consider the x-Bar and R chart where a pre-study has 10 subgroups of 5 samples each, and the sum of the measure $\bar{x}$ is $\Sigma\bar{x} = 26.8$, and the sum of the range is $\Sigma R = 31.2$. Find the lower and upper control limits for x-Bar and R. If the upper specification limit is 6.00, what is the process capability (cpk) for this item?

6. Consider the x-Bar and s chart where a pre-study has 10 subgroups of 5 samples each and the sum of the measure $\overline{x}$ is $\Sigma\overline{x} = 30.8$, and the sum of the standard deviation is $\Sigma s = 24.8$. Find the lower and upper control limits for x-Bar and s. If the upper specification limit is 20.0, what is the process capability (cpk) for this item?
7. Consider the median chart where a pre-study has 10 subgroups of 5 samples each, and the sum of the median is $\Sigma\tilde{x} = 28.1$, and for the range it is $\Sigma R = 30$. Find the lower and upper control limits for the median and for the range.
8. Consider the individual chart where a pre-study has 10 subgroups and the sum of x is $\Sigma x = 100.4$, and the sum of the range is $\Sigma R = 28.4$. Find the lower and upper control limits for x and for the range.

Solutions

Chapter 2

1. cov(A) = 0.20, cov(B) = 0.40
2.

t	x(t)	w(t)
1	3	0.66
2	2	0.73
3	5	0.81
4	4	0.90
5	6	1.00

   $\Sigma w = 4.10$ and $\Sigma wx = 17.09$ yields $a = 17.09/4.10 = 4.17$

   $f\tau = 4.17$ for $\tau = 1$ to 5 and integer forecasts are 4, 4, 5, 4, 4 for $\tau = 1$ to 5

3. $F_3 = 4.17 + 4.17 + 0.5 \times 4.17 = 10.42$
4. $\Sigma w = 4.10$, $\Sigma wx = 17.09$, $\Sigma wt = 13.15$, $\Sigma wxt = 72.1$, $\Sigma wt^2 = 50.27$

   $b = 0.82$

   $a = 1.53$, $a(5) = a + 5b = 5.63$

   $f1 = 6.45$

   $f2 = 7.27$

5. $a(t) = 0.10 \times 12 + 0.90 \times 10 = 10.2$

   $f1 = 10.2$, $f\tau = (10, 10, 11, 10, 10, 10)$ for $\tau = 1$ to 6

6. $a(t) = 0.10 \times 9 + 0.90 \times (10 + 1) = 10.8$

   $b(t) = 0.20 \times (10.8 - 10.0) + 0.8 \times 1.00 = 0.96$

f1 = 10.8 + 0.96 = 11.76

f2 = 10.8 + 2 × 0.96 = 12.72

7. a(25) = 0.1(28/0.58) + 0.9(41.71 + 0.29) = 42.63

   b(25) = 0.2(42.63 – 41.71) + .8 × 0.29 = 0.42

   r(37) = 0.3(28/42.63) + 0.7 × 0.58 = 0.60

   f1 = (42.63 + 0.42) × 0.66 = 28.41

   f2 = (42.63 + 0.84) × 0.80 = 34.78

   f3 = (42.63 + 1.26) × 1.20 = 52.67

8. fL(1) = 31.0

   fL(2) = 46.5

   fL(3) = 62.0

   fL(4) = 77.5

   fL(5) = 93.0

Chapter 3

1. Q = 100, K = 300, s = 0.025, c′ = 20.50, K(50) = 375
2. At A′ = 600, Q′ = 142. At A′ = 1800, Q′ = 244
3. Q′ = 142
4. Q′ = 81.6
5. Q′ = 81.6
6. At Q′ = 15, K′ = 217. At Q′ = 5, K′ = 250
7.

q	c	Q	K′	
1-10	100	7	138	
11-20	95	11	133	EOQ = 11
21-30	90	21	170	
31-	85	31	217	

8.

t	r	Q	K	K/Q	
1	24	24	22.5	0.937	
2	20	44	28.8	0.653	
3	20	64	39.2	0.612	LUC = 64
4	10	74	46.5	0.628	

9. Set Co′ = 0.25Co

10. Set h′ = 1.5625h
11. Q′ = 0.976Q
12. Q′ = 1.072Q
    Inventory increases by 1.072

Chapter 4

1. SS = 22 + 0.4 × 24 = 31.6
2. k = 1.476 and SS = 10.43
   OP = 30.4 and OL = 45.4
3. (a) MS = 0.20
   (b) σ_L = 7.07, k = 0.28, AV = 0.61
   (c) σ_L = 7.07, k = 0.28, E(k) = 0.215, SL = 0.87
4. E(k) = 0.149, k = 0.674 and SS = 4.76
   OP = 24.8 and OL = 39.8
5. F(k) = 0.975, k = 1.96, SS = 27.7 and SL= 0.99
6. (a) SS = 0.44
   (b) SS = 0.25
   (c) SS = 0.25
   (d) SS = 0.78

Chapter 5

1. F = 20/month, L = 1 month, M = 1 month, OH + OO = 45, SS = 10
   FL = 20, Q = 20, OP = 30, OL = 50

Month t	0	0.75	1.75	2.75	3.75	4.75	5.75
OH + OO	45	30	30	30	30	30	30
Buy q		20	20	20	20	20	20
OH + OO + q		50	50	50	50	50	50
Receive t		1.75	2.75	3.75	4.75	5.75	6.75

2. F = 10/month, L = 2 months, M = 2 months, OH + OO = 12, SS = 8
   FL = 20, Q = 20, OP = 28, OL = 48

Month t	0	2	4	6
OH + OO	12	28	28	28
Buy q	36	20	20	20
OH + OO + q	48	48	48	48
Receive t	2	4	6	8

3. F = 40/month, σ = 20, L = 2 months, M = 1, SL = 0.95

loc	d12	p	f1	fL	q	σ	σL	E(k)	k	ss	op	ol
1	50	.10	4	8	4	2.75	3.89	0.051	1.24	4.82	12.82	16.82
2	150	.30	12	24	12	6.66	9.42	0.064	1.13	10.64	34.64	46.64
3	300	.60	24	48	24	12.39	17.52	0.068	1.10	19.27	67.27	91.27

4. F = 20/month, σ = 6, L = 0.75 months, M = 1, SL = 0.90

size	p	f1	fL	q	σ	σL	E(k)	k	ss	op	ol
S	.20	4	3.0	4	2.15	1.86	0.215	0.44	0.82	3.82	7.82
M	.50	10	7.5	10	3.04	2.63	0.380	0.04	0.11	7.61	17.61
L	.30	6	4.5	6	2.72	2.36	0.254	0.33	0.78	5.28	11.28

Chapter 6

1. L = 0.25 months, d = 1, SL = 0.95
   Op = 1, OL = 2
2. L = 0.75 months, d = 4, SL = 0.90
   OP = 4, OL = 5
3. d = 4, L = 0.75, SL = 0.90, OP = 4, OL = 5
   m = d × L = 3/month
   E(s) = 0 × 0.050 + 1 × .149 + 2 × .224 + 3 × .224 + 4 × .353 = 2.681
   E(demand in order cycle) = OL – OP + m = 4.000
   E(sales in order cycle) = OL – OP + E(s) = 3.681
   Service level = sales/demand = 3.681/4.000 =0.920
4. D = 20/month, L = 1.0 month, SL = 0.90
   p = .20, d = 4/month, op = 4, ol = 6
5. d = 0.4/month, L = 0.50, SL = 0.95
   OP = 1, OL = 2

6.

Size	p	d	op	ol
S	.20	2	2	4
M	.50	5	4	5
L	.30	3	3	4

Chapter 7

1.

Location	p	f	lines	
1	.20	24	10.0	stock
2	.25	30	12.5	stock
3	.35	42	17.5	stock
4	.05	6	2.5	non-stock
5	.15	18	7.5	stock

2.

Location	OH′	Pre MS	Raw Allocate	Raw MS	Final Allocate
1	4	0.33	18.4	1.86	20
2	2	0.33	9.2	1.86	10
3	21	2.62	0.0	2.62	0
4	12	0.75	17.9	1.86	15
5	–2	–0.50	9.5	1.87	10
Sum			55		55

3.

Location	OH′	Pre MS	send	receive	Post OH	Post MS
1	30	3.56	12		18	2.33
2	19	1.58			19	1.58
3	4	0.40		12	16	1.60
4	23	1.64			23	1.64
5	16	2.00			16	2.00

Chapter 8

1.

Months (t)	0	1	2	3
forecast of sales (F)	–	200	240	180
desired ending inventory (I)	300	310	320	300
production plan (P)		210	250	160

2.

Months (t)	0	1	2	3
forecast of sales (F)	–	500	530	512
desired ending backlog (B)	270	310	270	320
production plan (P)		460	570	462

3.

Months (t)	0	1	2	3	4
forecast of sales (F)	–	360	340	380	420
desired ending backlog (B)	80	80	120	120	110
desired ending inventory (I)	370	400	420	440	480
production plan (P)		390	320	400	470

4. Q = 100 order size
OH = 80 on-hand
L = 0 lead time

t	0	1	2	3	4	5	6	7
F		10	0	0	10	0	0	10
PF		8	17	25	30	30	30	30
AD		22	13	5	0	0	0	0
R		40	30	30	40	30	30	40
PB	80	40	10	80	40	10	80	40
AP		58	82			100		
MPS			100			100		

5.

End item	Resource per unit		Months 1	2	3
A	1.2	planned order release	200	190	300
		resource usage	240	228	360
B	0.8	planned order release	250	300	300
		resource usage	200	240	240
		Load total	440	468	600
		cumulative	440	908	1508
		Capacity total	500	500	500
		cumulative	500	1000	1500
		Variance total	60	92	–8
		cumulative	60	152	144

Chapter 9

1. $\Sigma t = 100$, T = 440

N	n′	n	c′	c	d
50	11.36	12	8.80	8.33	.053
51	11.59	12	8.63	8.33	.034
52	11.82	12	8.46	8.33	.015
53	12.05	13	8.30	7.69	.073
54	12.27	13	8.15	7.69	.056
55	12.50	13	8.00	7.69	.038

2. Cycle time = 10.4 minutes

   Average operation time = 10.0 minutes

   Balance delay = (10.4 – 10.0)/10.4 = 3.85%

3. Station 1: elements (1, 2, 3, 4, 5, 6, 8, 9, 13) time = 19.2 minutes

   Station 2: elements (7, 10, 11, 12, 14, 15, 16, 17) = 18.6 minutes

   Balance delay = (19.2 – 18.9)/19.2 = 1.6%

4. Station 1: elements (1, 3, 5, 6, 8) time = 9.6 minutes

   Station 2: elements (9, 13, 14) time = 9.2 minutes

   Station 3: elements (2, 7, 10, 11) time = 9.4 minutes

   Station 4: elements (4, 12, 15, 16, 17) time = 9.6 minutes

   Balance = (9.6 – 9.45)/9.6 = 1.6%

5.

Element	A	B	time	total	station
1	1	0	0.7	7	1
2	0	1	2.0	40	1
3	0	1	1.8	36	1
4	1	0	1.0	10	1
5	1	1	2.0	60	1
6	0	1	1.4	28	1
7	1	0	0.8	8	1
8	1	1	3.7	111	1
9	1	1	3.5	105	2

10	1	1	3.0	90	1
11	1	1	3.6	108	2
12	0	1	2.5	50	1
13	1	1	3.1	93	2
14	1	1	2.6	78	2
15	1	0	2.8	28	1
16	0	1	1.9	38	2
17	1	1	1.4	42	2
Sum				932	Station 1: 468 minutes Station 2: 464 minutes

Chapter 10

1. K(order) = 328, K(hold) = 321, K(goodwill) = 944, K(excess) = 0, K(1.715, 2.248) = 1593
2.

J	p(j)	F(j)	H(j)
1	0.00	0.00	1.00
2	0.00	0.00	1.00
3	0.00	0.00	1.00
4	0.00	0.00	1.00
5	0.00	0.00	1.00
6	0.30	0.30	0.70
7	0.21	0.51	0.49
8	0.15	0.66	0.34
9	0.10	0.76	0.24
10	0.07	0.83	0.17
11	0.05	0.88	0.12
12	0.04	0.92	0.08
13	0.03	0.95	0.05
14	0.02	0.97	0.03
15	0.01	0.98	0.02

3.

t		x(t)	d(t)
1	p	1.00	
2	p	2.00	
3		2.00	
4		2.00	
5		2.00	
6		1.70	
7	d	1.19	200
8	d	0.83	140
9	d	0.58	100
10	f	0.41	69
11	f	0.29	49
12	f	0.20	34
13	f	0.13	22
14	f	0.08	14
15	f	0.05	8

X(3) = 1.19 + 0.83 + 0.58 = 2.60

D(3) = 200 + 140 + 100 = 440

a = 440/2.60 = 169

ATR = 69 + 49 + 34 + 22 + 14 + 8 = 196

Chapter 12

1. 1 day = 8 hours, λ = 6/day, μ = 8/4 per day ρ = 3.00, SL = 0.90, backorders, N = 6
2. 1 day = 8 hours, λ = 1000/day, μ = 48/day, ρ = 20.8, SL = 0.85, backorders, N = 26
3. λ = 5/hour, μ = 2/hour, ρ = 2.5, SL = 0.85, backorders, N = 5
4. λ = 5/week, μ = (7/1.5)/week, ρ = 1.07, SL = 0.95, lost sales, N = 4
5. λ = 2/month, L = 1.5 months, μ = 0.67/month, ρ = 3, SL = 0.99, N = 8, lost sales, N = 8, OP = 7, OL = 8

Chapter 13

1. $\overline{p} = 0.052$, $\overline{n} = 28.6$, $\sigma = 0.042$, (LCL, UCL)p = (0, 0.178), pc = 0.948
2. $\overline{np} = 0.67$, $\overline{p} = 0.067$, $\sigma = 0.79$, (LCL, UCL)np = (0, 3.04), pc = 0.933
3. $\overline{c} = 1.68$, $\sigma = 1.30$, (LCL, UCL)c = (0, 5.58)
4. $\overline{u} = 0.208$, $\overline{n} = 3.0$, $\sigma = 0.26$, (LCL, UCL)u = (0, 0.988)
5. (LCL, UCL) $\overline{x}$ = (–0.87, 4.49), (LCL, UCL)R = (0, 6.58)
   USL = 6.00, $\sigma = 1.32$, kU = 2.52, cpk = 2.52
6. (LCL, UCL) $\overline{x}$ = (–0.47, 6.63), (LCL, UCL)s = (0, 5.18)
   USL = 20.0, $\sigma = 2.638$, kU = 6.414, cpk = 6.414
7. (LCL, UCL) $\tilde{x}$ = (1.07, 4.55), (LCL, UCL)R = (0, 6.33)
8. (LCL, UCL) x = (1.64, 18.43), (LCL, UCL)R = (0, 10.33)

Index